To Change
Reels

Contemporary Film and Television Series

*A complete listing of the books in this series
can be found at the back of this volume.*

To Change Reels

FILM AND CULTURE IN SOUTH AFRICA

Edited by
Isabel Balseiro and Ntongela Masilela

WAYNE STATE UNIVERSITY PRESS   **DETROIT**

Library of Congress Cataloging-in-Publication Data

To change reels : film and film culture in South Africa
/ edited by Isabel Balseiro and Ntognela Masilela.
p. cm. — (Contemporary film and television series)
Includes bibliographical references and index.
ISBN 0–8143-3000–2 (alk. paper) —
ISBN 0–8143-3001–0 (pbk. : alk. paper)
1. Motion pictures—South Africa—History.   I. Balseiro,
Isabel.   II. Masilela, Ntognela.   III. Series.
PN1993.5.S6 T62 2003
791.43'0968—dc21   2002151896

The chapter "The Politics of Leisure during the Early Days of South African
Cinema" from *Monarchs, Missionaries and African Intellectuals* by
Bhekizizwe Peterson is published with the permission of Witwatersrand
University Press and Africa World Press.

In memory of
Lionel Rogosin
(1928–2000)

Contents

vii

Contents

Acknowledgments

We would like to gratefully acknowledge the many friends and colleagues who helped shape this book. We also wish to thank our editor, Jane Hoehner, at Wayne State University Press, and Judy King, our indexer.

I would like to express my gratitude to Jam Karanja (in memoriam), C. R. D. Halisi, Boyd James, the Masilela family, Ezekiel Mphahlele, Miriam Makeba, Hugh Masekela, Letta Mbulu, Thula Mndaweni, George Menoe, Caiphus Semenya, Peter Davis, Mark Beittel, Lucia Saks, Keyan Tomaselli, and the members of the Los Angeles School (Charles Burnett, Julie Dash, Haile Gerima, Larry Clark, Billy Woodberry, Teshome Gabriel, Yemane Demissie, Ben Caldwell, Melvonna Ballenger, Sharon Larkin, and Barbara McCullough).

NTONGELA MASILELA

I wish to warmly thank Tobias Hecht, Heidi Grunebaum, Pam Nichols, and Paul Wise. Mark Beittel, Edwin Hees, Bhekizizwe Peterson, and Lucia Saks made working collaboratively a pleasure. I was fortunate to receive encouragement and advice from members of a new generation of South African filmmakers that includes Zachariah Rapola, Sechaba Morojele, and Khubu Meth. Graham Goddard at the University of the Western Cape–Robben Island Mayibuye Archives/Film and Video Archives, Freddy Ogterop at the Provincial Government of the Western Cape, and Trevor Moses at the National Film, Video and Sound Archives in Pretoria helped make the search for archival resources a fruitful one, while Brenda Cooper offered a spirited working space at the Centre for African Studies, University of Cape Town. Awards from Harvey Mudd College, of the Claremont Colleges, generously supported this research through travel grants and other subsidies. Special thanks are also owed to the research assistance of a formidable team that included, at different times, Houston ("Troquero") Gilbert, Elise Lawson, Sarah ("Saartjie") Olmstead, Anne ("Annie") Short, Megan Thomas, and Mira Stoilova.

ISABEL BALSEIRO

Contributors

Isabel Balseiro is an associate professor of comparative literature at Harvey Mudd College, the Claremont Colleges, California. Recipient of the Arnold L. and Lois S. Graves Award for Teaching in the Humanities, she edited *Running towards Us: New Writing from South Africa* (Heinemann, 2000).

Mark Beittel has M.A.s in historical sociology and applied linguistics, and he has published on South African social history, literature, and film. Formerly a research associate at the Fernand Braudel Center, Binghamton University, he now teaches English at the University of Trent in northern Italy.

Haile Gerima is an Ethiopian filmmaker living in the United States. He teaches in the Department of Radio, Television and Film at Howard University. His films include *Child of Resistance* (1972), *Harvest, 3000 Years* (1976), *Bush Mama* (1978), *Ashes and Amber* (1985), *Sankofa* (1993), and *Adwa: An African Victory* (1999).

Edwin Hees is a senior lecturer in the Department of English at the University of Stellenbosch, Western Cape, South Africa. His main academic interests are the history of theater and the history of film, especially South African film. He has edited two special issues of the *South African Theatre Journal* on the South African film industry, and has published a number of related articles.

Kgafela oa Magogodi is a poet, songwriter, and film critic. He teaches African film studies and contemporary oral poetry studies and performance in the Wits School of Arts, University of the Witwatersrand, Gauteng, South Africa. Magogodi is also a Ph.D. candidate in the Department of African Literature at the University of the Witwatersrand, where he is studying the genealogy of black cinema in South Africa.

Contributors

Jacqueline Maingard lectures in film and television studies at the University of Bristol, England. She has published in a range of journals including *Screen* and the *Journal of Southern African Studies*. She directed a short video called *Uku Hamba 'Ze—To Walk Naked* and is currently writing a book on South African cinema for the Routledge National Cinema series.

Ntongela Masilela is a professor of English and world literature at Pitzer College and adjunct professor of African American studies at the University of California–Irvine. He edited *Black Modernity: Discourses between United States and South Africa* (Africa World Press, forthcoming) and is the general editor of a New African Renaissance imprint of Africa World Press.

Bhekizizwe Peterson teaches in the Department of African Literature at the University of the Witwatersrand, Gauteng, South Africa. He is a critic as well as a writer and playwright. His most recent works include *Monarchs, Missionaries, and African Intellectuals: African Theatre and the Unmaking of Colonial Marginality* (Witswatersrand University Press, 2000) and the screenplay for the feature film *Fools* (1997) by Ramadan Suleman.

Lucia Saks is an assistant professor in the Film and Video program at the University of Michigan. She was formerly program director of media communications at the University of Natal, Durban, South Africa. She is the author of a number of articles on transnational cinema and is completing a book on the reconstruction of national identity in post-apartheid South African cinema.

Laura Twiggs is features editor of *Femina* magazine, to which she also contributes articles and two columns. She received her M.A. (with distinction) in English from the University of Cape Town in 1997. She presents a weekly arts talk show on Cape Town's FMR radio station, reviews arts and culture for newspapers, and occasionally forays into filmmaking.

Introduction

Ntongela Masilela and Isabel Balseiro

During the nearly half century of apartheid, South African cinema was almost wholly excluded from larger discussions of African cinema; most texts on the continent's filmmaking make no more than passing reference to South African production. At the same time, no serious consideration of South African cinema in its own right emerged to make up for this silence; to date, only a handful of book-length studies on South African filmmaking have been published (Gutsche 1972; Tomaselli 1989; Hees 1991; Blignaut and Botha 1992; Botha and van Aswegen 1992; and Davis 1996). Of these, none offers a systematic approach to film history that problematizes the absence of black voices in South African cinematography and none takes account of the participation of blacks as other than background figures. Yet the cultural forces that made cinema possible in South Africa and made it what it is tell a larger story about South African cultural and intellectual history. This book, not limited to the treatment of film production, approaches cinema as a manifestation of South African cultural history. Hence, the chapters that follow are not narrowly about films made by South Africans in South Africa but describe the unfolding of film culture within a series of stages that have yet to give rise to a national cinema.

Dating back to the end of the nineteenth century, the South African film industry had an early start in the land once divided into two British colonies and two independent Afrikaner republics. But does footage from the 1899–1902 Anglo-Boer War taken by English cameramen constitute South African cinema? Are films made by non-South Africans part of national production? Or was South African cinema born only with the 1911 fiction film *The Great Kimberley Diamond Robbery,* which was produced by people who lived in South Africa? And what of apartheid cinema? Or the films made by South African exiles? Are these expressions of South African cinema? Where does one situate films that have a "South African theme," whatever that may be?

For the purposes of this book, South African cinema is understood to be made up of films with any of these characteristics and also encompasses the ways film is used, experienced, and apprehended in the country. Whereas production, until the last few years, has been almost exclusively in the hands of whites, white filmmakers could only work within a nascent or existing film culture: a film culture that, however reluctantly, took black South Africans into account.[1] It is thus with film culture that this book begins, and that idea is central throughout. How have the possibilities of cinema been viewed at diverse times in South African history, by different governments and social groups? What happens when whites aim to make "black" films? What is the relationship between film and a larger notion of leisure in South Africa? And what does all of this tell us about the larger picture of the South African society in which—and about which—these films have been made?

Paradoxically, to be original and imaginative is to be historical. And to be historical is to possess a "consciousness of precedent," as Thomas Crow (1999, 564) writes in an essay on the theoretical complexities of the history of form in conceptual art: "Almost every work of serious contemporary art recapitulates, on some explicit or implicit level, the historical sequence of objects to which it belongs. Consciousness of precedent has become very nearly the condition and definition of major artistic ambition." The first two presidents of a democratic South Africa, Nelson Mandela and Thabo Mbeki, have called for the forging of an "African Renaissance." But what is the precedent for this rebirth? It is unlikely to be found in the films made by South Africans.

A few years before the demise of apartheid, Lewis Nkosi (1990, xv), a South African writer and critic, suggested:

> A serious examination of South African culture must at some time come to terms with a fact that may be uncongenial to both black and white progressives, given our prior commitment to a non-racial democratic future, and that fact is the near total hegemony, within the various cultural practices of South African society, of an unrepresentative white minority, consisting not only of diehard upholders of the apartheid system but also of white liberals and progressives as well, in their roles as academics, as critics, as anthologists, as impresarios, as gallery owners and publishers and as consultants of those who own virtually all the means of cultural production.[2]

The unrepresentative nature of those who control the means of film production is, likewise, one of the factors bedeviling the making of South African cinema, to say nothing of a national cinema. The cultural historian Thelma Gutsche refused to engage with features made by white South Africans (most of whom saw themselves, in any case, as Europeans in Africa) in her seminal 1972 history of film in South Africa, *The History and Social Significance of Motion Pictures in South Africa, 1895–1940*. She presciently saw that unrepresentative white domination would prove disastrous for South African cinema, as indeed was the case for decades. In her reading of film history, Gutsche unquestionably believed that the cultural practice of making films should be at the service of democratic traditions. On the other hand, her refusal to engage with films made in South Africa as an autonomous representative form reflects the fact that, for her, film history should be written from the perspective of cultural history, from which cinema has become inseparable. Thus the founding text of film studies in South Africa does not treat films made in South Africa as autonomous aesthetic objects, concerning itself instead with the introduction of European modernity into the country through film culture. For Gutsche, South African cinema was not born with those films made by South Africans in South Africa but rather with the impingement of foreign films on the South African imagination and with the social and cultural institutions that made this possible.

This book both aims to set film in a social context, in the tradition of Gutsche's scholarship, and offers an examination of particular films as aesthetic objects, though never to the exclusion of the cultural forces leading to (and even emerging from) their production. The precedent, not only for any sort of African Renaissance but also, and more to the point, for an understanding of South African cinema, might be found in the intellectual and cultural heritage bequeathed by the New African Movement; it is there that this book begins.

Entitled "Historical Perspectives," part one concerns the early history of South Africa's film production. To understand film culture in South Africa, one must first understand the emergence of modernity in the country. The leaders of the New African Movement, which was born a few years after the Anglo-Boer War of 1899–1902, were deeply impressed by what the New Negroes had achieved in the United States in the short period since the abolition of slavery. These achievements "were taken by the New Africans as lessons they themselves had to learn in order to forge South African modernity"; in chapter 1, Ntongela Masilela suggests that the beginnings of a film culture for black South Africans can be found in the New African Movement. Solomon T. Plaatje, one of the founders of the movement, began showing documentary films about the achievements of the New Negroes in the United States, while his successors wrote about, extolled the virtues of, and poked fun at films that, often, they were not even permitted to see.

The New African Movement's failure to construct a national culture was due to its political defeat by the reactionary forces of white nationalism and white supremacy. Although 1994 represents a political triumph, it is questionable whether this turning point in South African history has been accompanied by commensurate intellectual and cultural achievements. Yet South Africa's present may find a dialectical connection with the past. Contemporary South African film practice and scholarship could certainly find a place for the past in the present.

In chapter 2, Bhekizizwe Peterson examines another site where early black film culture was being forged, here largely at the instigation of whites. Focusing on the period from 1920 to 1940, Peterson delves into how the promotion of cinema for blacks in South Africa was enmeshed in a larger social project of "moralizing" the leisure time of urban Africans. The discussion reveals how missionaries sought to instill "wholesome" cultural attitudes in blacks and how cinema was ambiguously a part of this exercise. While discouraging a *marabi* culture, which was organized around informal support systems, music, and parties and also involved liquor and prostitution, film was regarded as an agency of instruction that, as a visual medium, could reach the illiterate. At the same time, however, the visual nature of film aroused anxiety over the "negative" impact "bioscopes" might have on the morals of Africans. The historical and cultural contingencies and malleability that seemed to mark life in Johannesburg apparently confirmed the dangers and "diseases" of the city, as far as missionaries were concerned. They instead turned, in their writings and cinema, to fixing African identities, projecting them backward into the past by casting them in ethnographic templates.

Part two, "Cinema before and under Apartheid," opens with Edwin Hees's "The Birth of a Nation: Contextualizing *De Voortrekkers* (1916)." One of South Africa's first historical features, *De Voortrekkers* has often been likened, in passing, to D. W. Griffith's *The Birth of a Nation* (1915), as its epic scale and racist premises mirror those of the American film. Hees develops the comparison by placing the South African film in the social, cultural, and political context of the post–Anglo-Boer War period of reconstruction and, more specifically, the era of reconciliation politics in which a settlement was reached between the English and Afrikaners after the establishment of Union in 1910. The Act of Union deliberately excluded black South Africans from political participation, and some of the effects of growing black resistance politics on the film are considered. The chapter traces the way the film's screenwriter, Gustav Preller, selectively manipulated the history of the migration of Dutch farmers into the interior in the 1830s, in some ways even distorting his own pro-Afrikaner version of the myth of the Great Trek in what was, in effect, a nation-building enterprise. As in *The Birth of a Nation*, the defeat and suppression of black peoples is seen as the moment when a new nation is born.

No work of twentieth-century South African literature looms larger than Alan Paton's novel *Cry, the Beloved Country,* first published in 1948. The novel has been translated into many languages and sold millions of copies. It has also appeared in two cinematic versions, one released in 1951 and the other in 1995, both with important international casts. Both versions were generally credited with being faithful to the novel (Crowther 1952; Holden 1995); curiously, the first cinematic rendition was lauded by D. F. Malan, then prime minister and apartheid stalwart, the second by Nelson Mandela. To what forces can we attribute the staying power of this story and its ability to attract varied audiences? In chapter 4, Mark Beittel examines these two films as well as their reception and significance within the larger arena of South African cinema and politics. In comparing the two versions of the film, Beittel delves into the political context in which each was made and the meanings each took on in its time; the chapter also explores the differing narrative approaches each film takes to the 1948 novel. The comparison is useful not so much to see how each film interprets the book, but rather to see how these interpretations function culturally in the two different political and historical contexts that produced them.

In chapter 5, "*Come Back, Africa*: Black Claims on 'White' Cities," Isabel Balseiro examines a pivotal film in the history of South African cinematography. American director Lionel Rogosin's *Come Back, Africa* (1959), somewhere between fiction film and documentary, is a striking account of black urban life in the early years of apartheid. Filmed clandestinely in Johannesburg and Sophiatown in 1958, *Come Back, Africa* was perhaps the first feature film made with black South African scriptwriters (Sophiatown intellectuals Lewis Nkosi and Bloke Modisane wrote the 1958 script with Rogosin) and the only film from this period to treat urbanization from a black perspective. *Come Back, Africa* offers a glimpse at the formation, and affirmation, of a new African urban identity irrevocably severed from its rural origins. The film revolves around the experiences of Zacharia, a rural migrant to Johannesburg whose life tragically crosses paths with that of a local Sophiatown *tsotsi,* or gangster, and highlights the interlocking spheres of rural and urban identities.

One could argue that this book is mostly about the prehistory of South African cinema, about the "cinema of occupation," but to do so would imply a negation of the work already achieved. Worse yet, to speak about a "prehistory" raises the question: when does one get to the history? If the answer is that 1994, when the first democratic elections were held, is indeed the year zero, would this not imply complicity with the racialized politics apartheid sought to entrench so firmly in the country's psyche? If white nationalism wreaked havoc on the cultural production of South Africa in the predemocratic phase, might black nationalism not threaten to do the same in the postapartheid era? White nationalism—Afrikaner and British alike—has indeed debilitated filmic practice in the country from its inception by firmly grounding its ideological perspective in ethnocentrism. Present-day cinema in South Africa, one could argue, is what it is because of this. But not only that. Should a "true South African cinema" be one where the means of production are in the hands of the majority of South Africans—or, at the very least, in the hands of an intellectual black elite that claims to represent the interests of that majority more persuasively than has hitherto been the case? If the answer is yes, would it follow that "black films" would then be made? And would "black films," by virtue of being made by blacks, fit the bill of being part of a South African national cinema?[3]

South Africa won its freedom from white rule decades after nearly every other country on the continent and in unique circumstances. Africa changed dramatically during these decades, and so did cinema. In part 3 of this book, Jacqueline Maingard and Lucia Saks examine the idea of a national cinema in South Africa. A national cinema? For Maingard, at least, no such thing exists. Why, then, frame South African film and television as national? As she answers, and Saks would seem to concur, "democracy [or, for Saks, something we could at least call a new body politic] is being made in South Africa and is mediated through the images presented in film and on television." Cinema, as Saks notes, is enmeshed in the very idea of modernity, and in talk of an African Renaissance—whatever one takes that to mean—film is clearly a vital point of reference.

Jacqueline Maingard's "Framing South African National Cinema and Television" weaves back and forth between, on the one hand, larger ideas about cinema and the nation, policies in relation to cinema, and the idea of the "speaking subject" and of "voice" in documentary film and, on the other, a more specific analysis of documentaries made by

Video News Services (later known as Afrovision) and a series entitled *Ordinary People* produced by Mail and Guardian Television. A number of assumptions regarding national cinema and television in South Africa underlies her chapter. The first is that the boundaries between documentary and fiction film have become increasingly blurred. The second is that film and television are strongly linked. This is true universally, with films made as cinema being shown on television and films being made expressly for television. The third assumption is that there is no clear division between the apartheid era and postapartheid democracy. While there are moments and events that delineate points in history signifying change, there are ways beyond time in which, in the experience of life in South Africa, the fault lines of history overlap: in the 1980s the term "postapartheid" attempted to reach beyond apartheid and described the actions and movements toward it; in the early 1990s one spoke of the "transitional period," the historical interregnum in the political processes initiated and developed toward the first democratic elections in 1994; now there is talk of "democracy." But none of these are clearly demarcated and lines of these pasts cross through and are entangled with the present. Ultimately, Maingard views national film and television in South Africa from within a contemporary perspective, rather than reaching back to cinemas of the past.

But what about the future? What is the context in which a South African cinema might emerge? What is the role of the state, and what is the role of the market? How might a "cinema of its own" be legitimated in South Africa and where might black empowerment figure in its creation? What is the relationship of South African cinema to African cinema as a whole and to global notions of modernity? Is there any more value in discussing *an* African cinema than in debating *a* European cinema? And what is the point of promoting cinema when people lack adequate housing, health care, and nutrition? In "The Race for Representation: New Viewsites for Change in South African Cinema," Lucia Saks takes up these questions, suggesting that the country's cinema can usefully be viewed from three sites: first, by examining the role of the state, the market, and the independent filmmaker; second, through defining the problems and dilemmas of expressing cinema in a way that aims to carry the aspirations of an emerging and very diverse nation; and, third, by considering the intricacies of didacticism and pragmatism in the larger context of African cinema, or cinemas.

Cinema is a clearly less spontaneous, more capital-intensive form of art than, say, writing or painting, and the contours of cinema in South Africa have been shaped, in part, by the competing aspirations of diverse forces within the state and the market. It is thus no wonder that South Africa's *White Paper on the Film Industry* brings together the "fighting rhetoric one has come to associate with postcolonial academese with phrases that might be found in a reader on neoliberal economic policy," as Saks puts it. Between these contending forces of the state and the market figure, of course, the filmmakers themselves and the viewers—or those who might be viewers, if only all South Africans were participants in that form of modern life in which cinema has emerged as such an important icon.

The transition into democracy signals a shift from an emphasis on racial politics in South African film criticism. Questions of sexuality, for example, become foremost political questions and can no longer be ignored. Under the new dispensation, women's and gay rights have been institutionalized in the constitution. This alone politicizes gender issues. The constitution openly acknowledges that both groups in South Africa have in the past been treated differentially, and that, in this differential treatment, black women experienced apartheid policies and laws at their worst. Filmmakers now must take up the challenge and the initiative to demonstrate how black women are marginalized by and suffer under both white rule and discriminatory treatment at the hands of black men themselves. For South African filmmakers and scholars who claim to be radical, questions of sexuality and gender must be on the agenda. Releasing "black sexuality and gender portrayals from colonial, apartheid, and patriarchal imaginaries," to borrow from Kgafela oa Magogodi (whose chapter is discussed below), ought to be prioritized, most pressingly in terms of what it means for women and gays.

Part four, "Into the New South Africa," opens with a chapter by Laura Twiggs that examines early film practice in democratic South Africa, in particular Les Blair's *Jump the Gun* (1996). The film, Twiggs argues, suggests a model that could be revolutionary for the cinematic representation of women and for understanding the nexus between how women are represented by men and how they choose to represent each other and themselves. It also could point the way toward a criticism that incorporates differences of class and race at the same time as gender. When analyzed in the context of feminist psychoanalytical film criticism, *Jump the Gun* calls into question the spectator-text relationship based on the spectator's identification with the "male gaze."

Set in Johannesburg after the 1994 elections, the film exhibits a sociohistorical awareness far more progressive than any South African predecessors that have treated relationships between black and white characters. Until that time, in Twiggs's view, only films that focused on black people showed a degree of contextual awareness, yet seldom were they concerned with issues of gender representation or with any serious exploration of relationships between the races. *Jump the Gun* proposes a forward movement, a progression that is applicable not only to the South Africa represented in the visual text but to the country beyond the film. Its representational inclusion of the black male gaze, its representations of black (and specifically black women's) sexuality, its encouraging of the spectator to break away from an identification with the "male gaze," and its representations of interracial hetero- and homosexuality distinguish *Jump the Gun* from previous work. These features separate it too from any parallels between its representation of black women and the homogenizing "blind spots" in Western feminist discourse that too often lead to the suppression of black women's voices.

This last section ends with Kgafela oa Magogodi's "Sexuality, Power, and the Black Body in *Mapantsula* and *Fools*." Made during the political upheavals and racial tensions of the late 1980s, *Mapantsula* (1988) gave short shrift to the struggles of women in South Africa, and most criticism of the film has sidestepped the question of gender, according to Magogodi. *Fools* (1997), on the other hand, made after the end of apartheid, delves explicitly into the relationship between racism and sexism. Based on the eponymous story by Njabulo Ndebele, *Fools* tells the disturbing tale of a black teacher who rapes and impregnates one of his township pupils. The act, though set against the backdrop of pervasive state violence in the late 1980s, is not politically motivated per se, but it hints at the consequences of political and other forms of oppression, with the schoolteacher lashing out against one who is even more powerless than himself.

The teacher's violent act of rape, Magogodi suggests, needs to be seen, on one level, as symptomatic of the system of patriarchy in townships, where women's voices have traditionally been silenced. On another level, the film exposes the emasculation of the black man, himself subject to repressive white authority. During apartheid, notions of black masculinity often were built on female oppression. In fact, both *Mapantsula* and *Fools* raise the gendered metaphors that were born out of black nationalist discourse. Magogodi's analysis probes the idea that African nationalism has been constructed around masculinity, with the success or failure of the nation figuring around virility or the lack thereof. If, in nationalist parlance, Africa has been referred to as "Mother Africa" and colonialism has been understood as the political rape of the continent, the idea of the female body as victim continues to play a role in this construction of history. Magogodi persuasively argues that the sexual symbolism used to define the colonial encounter finds its counterpart in African nationalist rhetoric, which equates the lack of freedom to femininity. If political conquest over Africans by Europeans was marked by violence committed over the bodies of the conquered, women all too frequently bore the brunt of domination. The gendered metaphors Magogodi decries in *Mapantsula* and *Fools* call for a collectivity among women. As long as patriarchy remains dominant, as long as women continue to be violated, hope for social transformation will remain stunted. Historically oppressed groups, like women and gays, as the constitution legislates, must be equal partners in shaping the course of a new South Africa.

The book concludes with an afterword, a travel diary of three journeys to Zimbabwe and three to South Africa by Ethiopian filmmaker Haile Gerima, which sharply critiques cinematic practices in the region. Written from the perspective of a black director committed not to partisan politics but to people's need to tell their own stories, the essay spares no one: not the liberals who pretend to adapt to change, not the black artists whose creativity becomes curtailed by financial interests, not the nouveau riche bureaucrats who fight over jurisdiction of film festivals, not the foreign white producers who seek to mandate ideological content. At the crux of Gerima's argument lie a number of claims: in the South African context, nonracial cinema is an impossibility; white South African filmmakers, after almost half a century of benefiting from apartheid privileges, need to put their own artistic projects on hold and focus on the production, financing, and overall support of filmmaking by black South Africans; newly independent states cannot expect artists to be their propaganda puppets. Instead, black filmmakers need to express visually the long-repressed individual stories that make up a community. In a democratic and technologically advanced South Africa, filmmakers must recognize their historical debts, Gerima suggests, and lead the cultural struggle toward a continental African cinema aesthetic.

Lewis Nkosi makes an acute observation in the documentary *In Darkest Hollywood* (1993) that in all probability will influence the future reconstruction of South African intellectual and cultural history: "Although everyone agrees that apartheid is very much dead, the struggle for political and cultural autonomy would have been in vain if the black majority continues to be represented only by even well meaning whites. . . . we need blacks to recover our own history and represent it ourselves in the ways we want to become." This statement is in synchrony with an essay recently written by another major member of the Sophiatown Renaissance, Es'kia Mphahlele (forthcoming):

> South African white scholars as a cultural establishment, too, have until very recently generally failed to acknowledge the black man's humanity. They have lacked the "intellectual curiosity, a desire to analyze and understand the unique aspects of his culture and to study the answers he has offered to the timeless problems of the universe." White South African scholars footnote one another, have colonized the research territory, are endowed with bags of funding from the white cultural and financial establishments. . . . The crisis of the Black intelligentsia in South Africa as I see it is threefold: (a) because of our history of racism and dispossession, the Talented Tenth (to use W. E. B. Du Bois's famous phrase quoted by Gates [1989]) is still a tiny minority. In turn it has never been unified, nor strong, nor economically independent to be of much use to the lower underclass; (b) a significant portion of it has been preoccupied with resistance politics and keeping our political movements in shape; all of which has sapped their energy; (c) it is an intelligentsia without any capacity to accumulate capital and property and thus become a middle class after the pattern of its counterpart in the western world; a middle class on someone else's terms rather than on its own, which only means between the prosperous sheltered white population and its governing machine at the top and the dispossessed class; a middle class without any power to influence the political equation short of a revolution. . . . Black nationalism, otherwise called African nationalism, Black consciousness, are not dead issues in South Africa, contrary to appearances, riddled though they are with massive ambivalence among us. Yet the Black intellectual in South Africa is pathetically absent from the debate on nationalism and integrationism. Nor is he offering any guide as a basis for understanding or exploring the issues among the populace.

The need that both Nkosi and Mphahlele express unequivocally is not being met and will never be met until blacks in South Africa have in their hands the cultural means of its production. A new South African cinema will not materialize until the hegemonic power that controls artistic production is broken. Notwithstanding historical failures, such as the fact that a vigorous cinema did not flourish in exile, we suggest that South African cinema may be able to move forward through a gaze back to the pivotal, if largely ignored, role blacks have had in it from its beginnings. The current African Renaissance then may be seen as a call for completion of the modernist project started by the New African Movement. Although there was never unanimity among the major intellectuals of the New African Movement regarding the definitive nature of a modern national culture, they were in agreement concerning its components: the integration of modernity and tradition, the correspondence between the new and the old, the points of intersection between Africanism and Europeanism, the coexistence of African and European languages, and the mixture of revolutionary impulses and evolutionary imperatives. In other words, to the New Africans the making of a national culture was a dynamic project, defined by constant search and experimentation rather than certitudes. In this context, the New African Movement provides a historical precedent of national culture as a collective experiment. In our view, South African film practice, with its scholarship, "belongs to the historical sequence of objects" that should be in synchrony with the intellectual achievements and expressive forms attained by the New Africans.

Notes

1. By "black South Africans," we mean South Africans of all heritages except exclusively European.

2. Like the earlier generations of New African intellectuals within the New African Movement, such as R. V. Selope Thema, H. I. E. Dhlomo, and H. Selby Msimang, Lewis Nkosi was preoccupied with the historical ideas of the "New African" (see Nkosi 1981).

3. The question of what constitutes "black films" has preoccupied many scholars. See, for example, Martin 1995; Reid 1993; Lott 1991; Mercer 1988; Yearwood 1982; and Cripps 1979. For commentary on this subject in the South African context, see Tomaselli 1993.

PART 1

Historical Perspectives

1

The New African Movement and the Beginnings of Film Culture in South Africa

Ntongela Masilela

Film is an expression of the modernist experience in South Africa, and making sense of the country's film culture requires an awareness of the intellectual movements that informed its early reception and practice. The Sophiatown Renaissance, roughly bracketed by the Defiance Campaign of 1952 and the Sharpeville Massacre of 1960,[1] was, according to some, the apogee of modernist sensibility in South Africa; yet I would suggest that the Sophiatown Renaissance has been distinctly overvalued in relation to other cultural movements preceding it, in particular the New African Movement, of which the Sophiatown Renaissance can be seen as but the closing chapter. The beginnings of a film culture in South Africa rest partially on this vitally important—but little understood—intellectual history.

The New African Movement emerged a few years after the Anglo-Boer War of 1899–1902. The ideas of a "New Africa," a "New South Africa," and the "New African" were first theorized and articulated in the newspaper *Umteteli wa Bantu* (The Mouthpiece of the Native Peoples), on whose pages the first serious engagement with film culture by an African intellectual was mentioned. Solomon T. Plaatje, one of the founders of the New African Movement, was featured for showing documentary films about the achievements of the New Negroes in the United States. In addition to Plaatje, stalwarts of the New African Movement included Jordan Ngubane, R. V. Selope Thema, Allan Kirkland Soga, H. I. E. Dhlomo, Gerard Sekoto, and Rueben Caluza.[2] Inasmuch as the Sophiatown Renaissance is incomprehensible without the figures of the New African Movement, film culture in South Africa, as hinted at in the introduction, cannot be fully apprehended without exploring further the entrance of European modernity into African history. This chapter endeavors to make visible the beginnings of an African modernity and a film culture tradition among Africans.

The leading thinkers of the New African Movement were profoundly impressed by what the New Negroes had achieved in the United States in the short period since their emancipation in 1865. The achievements of the New Negro intelligentsia were taken by the New Africans as lessons they themselves had to learn in order to forge South African modernity. The New African was keenly interested in the trajectory of the New Negro. Indeed, the New Negro dominated the imagination of the New African. [3]

Beginning in the 1880s, the African intelligentsia around King William's Town and Alice in the Cape Colony—Walter Rubusana, Elijah Makiwane, Pambani Mzimba, John Tengo Jabavu, and others—debated the issue of how to appropriate the historical lessons of the New Negro modernist experience in the Lovedale Literary Society and in the Native Educational Association. These two organizations had been formed to express the African determination to participate fully in the making of modernity. Many of the principal essays touching on the "making of the new" were published in John Tengo Jabavu's newspaper, *Imvo Zabantsundu* (African Opinion). Newspapers founded later by other New African intellectuals continued to focus on the issue of constructing modernity in one form or another. For instance, in an anonymous article entitled "Booker T. Washington," published on 12 November 1901 in *Izwi Labantu* (The Voice of the People), we find the following statement: "There are many things in the life of this man both interesting and applicable to the natives of South Africa. Particularly is his attitude on the subject of manual labour to be commended to the serious consideration of our people. Mr. Washington lays great stress on work, and his latest utterances on this subject to the American negros can be fitly applied to our position in this country." [4] As though not to be outdone, a newer newspaper, *Izwe La Kiti* (Our Nation), under the management of Mark Radebe Sr., published a long sympathetic report (30 October 1912) on the International Congress on the Negro that Booker T. Washington had organized in Tuskegee in April 1912. [5] An editorial in Abdullah Abdurahman's newspaper, *A.P.O.*, leaned toward the position that there was not very much that the Old African could learn from the Old Negro, there being very little in common between them, given that the former lived in reserves and was governed by native customs and tribal law while the latter lived along the lines of white civilization and spoke English as his native language (*A.P.O.*, 12 February 1910). The paper soon took an abrupt turn, however, extolling the closeness between the New Negro and the New African.[6]

Harold Cressy, a brilliant intellectual who died tragically while still young, was among the first New Africans to address the historical rationale of New Africans identifying with the New Negroes. In a lecture entitled "On the Rise of the American Negro as a Landowner," published in *A.P.O.* on 25 March 1911, he made the acute observation: "In America, no people make a greater study of the Negro than the Negro himself. The same cannot be said of the Coloured and the Native races in South Africa." While the New Negro was preoccupied with race pride, national feeling, a study of the self, and a deep concern with the welfare of the race, there was a marked absence of this among the New Africans. Cressy made this observation approximately a year before the founding of the South African Native National Congress (later known as the African National Congress).

In his call for the African people to come together to found the South African Native National Congress, made a few months after Harold Cressy's lecture, Pixley ka Isaka Seme (*Tsala ea Becoana* [The Friend of Bechuana], 28 October 1911) echoed some of the issues raised by Cressy that had been preoccupying other New African intellectuals:

> There is to-day among all races and men a general desire for progress, and for co-operation, because co-operation will facilitate and secure that progress. . . . We are the last among all the nations of the earth to discover the priceless jewels of co-operation, and for this reason the great gifts of civilisation are least known among us to-day. I repeat, co-operation is the key and the watchword which opens the door, the everlasting door which leads into progress and all national success. The greatest success shall come when man shall have learned to co-operate, not only with his own kith and kin but with all peoples and with all life.

What better means of bringing about cooperation and progress among African people than national feeling, a study of the self, and race pride? In fact, these ideas were already present in Pixley ka Isaka Seme's landmark essay of 1906, in which he wrote:

> Yes, the regeneration of Africa belongs to this new and powerful period! By this term, regeneration, I wish to be understood to mean *the entrance into a new life,* embracing the diverse phases of a higher, complex existence. The basic factor, which assures their regeneration, *resides in the awakened race-consciousness.* This gives them a clear perception of their elemental needs and of their underdeveloped powers.

This entrance into modernity defined by a particular historical consciousness was paramount for successive generations of New Africans.

For Solomon T. Plaatje, this regeneration was inseparable from learning what the New Negroes had achieved within U. S. modernity, as his essay of 1904, "Negro Question" (*Koranta ea Becoana,* 7 September), amply demonstrates. He begins his reflections with the statement, "Among many important topics of today there is nothing more important than this one [the Negro question]." This is clearly an allusion to the famous sentence in W. E. B. Du Bois's *The Souls of Black Folk* (1989 [1903]), which had appeared the previous year: "The problem of the Twentieth Century is the problem of the color-line." Plaatje's allusion indicates his belief that there were profound affinities between the process through which the New Negro intervened in the construction of U.S. modernity and the means by which the New African should participate in the newly emergent South African modernity. The "Negro question" can be read as an incentive for the New Africans to emulate the New Negroes. Plaatje posits the historical similarities and the cultural and intellectual affinities among black people all over the world, which make understandable why the New Africans in South Africa would be impressed with the achievements and the cultural inventiveness of the New Negroes. What makes Plaatje's intervention crucial in the discourse between the two peoples on either side of the Atlantic is that whereas other New Africans were largely content with the emotive forms of this sense of historical identification, he appraised it as an intellectual process with historical resonance. This capacity to look at processes and discern their deeper historical context brought Plaatje to the forefront of the New African Movement.

It was Plaatje, as editor of *Tsala ea Becoana,* and F. Z. S. Peregrino, a Ghanian resident in Cape Town and editor of the newspaper *South African Spectator,* who in 1904 established the South African Native Press Association, which was modeled on the Negro Press Association in the United States. The other New African intellectual in the organization was its president, Allan Kirkland Soga, editor of *Izwi Labantu.* Plaatje's biographer, Brian Willan (cited in Plaatje 1997: 82), states that the constitution of the organization was in all probability written by Plaatje. It reads:

> The principles of this association will be, to encourage and to seek to aid all who are engaged in the laudable work of diffusing knowledge and in legitimate educational work among the Natives of South Africa, to seek to cooperate with the Government in the solution of the many difficult race problems by which we are confronted, and to help to bring about

understanding, and to establish amiable relations between the various Governments of South Africa, and the Native population.

It was this idea of transforming the African people into New Africans through knowledge and education that had been so central to Plaatje's concerns in *Tsala ea Becoana* (later renamed *Tsala ea Batho* [The Friend of the People]), and this idea that was to be central in his introduction of film culture among New Africans. Solomon T. Plaatje introduced film form to the New Africans as a pedagogical instrument compatible with a Christian civilizational interpretation of modernity. His decision to show films about the achievements of the New Negro was featured prominently in *Umteteli wa Bantu*.[7]

Plaatje's first trip abroad, from June 1914 to February 1917, had been confined mainly to Britain—he went as part of the South African Native National Congress (SANNC) delegation to protest the Natives' Land Act of 1913 to the British government. This visit resulted in the publication of *Native Life in South Africa* in London in 1916. After his second trip abroad with an SANNC delegation to England, from July 1919 to September 1920, Plaatje went to the United States, returning to South Africa in November 1923.[8]

Within a few months of his return, Plaatje traveled to the major cities of the country, showing short documentary films detailing what the New Negroes had achieved and were achieving, especially in the realm of education. What R. V. Selope Thema intended to accomplish through his writings in *Umteteli wa Bantu,* Solomon T. Plaatje aimed to realize through visual culture: to impart the social responsibilities entailed in the construction of modernity in South Africa.

Plaatje seems to have traveled the country for several years showing his "bioscope," as the exhibition was called.[9] An anonymous article entitled "The Plaatje Bioscope" was published in *Umteteli wa Bantu* on 5 December 1925:

> Mr. Plaatje was complimented on the excellence of his Show, and explained that many of his "topicals" were given him by Mr. Henry Ford, of motor car fame. Negro industrial films were given him by Dr. Moton of Tuskegee, while English and South African pictures were a gift by Mr. I. R. Grimmer of Kimberley. The De Beers Company helped Mr. Plaatje to acquire a portable generator which enables him to show cinema pictures at Native kraals and other places where electric light is not available.

Plaatje introduced two innovations with his bioscope: he complemented his pedagogical films with others that were for entertainment, and he did not restrict his audiences to Africans—"prominent Europeans" also attended his shows.

Plaatje's project of introducing some of the fundamental principles and achievements of modernity to Africans through film was perhaps destined to failure because of the activities of the American Mission Board. Through its leading ideologues, Dr. F. B. Bridgman and the Reverend Ray Phillips, the organization was already introducing films in the mining compounds of Johannesburg—films meant as entertainment but also as an instrument of white superiority and a means of controlling the morals of Africans (see chapter 2 in this volume and an anonymous article entitled "The Cinema Influence," *Umteteli wa Bantu*, 7 July 1923). Phillips and Bridgman called for the censorship of certain American films to African audiences, claiming Africans lacked the sophistication to interpret appropriately what they saw on the screen. Their primary concern, since they believed Africans did not possess the intelligence of Europeans, was to control the way Africans understood European civilization: only the good side of this civilization should be shown so that Africans would admit and submit to its superiority.

Phillips and Bridgman understood, as Plaatje did, the power of film to educate Africans—the difference being that Plaatje believed in the open enlightenment of the imagination through film whereas Phillips and Bridgman saw cinema as a controlling instrument. They believed in the necessity of "moralising the leisure time of the Natives" because otherwise the forces of modernity, which were beyond Africans' understanding, would corrupt their innocence and naïveté into haughtiness and criminality.[10] Phillips and Bridgman imported American films such as *Life of Christ* to prevent the awakening historical consciousness of Africans to the complexities of modernity. This process of pacification through film was undertaken at the same time that Phillips began writing a column in *Umteteli wa Bantu* on religious matters, with the same objectives.

Although they cannot be held directly responsible for the widespread feeling in white government circles that film was corrupting the African, Phillips and Bridgman's preoccupation with policing the African imagination sowed the seeds of distrust and fear, as can be observed from the following anonymous article published on 22 October 1926 in *Ilanga lase Natal*:

A new menace to European prestige has been discovered in the indiscriminate exhibition of films to Natives. *The Natal Witness* [a "white" Durban newspaper] is rousing public opinion to seriously consider the question whether a certain class of film called the social Drama should not be banned where the Native may attend. It is shown the witnessing of certain scenes depicting the seamy side in the life of the Europeans must have, and is already having an indescribable effect upon the Native mind. . . . A few are beginning to be aware that the white man is liable to err like the rest of humanity and their skins do not make them angelic.

Warning of the grave consequences this might entail, the author called for more teaching of Christian principles to the "child races" to counter the possible erosion of respect for European culture by New Africans.

Aware of the power of film to enlighten and inform, Solomon T. Plaatje (*Umteteli wa Bantu,* 18 July 1931) was equally aware of its possible detrimental effect. Vigorously protesting the showing of D. W. Griffith's *The Birth of a Nation* (1915) at the Johannesburg Town Hall, he asked why South Africa should show a film that was so hateful toward black people when in many parts of the United States, including certain southern states, it had been banned:

> The picture is based on *The Clansman* by Thomas Dixon, the avowed champion of American Negrophobes. It holds the abolitionists up to ridicule and glorifies the early outrages of the Ku Klux Klan. . . . The same film tried to sneak into Boston ten years ago, while I was there, and a public meeting of protest was called on the day of the show. . . . Some of us who saw it in England are surprised at the alleged Immortal Masterpiece. Ugly black peril scenes are shown until the emotions of white people are worked up to fever heat. Then follow masked night-riders who are vigorously applauded by the audience as they set out on the trail of Negroes.

Not only was this representation a distortion of American history during Reconstruction, it profoundly offended Plaatje who, like all the New African intellectuals, deeply admired the New Negroes:

> With 150,000 people in the centre of New York, Harlem is easily the biggest African city on earth. They own magnificent churches with gorgeous pipe-organs and beautiful choirs and a number of glittering chemists and barber shops and prosperous real-estate agencies all operated by Negroes. They have many splendid and well-furnished homes, with musical instruments (which the members of the family manipulate with remarkable skill), and commodious bathrooms replete with hot and cold water taps. . . . It was amazing to see the crowds of clean and well-dressed black men and women, issuing from the underground stations in the blare of the electric lights at night, and pouring through the streets of Harlem like Londoners in Oxford Street. (Plaatje 1997: 292–93)[11]

21

This modernity of the New Negroes, which Plaatje had personally experienced, was denied by showings of *The Birth of a Nation,* a film about an earlier period.

Solomon T. Plaatje's role in the dissemination of film culture in South Africa was profound; so much so that in 1933, a year after his death and nearly a decade after his tours of the country with films showcasing the achievements of the New Negro, the *Bantu World,* then the largest African weekly, made a similar tour, though it concentrated on rural areas (see the article published under the pseudonym "Joe" in *Bantu World,* 9 December 1933).

The appreciation of film culture extended even to those New Africans who had not initially embraced cinema. One of these was H. I. E. Dhlomo, arguably the greatest advocate of modernity in South Africa (see Masilela forthcoming a). Dhlomo's first comments concerning film culture, found in his voluminous writings in *Ilanga lase Natal* from 1943 to 1955, was not on the aesthetics of film form but rather on censorship and its psychological impact. This underscores the fact that New African Movement intellectuals and artists, from Pixley ka Isaka Seme through Dhlomo himself to Gerard Sekoto, had not as yet developed a historical consciousness of film as an art form. Dhlomo had a deep sensibility for drama, theater, opera, European classical music, and poetry. It was only with Sophiatown Renaissance writers like Lewis Nkosi, Bloke Modisane, and Ezekiel Mphahlele, or with artists like Lionel Ngakane, that a historical consciousness for cinema began to emerge. Given that in the United States serious New Negro film criticism emerged only in the 1930s with Sterling Brown's meditation on the work of Oscar Micheaux, the belated awakening to film aesthetics in the South African context is not surprising.

Dhlomo's first writing on the subject was a condemnation of the stricter and more elaborate censorship the government had imposed in 1947 concerning the categories of films that Africans were allowed to see. Ridiculing the government's argument that American films were making Africans social misfits and susceptible to having a low opinion of Europeans, he argued that although films may influence the behavior of individuals, it was the environment, the social and economic conditions, that was the more crucial determinant. In a sharp response, Dhlomo, under the alias of Busy Bee *(Ilanga Lase Natal,* 26 July 1947), noted: "A healthy mind in a healthy body in a healthy home in a healthy environment can see hundreds of gangster films and think of them as exciting or dull entertainment, without once thinking of emulating them. It is the social conditions that produce the criminal." In another context, under the same alias, he vehemently objected to Indians, Europeans, and coloreds being allowed to see certain films that were forbidden to Africans: "We believe that the African responds to the cinema as other human beings do. The subject as to whether the cinema has good or harmful effects on the character, morals and thought of the young or the old is a matter of serious research" (*Ilanga Lase Natal,* 7 April 1951).

The discrimination against Africans in relation to world film culture affected Dhlomo personally:

> One day you will arrive with your lady friend all spick and span or accompanied by many visitors whom you are entertaining, only to find that "No Natives" are allowed to see the picture that night. Your group might include graduates and wealthy African businessmen, but that will not help. As you stand helpless and humiliated, the disdainful glances and even the sarcastic smiles of non-African patrons will drive you mad.

On the two occasions when Dhlomo was in a position to view classic films, he made them the objects of his extraordinary critical imagination. It was not accidental that both were film versions by Laurence Olivier of Shakespeare's plays; as a playwright who considered the English bard the high point of human civilization, Dhlomo could only have been exhilarated by such an opportunity. Arguably these critical texts represent the founding moment of African film criticism within the New African Movement. In a way, the films, rather than being important in themselves as aesthetic forms to be studied, were a pretext for philosophical meditations on other matters.

Dhlomo begins by observing that segregation and discrimination made it practically impossible for Africans to view a film like Olivier's *Henry V.* He further notes that Africans were also barred from concerts and performances by great overseas artists. Dhlomo finds it tragic that African writers, artists, and intellectuals were prevented from experiencing work that could inspire them. Such discriminatory practices had the added consequence of diminishing the cultural and intellectual life of the country. For Dhlomo, this partly explained the presence of only a few writers and artists of international stature in South Africa. In an anonymous editorial, bearing Dhlomo's imprint, on Olivier's *Henry V,* the author confirms what Dhlomo had theorized a decade earlier, in the 1930s, as he was writing his major plays: that great plays are in themselves great literature and should be read as such, rather than experienced only in stage performance.[12] Since many plays are never staged, to wait until they are performed is to miss out on reading great literature. Although affirming his support for Kantian aesthetics, Dhlomo believed that one of the fundamental lessons Shakespeare teaches an artist is that the common people are the soil and soul of art. He urged African artists, writers, and thinkers to find material and inspiration in the New African masses.

Approximately three years after viewing *Henry V,* Dhlomo was to use Laurence Olivier's film version of Shakespeare's *Hamlet* in another editorial to reflect on the relationship between tradition and modernity and its possible ramifications in South Africa. To Dhlomo the poetic nature and the philosophical themes resonating in Olivier's *Hamlet* prove the unity of humanity, despite the divisiveness and hatred sown by political practices. The representation of the philosophy of human drama in the work of Shakespeare, Chaucer, Dante, Goethe, and other masters is applicable in all cultures and societies, Dhlomo believed. The singular achievement of Olivier's *Hamlet,* he wrote in an unsigned article in *Ilanga lase Natal* dated 18 September 1948, was to bring to the forefront the universality of great art:

> The mere fact of focussing the mind of the modern man to the beauty and the message of the great classics, is a necessary, wise and healthy thing. It is a fact that some of our troubles are the result of our neglecting some of the best things of the past. So-called primitive and elemental things . . . are the stuff of originality, progress and new forms of thought. . . . It is these and other truths that great classics like *Hamlet* teach and remind us. . . . [T]he whole Shakespearean idea of tragedy is that despite whatever Power that might be directing our lives, we too have a hand in it. We have our part to play. This is a scientific view showing that by understanding nature and himself Man can do much for himself. In a world torn by troubles and misery, this is an important message.

Africans in South Africa, in other words, could challenge white oppression by constructing a counternarrative, instead of believing that they were fated to be oppressed forever. Clearly Dhlomo was using film for purposes of reflection on the philosophy of history rather than looking at it in a Kantian mode, *Ding an sich.*

It was not until the emergence of the Sophiatown Renaissance that intellectuals began to examine film as an artistic object in and of itself. Although the historical and cultural distance is wide between Solomon T. Plaatje's effort, in the first generation of New African intellectuals, to use film as a pedagogical instrument and Bloke Modisane's effort, in the last generation of intellectual New Africanism, to articulate film as part of popular culture and entertainment, both used the African American experience as a touchstone. We have seen how Plaatje showed documentary films on Booker T. Washington's Tuskegee Institute and also how he protested the showing of *The Birth of a Nation* in an act of solidarity with the New Negro. For Bloke Modisane, according to Nkosi's article (1959) "Why 'Bloke' Bailed Out," the crucial figure was Canada Lee, the African American actor who, in the early 1950s, had taken a prominent role in the cinematic version of *Cry, the Beloved Country,* which had been shot in South Africa. After listening to a recorded interview of Canada Lee responding to questions posed by Bloke Modisane, Nkosi wrote: "The old man seemed to have sensed the hurt more deeply than any other visitor to South Africa and when he spoke of the degradation of human dignity he gave an emotional strength to these words which urged Bloke on to think that it was possible, like Lee, for human dignity to rise above the worst affronts the white people of this country were capable of giving." Canada Lee's empathetic voice had a profound impact on Bloke Modisane.

Modisane's writing on film culture in the *Golden City Post* focused mostly on the life of Hollywood stars. The idea of film criticism as a concept of historical appreciation had not, as yet, fully emerged within Sophiatown Renaissance intellectual circles; they were preoccupied with producing jazz criticism, a revolutionary undertaking given the hostility of an earlier generation of New African Movement intellectuals toward this form of music. Lewis Nkosi (1990) explained the importance of film for Bloke Modisane in his introduction to Modisane's autobiography:

> Bloke, like indeed many black writers in South Africa, was constantly irked by the barriers which prevented him from participating in the cultural experience of the country. There were moments of poignancy when the black man was constantly reminded of his position in society. In the company of whites, for instance, Bloke would join in the discussion of great films as if he had had the chance to see them. When asked if he had, in fact, seen them, he would reply rather shamefacedly that he had only read about them. They were mostly films banned to Africans.

Without the opportunity to see films, it is hardly surprising that this last generation of New Africans never fully engaged with serious film criticism. Lewis Nkosi was to explore this critical mode in appreciation of Lionel Rogosin's *Come Back, Africa,* to whose screenplay he and Bloke Modisane contributed. Both also acted in the film (see chapter 5 in this volume).

The political explanation for the absence of serious film criticism by African intellectuals is insufficient. Perhaps the historical conditions of the time dictated that African film criticism could emerge only from an encounter with films made by Africans themselves. Features such as *Jim Comes to Jo'burg* (a.k.a. *African Jim*, 1949), *Zonk* (1950), *The Magic Garden* (1951), and *Song of Africa* (1951) never elicited any critical responses from African intellectuals because, although the films had largely African casts, they were written and directed by Europeans. Typically of the early apartheid era, they were largely white films with a superficial coating of blackness.[13] Hence the silent rejection by African intellectuals.[14] This is not to say these films were unimportant; if nothing else, they have proven invaluable for capturing the social and cultural history of Africans at the height of the construction of modernity. It is no accident that *Come Back, Africa* (1959) and *Mapantsula* (1988), films about Africans in which Africans themselves played a major role in writing the screenplay, have proven to be the landmarks in the history of South African cinema. Yet they are not "black films"—whatever that means. As Fanon (1968, 212–14) rightly said: "In Africa, the native literature of the last twenty years is not a national literature but a Negro literature. . . . This historical necessity in which the men of African culture find themselves to racialize their claims and to speak more of African culture than of national culture will tend to lead them up a blind alley."

The kind of "Nite Life" column Bloke Modisane wrote in the Johannesburg-based *Golden City Post* in 1957 and 1958 was largely determined by the cultural politics of white oppression and exclusion. He responded creatively to the dilemma that history posed (it was no coincidence that he entitled his autobiography *Blame Me on History* (1990 [1963]). Modisane could not review and analyze the films he felt would enrich the cultural life of Africans, given that Africans were forbidden to see them, yet that did not stop him from writing on varied topics, from Indian film culture to Hollywood star gossip. Modisane seriously undertook to create a public sphere in the cultural politics of the 1950s. In a short article entitled "The Chinese Cheered 'Em" (6 July 1958), accompanied by a large photograph of Indian film stars, he wrote:

> "Mr. Beefcake" Nazir, idol of millions in Pakistan, gets the "unhand-me-Sir" look from sultry Sudhir. They appear together in the crackerjack film, *Baghi*, which has been flown from Pakistan as a special Eid attraction at the Khandaan Drive-In Theatre, Durban. *Baghi* snaffled the top honours at the Asian Film Festival held in Peking. The Chinese gave it the label "the finest film made in 1957." The Chinese were so impressed with this story packed with impact that they put it on in 22 cinemas simultaneously.

Writings like this were followed assiduously by a reading public that wrote to Modisane through a fan club ("Answering All Your Questions about Showbiz"). Some of the letters were published each week in his column. Modisane's example of active participation in forming a critical dialogue with the reading public partly explains why the Sophiatown Renaissance was so passionately embraced by its audience, as perhaps had never happened in South African cultural history before.[15] The Sophiatown Renaissance was experienced by audiences in the 1950s as their own particular historical creation.

The intellectual world of Modisane was altered by two invitations: one from Lionel Rogosin to assist him in the making of *Come Back, Africa* (see chapter 5) and one from an American professor he had met in Johannesburg to go to the United States. Rogosin's invitation led to Modisane's resigning from *Drum* and *Golden City Post* since neither would allow him to take a temporary leave of absence to assist in the writing of the screenplay for the film or to act in it.

In the documentary *In Darkest Hollywood* (1993), Lewis Nkosi, one of the other scriptwriters of *Come Back, Africa* along with Modisane and Rogosin, describes a moment in the making of the film that illustrates one of the major political themes of the 1950s: "In that scene in *Come Back, Africa* where we are all sitting around in the shebeen and discussing, there was still a tremendous feeling of hope that it was possible to change South Africa through a passive resistance, and through the moral force of one's argument." (This scene, discussed in chapter 5 of this volume, was wholly unscripted and involved the actors and scriptwriters, with the exception of Rogosin, simply speaking their mind.) In other words, this last intellectual generation of New Africanism still believed that rationalism, exemplified by the Enlightenment, could overcome irrational practices and obstacles. They were arguably the last generation of thinkers in South Africa to subscribe unreservedly, and perhaps uncritically, to the ideology of the Enlightenment. This subscription was reinforced by a political event that Nkosi alludes to: the Defiance Campaign of 1952.

The New African political leaders, such as Albert Luthuli, Nelson Mandela, Robert Resha, and Oliver Tambo, had initiated the Defiance Campaign believing that rationality would triumph over irrationality without the need to resort to force, what Fanon characterized as the cleansing force of revolutionary violence. Continuing with his observations, Nkosi notes: "The kind of racial cooperation exemplified in the making of *Come Back, Africa* became virtually impossible [after the Sharpeville Massacre of 1960]." The making of *Come Back, Africa* was part of the racial solidarity that had made possible the formation of the Congress of the People and the collective drafting of the Freedom Charter in 1955.

Given the echoing of these two major political events of the 1950s in the ideological makeup of *Come Back, Africa,* particularly in the discourse of the Sophiatown Renaissance intellectuals in the shebeen scene, it is no wonder that the film occupies a central position in South African film history. That shebeen scene shows the critical imagination of South Africa, not "merely" of New Africans, at its combative best. When Lewis Nkosi, in that sequence, castigates the racism-tinged hypocrisy of white liberals for their preference, in slothful ignorance of tradition, of the Old African over the New African, he is situating himself in a certain heritage of South African intellectuals. On the one hand, in this scene, as in his essay on *Come Back, Africa* and his participation in the documentary *In Darkest Hollywood,* Nkosi is following in the footsteps of Solomon T. Plaatje by using film as a pedagogical instrument. On the other hand, in discoursing on tradition and modernity, Nkosi is also upholding another aspect of a tradition that had been articulated by Xhosa intellectuals in the 1880s around John Tengo Jabavu's *Imvo Zabantsundu.* That tradition had largely begun with the pre–New African intellectual Elijah Makiwane, arguably the principal inspirer of this Xhosa cultural renaissance, when he wrote a seminal essay 26 January *(Imvo Zabantsundu)* seeking to understand why the Pondomisi were continually resisting modernity through an endless series of revolts. For both Makiwane and Lewis Nkosi, as for the African intelligentsia more generally, modernity was central to the survival of African people. And film was clearly a part of that survival.

Notes

1. The Defiance Campaign, launched in 1952 by the African National Congress (ANC) and the South African Indian Congress to defy apartheid laws, was the beginning of the triumph of the historical vision of the African National Congress Youth League within its parent organization, the African National Congress. The Youth League had been founded in 1943–44 by, among others, Anton Muziwakhe Lembede, Nelson Mandela, Oliver Tambo, Walter Sisulu, and Jordan Ngubane. The ideological struggle of the Youth League forced the ANC to adopt the program of action proposed by the youth leaguers at the 1949 annual conference. The program of action culminated in the Defiance Campaign, which, in a complicated and traumatic sense, paved the way for the great triumph of May 1994.

The Sharpeville Massacre took place in March 1960 in the midst of a protest against pass laws organized by the Pan Africanist Congress. This event led to the banning of the ANC and other nationalist political organizations, as well as to the exiling of most of the Sophiatown Renaissance writers: Ezekiel Mphahlele to Nigeria in 1957, Bloke Modisane to Britain in 1959, Alfred Hutchinson to Ghana in 1960, Lewis Nkosi to the United States in the same year, and Can Themba to Swaziland in 1963. The end of the great cultural experience and experiment known as the Sophiatown Renaissance, whose members were conscious of New African Movement ideals, coincided with the suppression of the national political practice of the ANC inside the country.

2. Elsewhere I attempt to draw the conceptual parameters of the New African Renaissance (see Masilela 1999).

3. For an in-depth study on this matter, see Masilela forthcoming b.

4. Seven years later the paper had completely changed its position, vehemently denouncing Washington in an article published on 4 February 1908: "We . . . believe Mr. Washington to be the most dangerous man in American to-day. . . . We know what the type has done for us in South Africa, the barbarian masquerading as the man of culture, a traitor at heart, ready to sell the race with Judas like treachery, and to thrive by the mess of pottage picked up from crafty white men on the ignorance and helplessness of their countrymen." This denunciation marks a shift from the ideas of Booker T. Washington to those of W. E. B. Du Bois. A cultural studies text could be written about the figure of Washington in the imagination of the New African.

5. The report lamented the fact that Booker T. Washington had prevented a presentation on Ethiopianism and on the role of African American missionaries in South Africa for fear of alienating the white South African missionaries who were attending the conference. Solomon T. Plaatje had published in a letter from Washington (*Tsala ea Becoana,* 18 July 1911) an invitation to the New Africans to participate in the conference. On 29 January 1913, *Izwe La Kiti* published an item entitled "College Trained Negroes" enthusiastically reporting a huge increase in the percentage of New Negroes attending colleges; the newspaper believed this was an example the New Africans should definitely follow.

6. The article, entitled "American and African: Two Outstanding Conclusions," lamented that no matter how much the New Africans acquired the new culture of modernity, whites still found ways of discriminating and oppressing them. In the same issue, the newspaper reprinted an essay by Booker T. Washington about his building a New South. The implied question here was, how would the "coloreds" as New Africans assist, through modernity, in building a New South Africa?

7. See, for example, the anonymous article entitled "Mr. Sol T. Plaatje's Bioscope" (*Umteteli wa Bantu,* 31 May 1924).

8. For a more detailed discussion of Plaatje's trips abroad, see Brian Willan's introductory remarks in Plaatje 1997.

29

9. A short film has been made about Plaatje's endeavors: *Come See the Bioscope* (1997).

10. For a lively discussion of this, see the anonymous article entitled "Native Leisure Hours" (*Ilanga lase Natal,* 8–15 August 1924).

11. Another indication of Plaatje's admiration for African American culture is evident in the obituary he published in 1927 of Florence Mills (*Umteteli wa Bantu,* 12 November 1927), which was in effect a celebration of New Negro Broadway musicals.

12. Most of Dhlomo's extraordinary essays on drama have been assembled in a special issue of *English in Africa* (Visser 1977).

13. Peter Davis (1996) has written a very instructive chapter on these films.

14. Curiously, however, Todd Matshikiza (1952) wrote enthusiastically of *Song of Africa:* "The most impressive musical of its kind ever made in Africa, *Song of Africa* has an entirely African cast and story. Most of the artists have never even been inside a cinema, much less had any experience of acting. The underlying theme of the film shows the influence of African tribal music on modern American jazz, and will therefore be especially interesting to those of us who study this type of music. It shows clearly that the beat of the drums of Africa was the forerunner of jazz as we know it today."

15. There was a time when Modisane threatened to quit because the audience either was not fully supportive of cultural programs or had become downright complacent. As an indication of how seriously the reading public took its historical role in the making of the Sophiatown Renaissance, several letters argued that in due course all other things would fall into place (see, for example, *Golden City Post,* 6 July 1958).

2

The Politics of Leisure during the Early Days of South African Cinema

Bhekizizwe Peterson

The introduction and promotion of cinema among the urbanized African population of the Witwatersrand has always been a complicated project. The period from 1920 to 1940 is particularly instructive since it highlights the myriad social, political, and economic variables that marked the arrival of film among urban blacks. The most sustained attempt to spread the "wholesome efficacies" of film was undertaken by missionaries and white philanthropists in a complex and wide-ranging project aimed at "moralising the leisure time" of Africans. Encompassing film, theater, music, dance, cultural and debating societies, pathfinder groups and sports, the missionary intervention in black recreation responded to what the church saw as harrowing developments in the slum yards: faced with poverty, disenfranchisement, and alienation, Africans—particularly those of the lower classes—had embarked on political campaigns and industrial action and created urban-based cultural practices that fused traditional and modern elements into striking, novel, defensive formations. This chapter examines the role of the American Mission Board (AMB) and the Reverend Ray Phillips, who headed its social work division, in laying the groundwork for a black film culture in South Africa. The endeavors of Phillips and the AMB led to the establishment of the Bantu Men's Social Centre (BMSC) and its tangential, but highly significant, interaction with the emergence of motion pictures in South Africa from 1920 to 1940.

Urbanization and Its Discontents

The initiatives around recreation on the Rand (the area situated along the Witwatersrand gold reef, including Johannesburg) came in response to the appalling social conditions among Africans living there. The industrial magnet of the Rand drew increasing numbers of Africans, both those displaced from the land and those escaping the growing impoverishment of the reserves. The number of Africans on the Witwatersrand by 1904 was estimated at 55,765, of whom 3,840 were women. In 1921 an official census put the African population at 115,120, and the presence of women had increased nearly fourfold, to 12,160 (Proctor 1979, 53–54). By 1930 it was estimated that approximately 300,000 Africans were living on the Rand (Phillips 1930, 60). The residential areas for Africans spread from the mining compounds to the adjacent urban slums and also included freehold areas such as Sophiatown, Martindale, Newclare, and Alexandra and the municipal locations of Klipspruit, Pimville, and Orlando.[1] Whether Africans worked in the mines or the industrial or service sectors, their average monthly earnings of four pounds, two shillings, and sixpence meant that Africans' wages were below the poverty line (Phillips 1930, 62). This economic frailty was further compounded by widespread unemployment, racial discrimination, and the absence of political rights.

The interplay between poverty and oppression led to the creation of a quilt of informal economic activities ranging from illicit beer brewing and street vending to self-help societies. Political activity expressed itself in the formation of the South African Native National Congress in 1912, the burgeoning movement of independent churches, and nascent forms of labor organization. The pursuit of socioeconomic and political aspirations in the slum yards was evident in emerging cultural patterns that were extremely complex in their encapsulation of the dwellers' experiences of alienation and resilience.

Living in Johannesburg soon brought new influences into the creative activities of migrant workers. On the Rand, Zulu migrants, *amagxagxa,* developed sophisticated networks based on kin that helped them to mediate the demands of urban life. Dance teams provided the camaraderie, identity, and status that others found in savings associations and shebeens (speakeasies). The clustering of Zulu clans in hostels served to intensify the rivalries that formed the cornerstone of dancing in traditional society.

Alongside the initiatives of migrant workers, the most vibrant cultural creativity was to be found in the slum yards, which housed urbanized, working-class Africans and where recreational life revolved around shebeens, which offered liquor, dancing, prostitutes, and *marabi* music.[2]

Life in the slum yards was without exception harsh and regimented. People lived in overcrowded, dingy corrugated-iron rooms amid poverty, squalor, and lack of sanitation. Life was lived under the constant threat of arrest, given the country's influx control legislation and numerous other discriminatory laws. As the writer H. I. E. Dhlomo observed in an unpublished essay entitled "Hats," "as a drunkard is to bar, bottles and bruises, so, in South Africa, is African to police, law courts and jail."

Survival in the slum yards had to be negotiated, not only with the police and other representatives of white power and supremacy, but also with gangsters and fellow yard dwellers with pent-up frustrations. The Rand and its slum yards were equally spaces of class solidarity and recreation and sites of violent confrontations with neighbors. The gangs, such as the formidable Ninevites and their young offshoot the Amalaita, showed that, whatever the destructive consequences for black slum residents, "crime became as effective a medium of protest and self-assertion as political organization" (Coplan 1985, 61). Alienation and violence were the pervasive themes of urban black experience, embedded in most areas of social interaction.

While both elite and *marabi* culture were intended, in their different ways, to alleviate social alienation, they also revealed that "there were sharp class differences amongst Africans," as H. I. E. Dhlomo observed in an anonymous essay entitled "Evolution of Bantu Entertainments" (*Llanga lase Natal*, 20 June, 1953). The relationship between middle-class and lower-class Africans in South Africa has always been a complex one. It is at once compatible and reciprocal, because of shared oppression and nationalistic aspirations, and antagonistic, because of divergent class and cultural interests. One should, however, resist romanticizing *marabi* and other forms of ghetto life. Although it had positive qualities, *marabi* culture was socially restrictive and in many respects dehumanizing. In the eyes of officialdom and sections of the African elite, the urban ghettos were nothing less than insanitary nightmares, incestuous dens of iniquity steeped in liquor, prostitution, violence, and crime.[3]

Religion and Leisure

The social problems on the Rand challenged the church in significant new ways. In 1913, 1915, and 1916 the mining industry was rocked by a series of strikes and, in 1917, by a boycott of mine stores by African mine workers. Municipal sanitation workers went on a "bucket strike" in 1918, and, two years later, Africans miners embarked on their most massive strike. Seventy-one thousand workers participated in the action, with about thirty thousand staying away from work for six consecutive days. The miners were joined in a solidarity strike by "houseboys" (Proctor 1979, 54). The upsurge in working-class militancy radicalized the Transvaal Native Congress in the period 1918 to 1920, compelling it to support worker demands for better wages and housing and for the removal of the pass laws and other discriminatory measures (Bonner 1982, 305).[4]

Sociopolitical developments in the 1920s brought to the fore the elements of race and segregation as paramount questions in addressing social phenomena. As Phillips (1930, 163) expressed it, "the question of health, as well as nearly every other native question, is intimately related with those basic considerations of housing, wages, and land." This focus presented unique ideological challenges to evangelism:

> Mission work is becoming more difficult than ever. The spirit of independence and freedom is spreading all over the world. The Natives want to have a share in the political and social adjustment of the world. . . . The rapid development of race consciousness seems characteristic of coloured races all over the world. It touches life in social, political and many other ways.
>
> (FIFTH GENERAL MISSIONARY CONFERENCE OF SOUTH AFRICA, 1922, 110)

The preeminence of race as the modality through which social conflicts were experienced by groups had important implications. It indicated that an educated, Christianized African elite was starting to coalesce and to perceive itself as a distinct social group with a messianic mission. The endeavors of liberal white philanthropists had to contend, more than ever, with the elite's relatively unusual readings of the "native problem."

Between 1919 and 1932, Phillips and the AMB were important catalysts of cultural initiatives. Phillips came to Johannesburg from America in 1918 after a brief spell in Natal, where he studied the Zulu language (*Phillips' Newsletter*, 17 February 1919; Phillips 1930, 93; 1936, xiii). A bachelor of divinity with a special focus on social service, Phillips advocated a social gospel that aimed to facilitate better race relations and to explore how Christianity could advance social welfare in an urban context. Urbanization threw economic and political contradictions into sharper relief, especially since Africans in the urban areas did not always determine their political status as the subjects of defeated monarchs. Instead, calls for the restoration of the monarchy were being made in tandem with demands for equality and justice on the basis of individual rights and the principles of the British protectorate. Phillips (1936, 52) abhorred industrialization, which placed "profits and dividends" above the welfare of Africans, as well as socialism and racism. As an advocate of a social gospel that emphasized the oneness of material and spiritual salvation, Phillips sought to change man and his surroundings so as to ensure "Abundant Life" as preached by Jesus, "the first great social worker" (*Phillips' Newsletter,* 18 June 1921).

Phillips had an astute appreciation of the role of culture in the construction of hegemony. His thinking on leisure drew on British and American responses to the challenges resulting from industrialization. Phillips cited George Eliot's creed, which was, according to the annual report for 1927 of the Bantu Men's Social Centre (BMSC), that rather than organizing industry, "it is more important to organize and direct the leisure of the world," since on the employment of the leisure industry "may be said to depend the whole destiny of man." Phillips was also greatly influenced by the analyses and recommendations of the Phelps-Stokes Commission (1922, 25) concerning the role of recreation in education and social welfare (see also Phelps-Stokes Fund 1925, 30–35). His other central tenets were based on Christian doctrine. Recognizing that the many new African inhabitants of Johannesburg found "themselves face to face with all the temptations of the white underworld," Phillips argued that "we must provide wholesome recreation as an antidote to the degrading influences of the slumyards and liquor dens, with vice and drink, where Natives drift in the absence of healthful leisure activities" (*Phillips' Newsletter,* 3 November 1925; BMSC 1927 annual report, 1). It is not surprising, then, that the trope of the "sanitation syndrome" heightened the social significance of leisure in the struggle over the body and soul of the African.

Phillips once described the condition of Africans in Johannesburg as one in which "the white man provides the work, and the Devil provides the recreation" (*Phillips' Newsletter,* 25 December 1919).[5] To Phillips, this highlighted the "great problem of moralising the leisure time of natives in city and country alike" and presented a challenge to the church to "capture the leisure of millions" (Phillips 1930, 58).[6] In accordance with his observations on how "wholesome" leisure activities were prerequisites for the subtle molding of "sound characters," Phillips (1936, 292) maintained that "whoever captures the leisure time of the people, gets the people. A people's character is molded by the kind of investment made of their free time."[7]

It was imperative, in Phillips's view, that the provision of recreation be fully institutionalized in order to have any noteworthy impact. With this in mind he encouraged an extensive and integrated approach to the provision of recreation to Africans on the Rand. He was supported by his superior at the AMB, Dr. F. B. Bridgman, who was responsible for evangelical work and had initiated a project in 1919 to acquire a building to house the various projects and programs run under the auspices of the board. Bridgman felt that the work done at the center would, on top of fulfilling the need for more organized recreation, "supplement the work of Native missions in the building of character, and will tend to the preservation of Native law and order and to their uplift" (*Umteteli wa Bantu,* 22 September 1923).

The campaign for a multipurpose center was initially overseen by a committee under the chairmanship of Sir Ernest Chappell, with members drawn from leading religious societies and the chambers of mines and commerce (Phillips 1930, 129). In his newsletter of 1920, under the heading "Bantu Men's Social Centre," Phillips announced to friends and potential funders overseas that Dr. Bridgman's dream of "a YMCA for the needy native men of the Town" was about to be realized. The "sorely needed" building was to be built at a projected cost of fifty thousand dollars (*Phillips' Newsletter,* 25 December 1919, 3). It was four years before the BMSC became a reality. On 25 October 1924, the building was officially opened by "His Excellency the Governor General" in front of a crowd of some four hundred Africans (*Umteteli wa Bantu,* 1 November 1924; *South African Outlook,* 1 August 1924; BMSC 1927 annual report, 1).

The opening address, delivered by Mr. W. Webber, chairman of the executive committee of the BMSC, sheds light on the sociopolitical aims of the institution. After elaborating on the evangelical roots of the center, Webber explained that it was intended "to surround the Natives in their spare time with wholesome influences, to build up character, to create ideas of decency and manhood, and to develop self-control and a sense of responsibility." Webber then proceeded to reassure whites that "we have framed the constitution of our Society so as to eliminate the possibility of this club being used for political propaganda" and that politics "were to be left outside." In a pious and grandiose tone recalling the model of the Hampton Institute in America, Webber declared, "here there is no Native problem. Here there is only education for life." The financing of the BMSC was a "good business investment" since the "moral and physical health" of Africans was viewed as paramount given their daily contact with white families. Furthermore, the club would exercise an important corrective influence on migrant laborers who, after coming into contact with "European civilisation," "very often return to their kraals to exercise an evil and not a good influence."

It was when Webber turned to address the African elite—"now a few words to our Native friends"—that the extent of political control and paternalism underlying the BMSC became apparent. The African elite was reminded that the project was funded "almost wholly" with money supplied by "Europeans" and that "it will be managed wholly for your benefit." The "noble career" facing the intelligentsia was to support the institution and to "teach your people how to use it" (*Umteteli wa Bantu,* 26 January 1924; see also *South African Outlook,* 1 August 1924, 189).

The significance of the BMSC in the social and political life of Africans was disproportionate to the relatively small numbers of active members (around three hundred to four hundred) between 1925 and 1940.[8] Notwithstanding the fact that the center, as a social space, was politicized by white attempts to control the recreational activities of Africans, attitudes among Africans toward the BMSC were diverse and predicated largely on class-related issues. Patrons of the BMSC were predominantly drawn from the elite sections of the African community on the Rand. Even before the official opening of the venue, the Native Mine Workers Association endorsed the project and donated one hundred pounds to its building fund, as reported in the newspaper *Umteteli wa Bantu* on 10 May 1924. African members of the executive board included some of the most noted members of the African middle class: R. V. Selope Thema, A. W. Champion, I. Makau, and Sol G. Senaoane, and the Reverends Robert Ngcobo and M. Maxeke. The symbolic import of the BMSC was encoded in its signification of the desired "high culture" amid the shacks and shackles of urbanization.

The announcement of the BMSC project in 1920 also elicited some skepticism, if not outright political cynicism, from the upper crust of the African community. In an editorial with the heading "Unbelief," published in *Umteteli wa Bantu* on 18 September 1920, the first paragraph ponders, "One would suppose that when the hand of the white man was extended in friendship and sincerity it would eagerly be grasped by the long suffering black." The conclusion more positively observes: "fortunately there are many Natives who have been quick to appreciate the worth of an institution such as the Bantu Men's Social Centre is designed to be, and have pledged themselves to support the institution."

The major issue of contention among some members of the African elite was the envisaged role for African leadership in a project that they regarded as paternalistic. Africans felt underrepresented in numbers and rank in the committees overseeing the running of the BMSC. Between 1926 and 1957 all the chairmen of the BMSC were white, while the position of secretary for the same period was inevitably held by a black (Mweli Skota 1966, 312–25). Some felt that the BMSC was nothing short of "a hoax devised for no other purpose than to hoodwink the Natives." Others felt that Africans should be organizing an independent initiative because the ideas behind the BMSC were exploitative and meant to "produce good boys who are traitors to their peoples" (*Umteteli wa Bantu*, 6 March 1926).[9] However, sections of the African intelligentsia favored the use of the BMSC, as is evident in the comments of H. I. E. Dhlomo's younger brother, Frank: "Let this building band young men in one solid mass. Some have criticized it expressing some hasty ideas against the Europeans. That is the reason why some of us are such hopeless cases" (*Ilanga lase Natal*, 27 March 1925).

The annual report for 1929 drew attention to the social significance of the BMSC, arguing that "the influence of the Club outside its walls is as important, if not more important, than its internal success." Recalling both the European and African detractors to the founding of the center, it notes that "a great change has come in the attitude towards the principle for which we stood" (*Umteteli wa Bantu*, 22 February 1930). By 1935 it could be claimed that "confidence in the Bantu Men's Social Centre continues to grow among Africans, and that those who formerly looked upon the Centre with suspicion, as the home of good boys, have now visited and held meetings there" (*Umteteli wa Bantu*, 23 March 1935).

The Fledgling Allure of Film

One of the first creative projects that Phillips initiated was to organize encounter sessions with mine workers using games such as Hunt the Thimble and Who's Got the Ring. Phillips soon supplanted games with the more cerebral experience of drama: film (Phillips 1930, 140–41).[10] From Johannesburg's first introduction to Thomas Alva Edison's kinetoscope in 1895 until the 1950s, cinema was targeted almost exclusively at white audiences (Gutsche 1972, 9; Tomaselli 1983, 38). Yet the basis for the subsequent spread and popularity of cinematic screenings among Africans can be traced back to the early 1920s, and in many respects it was due to the efforts of Phillips and the AMB. Even before the opening of the BMSC, Phillips and Bridgman were publicly acknowledged as "the pioneers of the pictorial education of the Native" (*Umteteli wa Bantu*, 7 July 1923). Phillips seems to have begun using cinema in 1919 or 1920; his first endeavor was an extensive screening program for African mine workers.

Advocates for the screening of movies to Africans argued that films were not only educational but also potentially useful in "sublimating potential criminal tendencies" (Gutsche 1972, 378). Phillips recounts how during the 1922 strike by white miners some two hundred thousand African miners were left "idle" with "their animal energies accumulating day by day." Apparently agents provocateurs were goading the miners to strike, loot, or plunder. When such actions seemed imminent, Phillips organized a screening of a Charlie Chaplin feature, which provided the necessary harmless diversion. Phillips (1930, 149–50) concluded the anecdote with the self-satisfied observation, "There was no murder that night at the New Primrose." The turning point in the promotion of screenings came when Phillips managed to secure the support of the chamber of mines, which believed that "this is a good investment of funds, an investment in contentment for their workmen" (*Phillips' Newsletter*, 18 June 1921). The chamber of mines eventually supported the program to the tune of £1,500 for equipment and an annual grant of £5,000 to cover running costs (Phillips 1930, 145). At its height, the screening circuit supervised by Phillips included sixty-nine compounds and eighty-three exhibiting centers outside the mines (Phillips 1936, 315).[11]

Entrepreneurs and others recognized the untapped market of African spectators. In 1920 a Mr. Dan Thomas was granted permission by the Transvaal Chamber of Mines to exhibit films on the mines using a portable system (*Umteteli wa Bantu*, 2 October 1920). The following year another license was granted to one Frank Cohen to "open and conduct a Bioscope show for Natives at Booysens." Sol T. Plaatje operated a mobile cinema within months of his return from America in November 1923 (*Umteteli wa Bantu*, 31 May 1924).[12] But by 1936 there were no more than four theaters licensed to show heavily censored movies to Africans (Phillips 1936, 293, 318).[13] (Elsewhere Africans were allowed to occupy only the gallery sections of bioscopes.) The small number of cinemas for Africans reflected the financial instability of the enterprise since admission had to be set at a level commensurate with the low wages paid to Africans (Gutsche 1972, 379). Phillips (1936, 324) acknowledged the receptivity and enthusiasm of Africans toward cinema and saw that the "lack of money" was behind their poor patronage. The financial viability of taking films to Africans was dependent on the philanthropic support of corporations such as the chamber of mines. It was only from the late 1940s, with the production of *African Jim* (1949), that a concerted drive was made to produce films with black performers and aimed at black audiences (Tomaselli 1989, 56–59; Davis 1996, chapters 3–4).

The paucity of venues did not stop missionaries and the media from inventing moral panics about the possible "pernicious effects" of the cinema on children and Africans. *Umteteli wa Bantu* (9 July 1921), in its announcement of the license granted to Cohen, could not resist asking whether the Johannesburg Town Council "has made provision for an effective supervision of Mr. Frank Cohen's entertainments." A few months earlier *Umteteli wa Bantu* (5 March 1921) gave vent to its consternation in an extensive editorial, "Bioscopes and Morals."

> The most deplorable feature of this class of film is their portrayal of white sordidness. The bully, the prostitute, the thief and the murderer are all prominent in these pictures, and it is not uncommon to see the semi-nude lady of fashion. . . . Such pictures are as bad for Natives as they are for Europeans. Probably Natives' morals suffer in a greater degree because they witness and are often imbued with a desire to emulate the baser passions of the race to which they normally look for their enlightenment and uplift. . . . We would ask our Government to . . . go further and prohibit the public screening of any picture which is likely to dull the moral outlook, or to blunt the finer perception. In this category we place the nauseating sex problem which the mawkish rush in crowds to see. . . . Such pictures are especially harmful to the Natives in the Transvaal where scores of thousands of them are separated from their women folk, and are for varying periods enduring an enforced celibacy.

The editorial concluded by welcoming the efforts of Phillips, advising him to secure "the production of films to picturise stories of Native life, with Natives for their characters": in short, "the clean and bright pastoral play or comedy, locally produced by Native artists" (*Umteteli wa Bantu*, 5 March 1921).[14]

Opinions were divided among the African elite. Peter Abrahams (1954, 110–11), the noted South African novelist, frequented the BMSC. He regarded the bioscope as a means for slum dwellers to keep in touch with developments in the world, but he also viewed it as a space where "illusion and reality often merged" in the minds of many frustrated young people. Ironically, Modikwe Dikobe (1981, 72, 75), another novelist and patron of the center, wrote that Black Cat and his other fictional hooligans "had learned the techniques of gangsterism at the free 'bio' operated by the Bantu Men's Social Centre."

The films screened by Phillips were generally procured from African Films, Ltd., a subsidiary company of the monopolistic empire run

40

by Isadore William Schlesinger, which dominated film production in South Africa for almost half a century.[15] Phillips also worked with that company's production unit, African Film Productions, in the making of a number of motion pictures during the interwar years. World War I had disrupted the regular supply of American movies, which by then also commanded prohibitively high prices. The scarcity of films and high charges led to a surge of local productions, which resulted in thirty-seven feature films being made from 1916 to 1922 (Gutsche 1972, 310–11; Tomaselli 1983, 95–96). A number of the features, made locally or in Britain, were reconstructions of "frontier" history, representations of the onward march of civilization under the unlikely alliance of the British and Afrikaner. The "natives" were portrayed as either menacing savages or faithful servants, the latter being a variation on the "noble savage" (Davis 1996, 8–9).[16]

This tradition was first manifest in *The Zulu's Heart* (1908) by D. W. Griffith, probably the first feature set in South Africa and expressing the paradoxical iconography of the Zulus, who "either threaten whites, or serve them." Key feature films made in South Africa from 1916 to 1940 include *A Zulu's Devotion* and *De Voortrekkers* (a.k.a. *Winning a Continent*) (both 1916); *Symbol of Sacrifice*, *Allan Quatermain and the Lost City of Gold* and *King Solomon's Mines* (all 1918); and *Prester John* (1920). Another version of *King Solomon's Mines*, starring Paul Robeson, was shot in South Africa and America in 1936.[17] The years 1937 and 1938 saw African Film Productions' monumental documentary commissioned by the government, *They Built a Nation* (a.k.a. *Die Bou van 'n Nasie*)—a nation that, like pictures of the empire, had as its cornerstone the apparent absence of Africans (Gutsche 1972, 327).

The only deviation from the "frontier" features was the emergence, from 1927, of "authentic African documentaries" filmed by Europeans. *Africa Today* (1927), which explored "the impact of Western Civilization on the native," was commissioned by missionary societies in Europe and directed by Britain's T. H. Baxter. June of the same year saw the arrival of an expedition, led by Professor Lidio Cipriani of the University of Florence, to make a "scientific study of the Zulus from anthropological and ethnographic points of view." The result was a full-length "native film" entitled *Zeliv* (1927), a drama dealing with witchcraft, which was screened in Johannesburg in December 1929 under the title *Witchcraft*. It also went under the title *Siliwa the Zulu*. American cinematographer and lecturer Captain Carl Hoffman came to South Africa in 1929 to document aspects of Zulu life for his classes.

Two years later, a German documentary producer, Major Hans Schomburgk, completed a project looking at "the development of the African native from the pygmy in the wilds to the worker in the skyscraper." The preoccupation with the perceived threat of industrialization to African life and society was passionately pursued by the British Drama League in the 1930s.

In 1938 Leon Schauder, a South African cinematographer who had been based in Britain for some time, returned and produced *Nonquassi [sic].*[18] The British Ministry of Information bought the world rights of *Nonquassi* in 1940, hoping, in Thelma Gutsche's words (1972, 334), "to exploit the propaganda effect of establishing a parallel between the Xhosa self-destruction through implicit faith in a fanatical prophetess and the imminent Nazi self-destruction through implicit faith in the fanatical Hitler."

Phillips was involved in 1921 in the production of two educational documentaries, *Dust That Kills* and *Safety First,* directed by Dr. A. J. Orenstein. The films dealt with working conditions underground and tried to promote safety among miners (*Umteteli wa Bantu,* 7 January 1922; Gutsche 1972, 321). Projects in which Phillips was involved between 1925 and 1934, coproduced by African Film Productions and either the Transvaal Chamber of Mines or the South African Railways and Harbours, included *Lovedale Missionary Institution, Industrialization of the African, The African Witch-Doctor, The Way Out: From Red Blanket to Civilization,* and *From Kraal to Mine* (Phillips 1936, 425). These films were probably documentaries of a quasi-ethnographic nature. Phillips (1930, 153–58) gives an account of going to Natal to "capture on cinema film, if possible, some of the daily doings of a native medical man" to be included in a promotional film titled *Mission Work among the Zulus.*

Some of the images gathered on this expedition were reproduced in a poster publicizing the BMSC. On the two sides of the poster are photographic stills with captions that describe the African experience in terms of two phases. The first is "The Old Days of the Bantu People, viz., The Chief at Home, A Group of Warriors, Applying Bitter Medicines to a Tubercular Knee (note the pain on the patient's face)." The second phase is "The New Day! A Time of Change and Transition, viz., A Compound Group, Slumyard in Doornfontein, The Bantu Men's Social Centre Building, Evening Sports and Games, All Enjoy the Weekly Programmes of Clean and Wholesome Films." The text on the central spaces of the poster contains dire warnings:

Industrialization and town life bring some of the good and much of the worst of civilization to the Bantu people / The Manhood of the Black Race is here—learning to work—that is good / But when their work is done, their recreation is the slumyard / their only sports—poisonous liquor drinking and vice / their athletic teams—the *amalaita* gangs / the resulting disease and degeneracy is a growing danger to all / An extension of the recreation and social work of the Bantu Men Social Centre is a challenging need! A sound investment—guaranteeing a wholesome and vital contribution to our grave city problem along sane lines.

(BMSC 1928 ANNUAL REPORT AND ACCOMPANYING POSTER)

Phillips (1930, 146) hoped that Africans who watched his movies would "acquire a sense of discrimination." The viewer was expected to distinguish between good and bad characters, between heroes and the many "villains in real life who are out to fleece him—and there are many such in this land—white in skin but ink black" (*Phillips' Newsletter*, 23 January 1929). The screenings, as we have seen, were also meant to challenge the appearance of "little dirty Movie houses . . . catering to the native people and pandering to the lower instincts." Phillips argued that "we can't kill this sort of thing by preaching against it, nor by demanding censor bodies to inspect films." By building the BMSC and initiating the mobile cinema project, Phillips and the ABM were "meeting the Devil on his own ground" (*Phillips' Newsletter*, 18 June 1921).

Phillips's assessment of the drawbacks and benefits of motion pictures reflected a broad consensus among whites and sections of the African elite. And yet, as evidenced in Dhlomo's repudiation of the links drawn between "idle minds" and crime, Africans on the Rand were just as dexterous in grappling with the multifarious contradictions of colonialism. As for the negative influence of the cinema, Dhlomo (*Ilanga lase Natal*, 5 May 1943) was emphatic that "not films or obscene literature, but the social and economic conditions gave birth" to black criminals and that, at worst, "films may encourage the already poisoned or converted." In any case, not only was Dhlomo aware of the peripheral role of Africans in movies, he was also very cynical of mass-produced art, particularly cinema, which he faulted for limiting participation "to mental exercise only" (*Umteteli wa Bantu*, 18 August 1931).[19]

The double standards that typified the application of film censorship did not escape the notice of the intelligentsia. To cite one example, Plaatje was outraged by the screening of an American production, *The Birth of a Nation*, based on *The Clansman* by Thomas Dixon, "the avowed champion of American Negrophobes."[20] Seizing on the irony that the movie had been either severely censored or banned in most states in America, Plaatje asked whether it was "licensed to fan the embers of race hatred in South Africa." The answer, Plaatje intimates in an article published in *Umteteli wa Bantu* (18 July 1931), lies in the movie's evocation of "ugly black peril scenes . . . until the emotions of white people are worked up to fever heat." It is only a matter of time, then, before the cavalry—"masked night riders"—come charging to the rescue, "vigorously applauded by the audience as they set out on the trail of Negroes." It was such sharp appraisals of the constitutive interaction between art and life that obliged the African intelligentsia to exploit the fractures between the myriad depictions of black subject positionalities and their social status as "natives at large" (Plaatje 1982 [1916], 197).

Conclusion

The emergence of cinema toward the end of the nineteenth century expanded the generic options available to dramatists and also gave a second lease on life to key texts in the fictional canon of empire. Since the making of motion pictures required extensive capital and because the technology was beyond the means and control of Africans, the ultimate effect was to locate Africans on the margins in all areas of filmmaking. Screenplays produced in South Africa celebrated the adventures of the empire or the post-Union oligarchy. The African entered the narrative frame as a one-dimensional subject, always as the amoebalike Zulu ogre, who served to signify the horrors that needed to be conquered and domesticated if the aims of the empire were to be achieved. Thus, despite its potential to reach a larger audience than theater, cinema's expense and its preoccupation with consecrating white supremacy and fixing Africans as primitive pastoral people meant that it was actually less accessible to the African intelligentsia. At any rate, the African elite would have found it difficult to perform in films such as *De Voortrekkers*, even as extras.

As indicated in Plaatje's critique of *The Birth of a Nation*, African intellectuals were cognizant of the historical distortions enshrined in the paeans to the white heroes of the contact zones. It would seem that even among the lower classes and whites, all participants were aware of the political symbolism involved in the reenactment of "frontier" encounters. In at least two cases, during the staging of the musical pageant *The Dawn of Union* in 1910 and the filming of a battle scene in *De Voortrekkers*, the warfare became real as black and white actors abandoned their scripts! The *De Voortrekkers* fracas left 1 worker dead from drowning, 122 injured, and 35 hospitalized (Hofmeyr 1991, 61; Gutsche 1972, 314–15; Stodel 1962, 53–54). While such scenes would be unheard of today, the making of cinema in post-1994 South Africa is still bedeviled by instances of race and class, just as it was at the beginning of the twentieth century.

Notes

1. Freehold areas were urban areas where blacks were permitted to own property under the terms of apartheid legislation.

2. *Marabi* was a modern, urban, syncretic, piano-driven musical style that mixed African music, the Cape colored tradition, ragtime, and jazz. As dance music, *marabi* eschewed improvisation in favor of melodic repetition. Although "*marabi* retained traditional musical practices and elements, its ultimate form reflected the desire of the largely unschooled and un-Westernized urban Africans to modernize by absorbing new cultural elements within a familiar structure" (Coplan 1985, 107).

3. For a discussion of the impact of urbanization on African family life, morals, and crime, see the chapters "The Bantu Home in the Town" and "Crime and Delinquency" in Phillips 1936, esp. 89–105.

4. For a list of grievances presented to the prime minister, see Bonner 1982, 297–98; see also Couzens 1976, 68.

5. For a description of the devil at work, see Phillips 1930, 124–25.

6. The delightful phrase "moralising the leisure time" is already present in BMSC 1927 annual report. See also Couzens 1982.

7. The kernel of this idea was already expressed in Phillips's earlier work *The Bantu Are Coming* (1930, 124): "Now, whoever captures the leisure time of the people gets the people in the long run." The same assumption is articulated in Phelps-Stokes Fund 1925, 25. A participant in a conference in what was then Rhodesia, a Mr. B. Mnyanda, is credited with the following statement, which is remarkably analogous to Phillips's observations: "for those who control the leisure of a people control the people themselves." See the editorials "The Natives' Leisure" and "Recreation for Natives in Towns," *Umteteli wa Bantu*, 1 August and 20 December 1924.

8. The following are examples of the total membership during those years. 1929: 330; 1934: 341; 1935: 408 (see *Umteteli wa Bantu*, 22 February 1930 and 23 March 1935).

9. For defenses of the BMSC, see Phillips's response in *Ilanga lase Natal* (19 June 1925) to criticism leveled in the Industrial and Commercial Worker's Union's the *Worker's Herald,* and Plaatje's rebuttal of H. D. Tyamzashe in *Umteteli wa Bantu,* 28 February 1925. Tyamzashe restated his views in *Umteteli wa Bantu,* 14 March 1925.

10. Phillips was involved in setting up numerous other projects targeted at African youth, including athletic leagues and the Pathfinders and Wayfarers movement. He saw the latter two initiatives as taking "the place for the strong craving for rhythmic expression, musical games and folk-dances" among the youth. (See Phillips 1930, 93–95 for a discussion of the allure of African dance for Christian children.)

11. For an account of a similar experiment with cinema among Africans in Tanganyika, Kenya, and Uganda from 1935 to 1937, see Notcutt and Latham 1937. This report was most probably the result of an outlay of forty thousand dollars by the Carnegie Corporation in 1935 for "the carrying out experiments on African films for Africans." See *Bantu World*, 29 June 1935; Davis 1935.

12. Plaatje tended to screen a variety of shorts, but prized among his library was footage on the Tuskegee Institute in Alabama that celebrated the achievements of African Americans in the fields of education and business (see chapter 1).

13. In Johannesburg the principal halls were Springbok Hall, Vrededorp, and the New Inchcape Palais de Dance, also known as the Ritz.

14. See also *Umteteli wa Bantu*, 7 July 1923. Just about anything was blamed for the perceived criminal behavior of urbanites. On the influence of "poor" literature, see the letter by Esau Mazibuko, "Detective Story Books and Love Novels," *Bantu World*, 2 October 1937.

15. For accounts of the significance and machinations of Schlesinger in the development of the cinematic industry between 1913 and 1940, see Gutsche 1972, chaps. 6, 8, 9, and 12; Tomaselli 1983, chap. 2.

16. For example, *A Zulu's Devotion*, written and directed by Joseph Albrecht, shows "how a Zulu farmhand frustrates the designs of two half-caste stock-thieves and rescues his little mistress from their clutches" (Gutsche 1972, 312). Phillips (1930, 144) described *A Zulu's Devotion* as "a native sketch with fine appeal."

17. For a detailed synopsis and discussion of the films mentioned here, see Gutsche 1972 313–21; Davis 1996, 15–17, 124–41. For a discussion of the 1918 and 1937 versions of *King Solomon's Mines*, see Cameron 1994, 23–32; Dunn 1996.

18. Nongqawuse was a sixteen-year-old Xhosa girl who prophesied in 1856 that the ancestors would rise from the dead and a new millennium would dawn if her people slaughtered their cattle.

19. Theodor W. Adorno and his associate Max Horkheimer, in their *Dialectic of Enlightenment* (1944, chap. 2), were just as dismissive of the "culture industry" and "mass deception." For salutary critiques see Eagleton 1990, chap. 13; Jameson 1992, 145–56.

20. Davis (1996, 132) suggests that the title of Griffith's *The Birth of a Nation* could have inspired Gustav Preller's writing of *De Voortrekkers*. See also chapter 3 of this volume.

PART 2

Cinema before and under Apartheid

On the preceding page:
LIONEL ROGOSIN. With permission of the Rogosin family.

3

The Birth of a Nation
Contextualizing *De Voortrekkers* (1916)

Edwin Hees

In 1916 the newly established South African film company African Film Productions made a historical epic based on an event that has been labeled—and indeed institutionalized—in South African historiography as "the Great Trek." Undertaken by a fairly small band of hardy pioneers called Voortrekkers, this was the migration of Dutch farmers, or Boers, away from British rule at the Cape Colony in the 1830s. The first half of the nineteenth century was a turbulent time generally on the subcontinent, but the most devastating upheaval in terms of the sheer scope of destruction and uprooting of peoples was the *mfecane*—the violent and profoundly destabilizing series of military, social, and political crises among the African tribes of the region, in which Shaka, the Zulu king, gained such preeminence. Yet it is the Great Trek that has, until recently, occupied a predominant place in the writing of South African history—to the extent that it has been referred to as the central constitutive myth of Afrikaner nationalism.[1] The African Film Productions film *De Voortrekkers* (1916) played an important role in generating and sustaining that myth.

The film was financed by the head of African Film Productions, I. W. Schlesinger, an American with extensive British-based business interests in South Africa. It was directed by Harold Shaw, producer for Vitagraph and London Films, who was brought to South Africa by Schlesinger to direct films, including *De Voortrekkers,* the first major epic to be produced in South Africa.[2] The popular journalist and historian Gustav Preller, a zealous champion of Afrikaans, a young and as yet unofficial Dutch-based language, wrote the screenplay (including presumably the very first Afrikaans intertitles) based on his own interpretation of one critical military engagement between blacks and whites in the interior during the course of the Great Trek.

In many ways this film occupies a position in South African film history analogous to that of D. W. Griffith's *The Birth of a Nation* in the United States. Commentaries on *De Voortrekkers* have often made passing references to *The Birth of a Nation,* but I am not aware of any sustained comparative analysis.[3] In the following comparison between the two films, it will become clear that their differences—not just technically, but in cultural historical importance—are as significant as their similarities. It is not possible, I think, to speak of Griffith's film as an "influence" on *De Voortrekkers,* though *The Birth of a Nation* had reached as far as London by the end of 1915. It is more likely that both films are indebted to the spectacular Italian epics that had appeared since about 1912, especially the highly acclaimed *Cabiria* (1914).[4] Griffith was certainly determined to outdo the European epics, but further investigation is necessary before one can make the same claim for Shaw[5] or Preller. The proposition I would like to demonstrate here is that the "epic impulse" behind the South African film, and Preller's screenplay in particular, derives from a nationalistically orientated reading of a few specific events of the Great Trek and an attempt to apotheosize the Boer leaders involved. In the first part of this chapter, I will focus on the social, political, and cultural context in which *De Voortrekkers* was made, and the second part presents some extended comparisons with Griffith's film.[6]

In considering the early South African film industry, one needs to remember that "South Africa" did not exist as a state for the first dozen years or so of the new art form. At the turn of the century two independent Boer republics and two British colonies constituted the geographical area we call South Africa today. At this time the two republics were engaged in a fierce war against the British Empire, after it became obvious to the Crown (more specifically to Cecil Rhodes) that these two sovereign states were also the owners of what were potentially the world's richest gold and diamond mines. The two republics were defeated after a bitter struggle in the Anglo-Boer War (1899–1902), and by 1910 the two colonies and the two republics were amalgamated into one state called the Union of South Africa. The period of reconstruction after the war was followed by a period of consolidation of predominantly white power after Union. It is in this context that *De Voortrekkers* occupies such a significant place in South African political and cultural history.

Films had been made in South Africa at least as early as the Anglo-Boer War, when a number of prominent English cameramen and film-makers came to the subcontinent to satisfy public demand in Britain for visual images of the war in what was still a novel medium with a potential for enormous "realism." This had the effect of stimulating the industry in England, but also meant that the material was shot from an exclusively British point of view.

A practical and logistical difficulty for cameramen was that there was no clear front line of battle; the Boers were highly adept at guerrilla warfare. The result was a great deal of footage of "official" occasions and set pieces: senior military personnel disembarking at Cape Town harbor, troop movements, cannons being fired, Boer prisoners, and panoramic shots of Cape Town, Table Mountain, or Africans dancing. One way of dealing with this inconvenient scarcity of dramatic material on the conflict was to make "fakes"—reenactments of skirmishes and other incidents, which appeared in abundance to satisfy the curiosity of the new film audiences in Britain.[7] The potential for propaganda was thus enormous. Elizabeth Streble (1977, 45) points out that "since the Boers had no photographers," these films are "undoubtedly more revealing of Victorian England than of South Africa, full of the myths and symbols of British imperialist iconography."

Two points about these Boer War films are particularly relevant here. One is summed up as follows by Keyan Tomaselli (1986, 35):

> Ideologically projecting the imperialist interests of international capital, the British Tommy is portrayed as "fighting for a trinity of God, Motherhood and country." The British are heroic; the Boers are the villains. Paul Kruger, President of the independent Transvaal Republic before the British conquest, is the embodiment of evil, completely lacking in morals or a sense of justice. . . . Typical of many of the British-made anti-Boer films was the "all-encompassing mystical power of the Union Jack, symbol of the all-powerful British Empire."

This suggests the intensity of the emotional dimension of the conflict, but even more to the point here was the alliance of British capital and Afrikaner interests in the immediate aftermath of the war. This was to have a decisive influence on Preller's account of the heroic trekker leader Piet Retief on film in 1916.

A second relevant point about the Boer War films is well made by Peter Davis (1996, 2–3), who notes that motion pictures were invented at the apex of the age of empire:

> The invention of the movie camera began a second conquest of Africa, not merely in the acquisition of images, but in the way these images were represented. . . . This war [the Anglo-Boer War], after all, was *about* the

soil of Africa, but in it the principal inhabitants of the land have been reduced to worse than irrelevance—if they participate at all, they do so as servants of the white combatants on both sides. The camera casually reveals a significant fact: by 1900, the political decisions about South Africa were being made exclusively by whites, shutting out the African majority.

In this instance too, the relationship between imperialism and representation was to have a fundamental influence on the way Preller's screenplay depicted the relationships between the Voortrekkers and the black inhabitants of the interior whom they encountered.

After the Anglo-Boer War, short films and documentaries were made in South Africa, and the formation of African Film Productions in 1915, specifically to promote the industry in South Africa while Europe was at war, stimulated a burst of activity lasting into the early 1920s. The making of *De Voortrekkers* was undoubtedly the moment when the silent film came to maturity in South Africa. In spite of its title, *De Voortrekkers* (or, as it was known in English, *Winning a Continent*) deals almost exclusively with the last years of the trekker leader Piet Retief, who had signed a land treaty with the Zulu king, Dingaan. After the massacre of Retief's men by Dingaan—an act of barbaric treachery according to the myth—the trekkers vowed to avenge Retief's death and to keep sacred the day of their victory (by the grace of God) over the Zulus. This they achieved on 16 December 1838, in the Battle of Blood River, which was won by the trekkers under Andries Pretorius, demonstrating their military superiority in the face of a massive Zulu force. For more than 150 years the "Day of the Covenant" or, as Preller popularized it, "Dingaan's Day," was a religious public holiday in South Africa and church services were held on the "sacred ground" at Blood River.

Other important characters in the film are the Reverend Owen, the missionary who was trying to convert Dingaan, and the two Portuguese traders who turn Dingaan against the white settlers because they fear the economic competition. The film also includes a wholly fictional black character, Sobuza, who turns against his king, Dingaan, and assists the trekkers. In spite of Preller's almost obsessive attention to detail for the sake of authenticity (there is even some historical basis for the two Portuguese traders), it is this character, created specifically for the film, that enables him to promote the nascent postwar Afrikaner cause without subverting the tenuous and fraught unity among whites achieved since Union.[8]

In many ways, then, Gustav Preller is the central figure in this discussion. If any single writer created the popular image of the Great

Trek and, in fact, gave it its heroic, mythical, almost sacred dimension, it was Preller. His first version of the biography of Piet Retief (based on a series of Afrikaans articles intended to demonstrate the effectiveness of the young language for historical writing) appeared in 1906 and was immensely popular, running into ten editions by 1930. For Preller, the migration of the white farmers away from imperial control at the Cape Colony was a deliberate act of nation making, and Piet Retief was without question the founding father of a new nation.[9] Isabel Hofmeyr (1988, 522) appropriately dubs such enterprises as Preller's "the cultural fabrication of nationalisms." Preller's book on Retief (1988 [1917]) is hardly a biography in any traditional sense: it is shaped—"driven" might be a better word—by Preller's anticolonial stance and deals predominantly with the last years of Piet Retief, his treaty with Dingaan, the massacre of Retief's men, the Covenant, and Andries Pretorius's conquest of the Zulus at the Battle of Blood River.[10] In Preller's version of the story, one witnesses the conquest of black "barbarism" by the forces of white, Christian—specifically Boer—civilization.

But the significant point here is that any hints of anticolonialism or anti-British sentiment in the book are suppressed in the film, as we shall see. As an admirer and friend of the prime minister, General Louis Botha, Preller was at this stage sympathetic to Botha's policy, adopted by the South African Party (SAP), of national reconciliation between the English and Afrikaans sections of the population. By the time Preller's biography (1988 [1937]) of the hero of Blood River, Andries Pretorius, came out in 1937 (in anticipation of the 1938 Trek centenary celebrations), however, his thinking had moved decisively in the direction of those Afrikaners who were sympathetic to the racial ideals of national socialism. White superiority and supremacy were issues he was beginning to take more overtly[11] for granted (they were always implicit in his work), and there is clear evidence that Preller's version of racism as expressed in the Pretorius biography found its way into the 1938 film *They Built a Nation,* commissioned by the government to celebrate the South African nation in the Great Trek centenary year and covering much the same ground as Preller's earlier screenplay.[12] During the 1938 centenary, the story of the Great Trek and its commemoration in a symbolic ox wagon trek from Cape Town to Pretoria achieved such resonance that the resulting mood of nationalistic euphoria provided much of the dynamism for the National Party election victory in 1948 on its apartheid platform. (It would be quite wrong, however, simply to equate Afrikaner nationalism and segregationist thinking.)[13]

Clearly, Preller's influence as a popular historian was decisive in *De Voortrekkers* and *They Built a Nation*; there is even a sense in which A. A. Pienaar's screenplay for *They Built a Nation* is truer to Preller's own ideals than Preller's screenplay for *De Voortrekkers* was. The virtual elimination of the British from *De Voortrekkers*, for example, makes it a text more untypical of Preller's work than has been acknowledged. I want to show that the screenplay for *De Voortrekkers* is a carefully adapted version of Preller's story of Piet Retief—adapted in order to bring the film more into line not only with the British imperialist ideology of its financial backers but also with the accommodating stance of General Louis Botha, whose South African Party was eager to promote reconciliation between the English-speaking and Afrikaans-speaking sections of the population after Union. The South Africa Act of 1909, promulgated at Westminster, had deliberately excluded black people from the political settlement reached between whites, postponing discussion of this fundamental issue to an unspecified later date. Several historians (Liebenberg 1975; Lombaard 1975; Du Plessis 1988) have pointed out the flaws in Preller's historical works—and Isabel Hofmeyr (1988, 526) adds the important point that he "synthesises historical data through the formulas of the news story and the popular novel." But what is pertinent here is not so much the quality of Preller's scholarship as the use he makes of one of his major acknowledged sources.

Behind Preller looms the figure of George McCall Theal, a Canadian historian who settled in South Africa; Preller frequently expresses his indebtedness to Theal's work. Theal's eleven-volume *Compendium of South African History and Geography* (1877) provided the first detailed account of what he called "the great emigration of Dutch farmers"; the series was started in the 1870s, when white rule was beginning to be consolidated throughout South Africa. According to Christopher Saunders (1988), Theal's version of the trek depicted the triumph of civilization in a country where the few, scattered white settlers had two enemies: the British imperial government, which was being misguided by meddling missionaries, and the "barbarous" black population, which the settlers were entirely justified in subjugating. As Saunders (1988, 29) argues: "Theal did more than anyone else to establish a tradition of strongly pro-colonist [that is, pro-trekker, anti-British], anti-black historical writing, and to create the racist paradigm which lay at the core of that tradition." In his writings, Preller combines Theal's historiography and a romanticized version of the Great Trek to create what was to become white South Africa's key myth for most of the twentieth century.

In 1916 an adapted version of this myth was put to the task of unifying Englishmen and Afrikaners, mortal enemies at the turn of the century, into a nation facing the dangers of the "dark continent" as Retief and Pretorius had done. Clearly, under the circumstances depicted in the film—quite apart from the issue of British-based funding—British imperialism could not be held responsible for the tribulations the trekkers had to endure. In his screenplay, Preller's strategy for promoting unity after 1910 was essentially to ignore the imperial dimension of the story and emphasize the threat posed by the indigenous black population. He further deflected anti-British sentiment by depicting the two Portuguese traders as melodramatic villains who precipitate suspicion, hatred, and even murder in their fear of economic competition from the Boers. By 1938 many historians had absorbed Preller and Theal's version of the story with its racist assumptions and, following their lead, blamed the interfering missionaries for what had gone wrong. One notes, for example, that the Reverend Owen is a rather less saintly figure in *They Built a Nation* than he is in *De Voortrekkers*.[14] The moral and historical perspective is wholly orientated toward the needs of the white settlers.

It is also useful to remember that in the 1930s the study of African societies was regarded as the province of anthropologists, not historians.[15] John van Zyl (1980, 32) makes a relevant point with reference to most early ethnographic films: black societies were regarded as having "no God, no morality, no history." The notion that African societies were ahistorical (to say nothing of immoral) was an important aspect of the settler myth.

Paul Coates (cited in Sobchack 1990, 40) points out that epics are produced when a country's national myths are still believed. In the case of *De Voortrekkers,* the film created and sustained the myth of the trekkers as founding fathers of a new nation as much as it reflected emerging historical beliefs. It has much in common with the "plantation myth" of postbellum America as portrayed in *The Birth of a Nation*: an Edenic state has been found, fundamentally jeopardized (by black people), and restored again. Perhaps the overriding feature that the two films have in common—and which provides them with their particular dynamism—is that they both use black people to represent the negative qualities against which whiteness and true civilization are defined. In this mythology these terms obviously overlap with ethnic purity and nationality, fairly narrowly and exclusively defined. Stoneman is the "anti-Lincoln" and Dingaan is the "anti-Retief," not in the sense that these figures were political protagonists, but in that Stoneman and Dingaan on one hand and Lincoln and Retief on the other represent mutually exclusive ideals. The two white leaders were determined to deal fairly with the black populace, but were destroyed, indeed martyred, in the process by a lethal alliance of generalized black iniquity and individual white villainy. Among whites evil is an aberration; among blacks it is virtually endemic. The "nation" can be "born" only once the forces of darkness have been vanquished. But this ideal requires such a highly selective reading of a heritage that one could appropriately describe it as a kind of collective amnesia. Ernest Renan has pinpointed the significance of such "absences" in historical narrative: "Forgetting history, or even getting history wrong, is an essential factor in the formation of a nation" (quoted in Van Rooyen 1994, 39).

For Preller, "history" is deliberately functional in this nation-building sense. It is irrelevant that objectivity is unattainable; in fact, it is undesirable. Nation building is not a science; it is an act of the imagination (in the creative romantic sense of the term). In that context, one of the central aspects of popularizing history for Preller is memory, which enables him to create what Isabel Hofmeyr (1987, 110) has called "a semiotics of Afrikaner history." The key negative elements in this system are the black hordes and British perfidy. We have seen that Preller felt compelled to eliminate the issue of British oppression and betrayal from the screenplay of *De Voortrekkers*, with possibly a single exception. The opening English title reads: "Piet Retief, a farmer in the Cape Colony, has planned a great emigration to the Unknown North for the purpose of buying territory from the natives upon which to establish a Free Dutch Republic." The parallel Afrikaans title (translated here) is clearly intended for a less neutral audience: "Despondent and dissatisfied with a bad government, Piet Retief, a commandant at the Cape, prepared to lead a Great Trek to the unknown north, where they would buy land from the kaffirs in order to establish a Free Republic."[16] This is a more highly charged description for a receptive audience, both in its hints of anti-British sentiment and its elevation of Retief's status from farmer to commandant. But Preller's SAP sympathies have been noted, so it remains to be seen how he uses "blackness" as a "cultural indicator"[17] in his film depicting the birth of a nation.

Three aspects of the film are discussed here: the depiction of the Zulu king, Dingaan; the function of Sobuza, Preller's wholly fictional character in this "history"; and the way the Zulu warriors are filmed.

Dingaan is presented in the film as the archetypal savage ruler; the initial images of him are the defining ones—first the total submission to his will of all those around him, followed by what the Afrikaans title refers to as "Dingaan's Justice." An old woman brings a child to him; he angrily reminds her that no child of his is to be allowed to live (a later sequence in the film shows seven or eight "wives" emerging from his hut). He takes the infant by one leg, waves it in the air and says, "Take him away. The birds want food." Significantly, the infanticide does not take place offscreen but is dramatized for the audience in a medium close-up of warriors thrusting their spears into the unseen child. Not only does this signify Dingaan's extreme brutality in preserving his power, it is the obverse of the romantic interest in the film, in which the young Voortrekker Jan Faber courts, rescues from disaster (twice), and marries Johanna Landman. The final shot in the film is of the two proud parents sitting in the church of the Covenant with a smiling infant on the mother's lap. As in *The Birth of a Nation,* the creation of a new nuclear family (two in Griffith's film) is the culmination of the personal and the political stories. Dingaan's tyranny, on the other hand, comes to an end with his wives weeping over his body, after he has been slain by Sobuza, the deserter from Dingaan's camp. Even more stereotypically, Dingaan is shown greatly appreciating, Calibanlike, the gin that the two Portuguese traders bring him.

The Reverend Owen clearly fails in his missionary task with Dingaan, but he succeeds with Sobuza. The terms on which he does so, however, are worth examining in detail. As Dingaan is ordering the infanticide, Sobuza and two other warriors are visiting the reverend at his hut outside Dingaan's kraal. Owen breaks bread with them in a kind of communion and reads from the Bible. But the two commandments that he reads appear to be pointedly selected and rephrased by Preller: "Honour thy father and thy mother that thy days may be long in the land which the Lord thy God giveth thee." This much is true to the Authorized Version, but the lines resonate in interesting ways in this film. The title continues: "desiring that all men, black and white, should live peaceably and without strife, God said, Thou shalt not kill." This commandment causes a great deal of inner turmoil in Sobuza, not because of the racial dimension Preller seems to have imposed on it,[18] but because it defines killing as inherently wicked and unchristian. He returns to Dingaan's kraal and is ordered to participate in the infanticide; when he refuses, one of the other warriors taunts and threatens him: "We shall see what the Great Elephant has to say to a white heart in the body of a Zulu warrior." The "whiteness" of his heart is accounted for in an earlier title describing the effect on him of the reverend reading aloud from the Bible: "The words of the Saviour awaken gentleness in the heart of Sobuza." His adherence to the sixth commandment by refusing to kill the child defines Sobuza as essentially "white," but the ultimate fulfillment of the fifth commandment intensifies an ideological point Preller is trying to convey.

Sobuza is banished by Dingaan and taken in by Retief, whom Sobuza calls his true "father" and vows to honor as an obedient subject: "Thou art my father and my chief and thy people shall be my people." He adopts European clothing in his role as Christian cook and childminder, though he retains his "primitive" skills—exemplified at this point in his rubbing sticks together to start a fire. But after the massacre of Retief and his men, Sobuza vows vengeance on Dingaan and reverts to traditional Zulu warrior garb. He says to Mrs. Retief: "Until the white Inkoos, my White King, is avenged, thou shalt see me no more." Clearly vengeance raises a moral dilemma in terms of the sixth commandment and Sobuza kills Dingaan as a "non-European." The moral imperative to assassinate Dingaan is satisfied, yet no taint of vindictiveness adheres to the Boers. When he sits outside the church of the Covenant at the end of the film, Sobuza is once again neatly dressed in European clothes, ecstatically pointing to the simple wooden cross built into the wall of the church.

The nation has been preserved but—and this is a paradox the film evades entirely—it has also just been born, signified strongly by the smiling Landman infant in the final shot of the film. The concluding title of *De Voortrekkers* confirms the vow made by the trekkers, thanking God "for the preservation of our Race and Country." The reference to "race" here is not primarily to whites as opposed to blacks, but to (white) Afrikaners—in other words, to a nation, as is confirmed in the parallel Afrikaans title: "vir die bewaring van ons Volk en Land." It was common usage at the time to speak of the English and Afrikaans "races," which had to deal with the "native problem."[19]

The similarity, ideological and otherwise, of the ending of *De Voortrekkers* to that of *The Birth of a Nation* is striking, except that in the conclusion of *The Birth of a Nation* there is not a black face in sight. The original epilogue apparently showed the Negroes being sent back to Africa, with Lincoln's blessing.[20] Part 2 of Griffith's film opens with a title referring to Reconstruction as "the agony which the South endured that a nation might be born." It ends with the double honeymoon and then shifts, somewhat surrealistically, into allegorical mode to depict visually, point for point, the penultimate title: "Dare we dream of a golden day when bestial War shall rule no more. But instead—the gentle Prince in the Hall of Brotherly Love in the City of Peace." Both films end with a clear religious sanction for a new "nation."

The obedient servant, Sobuza, is permitted onto the porch of the church of the Covenant—but not inside; that sacred space is reserved for the white families. The film is obviously participating in the developing discourse on segregation, as will be seen below. But in its valorizing of Sobuza's total subjection to white authority after the defeat of the Zulus at Blood River, the film is either ignoring growing black resistance in the country (which is unlikely) or attempting to suppress an anxiety about signs of black self-assertion. This anxiety, of course, manifests itself indirectly in the emphasis on the staggering number of black warriors who attack the white laagers. There is a complete absence in *De Voortrekkers* of the sexual paranoia that pervades *The Birth of a Nation* (although the Portuguese trader's leering at the virginal Johanna Landman signifies his villainy); the paranoia instead has its roots in fear of the possible obliteration of identity through the sheer force of numbers of the "other," who were showing signs of resistance at being relegated to the sidelines of national life. The increasing force that was required to impose this subjugation is itself evidence of the groundswell of resistance that was to characterize political life in South Africa so fatefully throughout the century.

The incident known as "Bambata's rebellion" in 1906, in which a Zulu chief and some four thousand of his followers were massacred by imperial forces in the forests of Natal for refusing to pay a new poll tax, was in many ways the last act of "tribal" resistance and the final military defeat of the Zulu nation. But black popular opposition was taking on other forms. In a television series, *Ulibambe Lingashoni—Hold Up the Sun: The ANC and Popular Power in the Making*,[21] made in South Africa just before the 1994 founding elections, a number of ANC veterans— including Nelson Mandela, Govan Mbeki, Walter Sisulu, and Harry Gwala—are interviewed about the founding of the ANC in 1912 (then called the South African Native National Congress). They all make the point that the Bambata rebellion was an inspiration for the formation of a "parallel" parliament in response to the settlement reached between whites in establishing Union and postponing the "native question."[22] These years of reconstruction and consolidation in white politics were thus also formative years of political activism in South Africa. For example, it was during this period that Gandhi, practicing law in South Africa, developed the philosophy of satyagraha in response to increasingly discriminatory legislation.

From this perspective of growing black nationalism, Sobuza's incorporation into white society (while being kept out of its institutions) could best be described as part of a white fantasy, reinforced by the trekker myth (and also by the notions of white "South Africanism" advocated among Lord Milner's protégés in South Africa).[23] In this context Sobuza's newfound psychological and physical contentment has its counterpart in the plantation ideal of the South, on which Everett Carter (Silva 1971, 138–39) comments wryly:

> The illusion maintained itself by explaining that the true Southern, full-blooded negro remained loyal throughout and after the war. It expanded the truth of individual instances of this kind into a general rule. In the Civil War sequences of *The Birth of a Nation*, the Camerons' slaves are shown cheering the parade of the Confederate soldiers as they march off to defend them against their freedom. . . . As a record of a cultural illusion *The Birth of a Nation* is without equal.

It should come as no surprise that by the time *The Birth of a Nation* was made, there had already been four film versions of *Uncle Tom's Cabin* (Bogle 1974, 3). What may be rather more surprising is that Griffith made probably the first fictional film about South Africa, *The Zulu's Heart* (1908). It is a melodramatic story of a Zulu chief who murders a Voortrekker man but, after the death of his own child, shows great kindness to the surviving mother and her child. The chief thus combines two stereotypes: the brutal savage and the noble savage. Peter Davis (1996, 9) sums up the implication of this: "After this, in film after film, Africans would be defined as either good or bad by their actions towards whites, which determined whether they were the Faithful Servant or the Savage Other."

In *De Voortrekkers,* the "alternative" to the loyal, submissive Zulu servant Sobuza is represented by Dingaan—a ferocious Zulu tyrant in command of dreadful forces. In terms of the myth, Dingaan *had* to die if whites were to survive with their identity intact. Manthia Diawara (1995, 405) notes a similar "necessity" and dynamism in the historical representation, and indeed distortion, of race and history in Griffith's film:

> *The Birth of a Nation* constitutes a grammar book for Hollywood's representation of Black manhood and womanhood, its obsession with miscegenation, and its fixing of Black people within certain spaces, such as kitchens, and into certain supporting roles, such as criminals, on the screen. White people must occupy the center, leaving Black people with only one choice—to exist in relation to Whiteness. *The Birth of a Nation* is the master text that suppressed the real contours of Black history and culture on movie screens, screens monopolized by the major motion picture companies of America.[24]

As Diawara suggests here, films not only "embody" ideologies, they also have histories of reception in which their contents are appropriated to suit diverse and even divergent needs. *The Birth of a Nation,* for example, had a decisive influence on the way black people were subsequently presented in the Hollywood product or in the "race films" made by black filmmakers. But if Griffith's film was increasingly marginalized, *De Voortrekkers* and its ideology were gradually incorporated into the ideals of the group that was to dominate South African political history for much of the twentieth century.[25]

Dingaan and Sobuza represent two alternative visions of the black presence in South Africa from a popular white perspective. This particular binary opposition was acceptable to the supporters of General Botha's SAP, as we have noted, but it also meshed very well with the racial ideals of the members of General Barry Hertzog's new National Party (established in 1914),[26] which was much more preoccupied with a narrowly focused Afrikaner nationalism and an intense and explicit conviction that segregation was essential for the survival of the Afrikaner.[27] In this respect the filming of the Zulu hordes made the appropriation of *De Voortrekkers* by the "new" Afrikaner nationalists virtually inevitable, as the camera style favored was the extreme long shot to emphasize repeatedly that the Africans were a vast, anonymous multitude obeying a blind impulse to destroy. Davis (1996, 133) describes them as "an ant-like mass," which is certainly the visual impression, but the description perhaps leaves the ideological point undeveloped.

This use of the camera may be contrasted with the camera's "passivity" (Rogin 1992, 211) in *The Birth of a Nation* when portraying the antagonists in the battle scenes of the Civil War: the general point that the differences between North and South are inessential is underlined by the depiction of the death of the Cameron and Stoneman boys in a virtual embrace on the battlefield. The true antagonists as far as both the North and the South were concerned, in the film's bizarre logic, are still to be identified, and they too will demonstrate (on a social and political rather than military level) the same kind of mindless and destructive irresponsibility in wielding power.

Among the very few close-ups in *De Voortrekkers* are those of Retief and his son in Dingaan's kraal just before the massacre, individualizing them and thus drawing the audience's sympathy. The one extreme close-up of Sobuza shows him enjoying the antics of two young Voortrekker boys in his care mischievously puffing away at a stolen pipe; his identification with them is clear. But this level of individual attention is reserved for the "white" world—a point that has considerable ideological implications. The major "problem" that segregation could not solve in South Africa was one of demographics; the film "solved" the problem of the huge demographic imbalance, as it were, by making its climax the humiliating defeat, with God's help, of overwhelming numbers of armed and dangerous black warriors. It was obviously discursively impossible for the film to represent the trekkers as land invaders with technologically superior weapons.[28] The rhythm of the film's editing in places also establishes the fact of the imbalance in numbers as inherently threatening. The sequence showing the arrival of Retief's party at Dingaan's kraal and the preparations for the signing of the "treaty" is intercut with a repeated shot of ranks of Zulu warriors; this belittles the formal protocols and prepares the audience (who know the story well) for the coming violence, which is to be met by righteous counter violence.

Both *De Voortrekkers* and *The Birth of a Nation* finally celebrate the establishment of white supremacy by violence. Reconstruction in the United States after the Civil War and Union in South Africa after the Anglo-Boer War unavoidably made black people visible and powerful and hence, in the logic of white supremacy, menacing. This suggests a structural parallel in the films (although I make this point tentatively because of the poor condition of the print of *De Voortrekkers* I viewed). In the first part of both films black people are almost invisible or very much part of the background, figuratively and literally. But the unstated premises in the films are the historical resistance to the emancipation of slaves (particularly in *The Birth of a Nation*) and the struggle for the ownership of land (especially in *De Voortrekkers*). Sorlin (1980, 93) makes this point (which is, in essence, applicable to *De Voortrekkers*) by saying that in *The Birth of a Nation* the Civil War is depicted as a "war with no cause." One takes the point that slavery is nowhere discussed, although a troubling aspect of Sorlin's analysis is that he seems to underestimate the knowledge that an audience brings to a film. If slavery is the unarticulated basis of the anxiety about miscegenation in *The Birth of a Nation*—white supremacists "create" the black rapist to keep white women in their place (Rogin 1987, 207)—then desire for possession of the land and fear of being "swamped" by black people (a fundamental anxiety in white right-wing politics in South Africa at least since Hertzog established the National Party in 1914) are the equivalent generators of racial violence in *De Voortrekkers*.

Sol Plaatje (cited in Dreyer 1980, 104) wrote bitterly after the promulgation of the notorious Natives' Land Act in 1913: "Awakening on Friday morning, June 20, 1913, the South African Native found himself, not actually a slave, but a pariah in the land of his birth." In the two films the issue of white supremacy has become totally fused with the issue of nationhood, and this has an important generic implication. The importance of the historical epic as a genre "is not that it narrates and dramatizes historical events accurately according to the detailed stories of academic historians but rather that it opens up a temporal field that creates the *general* possibility for recognizing oneself as a historical subject" (Sobchack 1990, 29).

It has been suggested above that *De Voortrekkers* was a part of the developing discourse on segregation, however unconscious its makers may have been of this dimension of their film. But the terms in which it conducted that discourse suggest that the "historical subjects" which it interrogated engaged with the issue of segregation not so much as an ideology arising out of "the modernizing dynamics of a newly industrialised society" (Beinart and DuBow 1995, 1), but rather more as subjects who feared and resisted modernity. For them,

> Segregation encompassed a backward-looking horror at the levelling and atomising consequences of capitalism. As a policy it therefore appealed to conservatives who were inclined to romanticise the countryside as a source of social order, tradition and deference. The developing anthropological notion of cultural relativism was readily adopted by segregationist ideologues who proclaimed the need to preserve the distinct identity of different cultures and the internal coherence of African societies. . . . [A]partheid thinkers went further than segregationists in equating cultural differences with national, ethnic and racial identities.
>
> (BEINART AND DUBOW 1995, 11)

Without wanting to suggest in any simplistic way that Preller was a "proto-apartheid" thinker, a relevant point has emerged: Dingaan had to die and the Zulus had to be vanquished, not because the film wished to demonstrate that this was historically true in an objective, disinterested sense, but because the identity of the "nation" (increasingly understood in the film's later appropriations as white and Afrikaner) was in jeopardy. This point can be developed with reference to Kinghorn's discussion (1994) of Afrikaner politics in the 1930s, particularly his introduction of another "myth" that has a bearing on this discussion. Making the point that debates in Afrikaner circles on social issues since the 1930s have drawn heavily on the Old Testament, Kinghorn highlights the story of Babel as particularly influential in determining policy, in a way that the secular myth of the Voortrekkers never was; the main function of the latter narrative was to sustain group solidarity. But this preoccupation with group-centeredness is precisely the link between the secular and the biblical stories. The Babel story enabled policymakers to justify "separation" as part of God's will, thereby elevating it beyond the reach of moral debate and validating their own identity as nation. The confusion at Babel made it sufficiently clear that "God was the anti-modern, the anti-cosmopolitan, the anti-plural force in this story . . . the ideal world is one which is static" (Kinghorn 1994, 403).

It seems to me that this deeply conservative impulse lies behind the final sequence of *De Voortrekkers*, with the whites occupying the sacred space inside the church of the Covenant and Sobuza worshiping the same God outside. Interestingly, Griffith is more obsessed with ethnic purity in *The Birth of a Nation* than the Afrikaners (or the English) in South Africa appeared to be at that time; the ending of *De Voortrekkers* has more to do with the imposition of control over labor and land,[29] by force if necessary, as the Afrikaner was confronted with modernity in the shape of a new nation-state (the Union of South Africa), capitalist pro-duction (particularly gold-based), liberal education, and European ide-ologies. Kinghorn's (1994, 402) summary of the Afrikaner response to modernity can also serve as a reading of the subtext of *De Voortrekkers*: "In their efforts to reconstruct their social cosmos, the combination of nationalist politics and a religiously constructed pre-modern social cosmology seemed to provide an answer."

In Preller's work this construction of a cosmology includes a great deal of violence, which is much more explicit throughout *De Voortrekkers* than it is in *The Birth of a Nation*.[30] This quality is proba-bly partly an aspect of the imperial myth of "dark Africa" as a place of endemic violence, but more specifically it is an integral part of Preller's screenplay, being an inherent element of the definition of the "other" in trekker mythology and hence of the identity of the group, whose most sustaining values are to be found in the family. Isabel Hofmeyr (1988, 534) has noted the conjunction of violence and memory as a typical feature of Preller's writing: "Virtually all of Preller's texts read as an inventory of atrocities which eventually calcify into almost a set of legendary codes: the battered baby skulls, the dead women, the drifting feathers, the skinning alive, and so on. All these shorthand images in turn acquire the status of implicit historical explanation and justifica-tion." In this enterprise Preller was as eager to use modern technol-ogy in exploiting "film's documentary pretense" (Rogin 1987, 228) as Griffith was.

Both Griffith and Preller insisted on the "realism" and authen-ticity of their stories.[31] Their extreme care and almost obsessive attention to detail have been well documented, but it is their understanding of the concept of "authenticity," namely that it somehow circumvents ideology, that is revealing about the operation of social and cultural dynamics. Preller (cited in Hofmeyr 1988, 525) declared with some satisfaction in 1917 that "People apparently imagine—so realistic are my representations—that they are seeing a real, photographic reproduction of the actual events as they happened in 1838"; the real and the represented are virtually elided in this statement. But a comment by Griffith takes one closer to the heart of the problem raised by cinematic representation. He claims that if children could watch moving pictures they need never read history again; all they would have to do is "press the button and *actually see what happened. There will be no opinions expressed*. You will merely be present at the making of history" (Silva 1971, 10; my emphasis).

Preller includes a shot of a copy of the Retief-Dingaan treaty in the film and Griffith presents a series of "historical facsimiles" (documents and tableaux) to guarantee, as it were, the truthfulness of their stories, but Snead's point (1994, 41) that these "historical facsimiles" serve ideological rather than narrative aims applies equally to Preller's naive realism, in which the distinction between fact and fiction, code and message, is taken as unproblematic.[32] It is easy enough to show how partial (in both senses of the word) their reading of history is; it is more unsettling to contemplate the cultural, social, and political implications and consequences of their work.

Ultimately, *De Voortrekkers* provides a vivid illustration of the multifaceted nature of a text. It stands as an icon in a nation-building enterprise, and is thus comparable to a film such as *The Birth of a Nation*. More specifically, it represents Gustav Preller's gesture of historical accommodation and came to be appropriated more exclusively as an Afrikaner epic on coming to terms with a negotiated Union. Looking at the film from the other end of the century, *De Voortrekkers* can be seen as a text that portends a fateful history of oppression, appalling suffering, and human rights abuses—and a violent struggle for liberation.

Notes

1. The Great Trek is a classic political myth in Henry Tudor's terms (1972, 138–39): it preserves the past; it focuses on the nation; it renders national experience more coherent; it helps to establish hegemony and strengthen solidarity. The extent to which it actually determined apartheid policy has been questioned by Kinghorn (1994).

2. In this respect it is worth quoting Thelma Gutsche, whose study, based on research conducted in the late 1930s and early 1940s, remains virtually the only major source of reference for films of this period: "The magnitude of *De Voortrekkers* was totally out of proportion to the reputation of the nascent film industry and gave evidence of the courage, confidence and optimism which attended its launching. Conceived on a grand scale, this ambitious historical film would have demanded the full resources, both financial and technical, of the best-equipped Hollywood studio of the day" (1972, 333 n. 22).

3. The first sustained recent attempt (after Gutsche's in the 1930s) at a critical engagement with *De Voortrekkers* is by Streble (1979, 25), who refers to it as "very much a South African *Birth of a Nation*," but the comparison is not developed beyond a few general points. The same can be said of Davis's interesting discussion of *De Voortrekkers*; Davis suggests the film was "probably inspired" by *The Birth of a Nation* (1996, 128).

4. *The Birth of a Nation* was explicitly compared to *Cabiria* at its opening (Silva 1971, 22, 26). Although Griffith's other films had been shown in South Africa, it seems that *The Birth of a Nation* did not reach the country until 1931. Gutsche is oddly quiet about such a famous film. She simply lists the title as having been screened in 1931, without even mentioning Griffith's name, as she does for his other films. It is also not clear whether this version is the one with sound that Griffith released in 1930 (Rogin 1987, 215). Gutsche (1972, 230) lists it as "silent," though this in itself does not exclude the possibility that she is referring to the 1930 version. Sorlin (1980, 113 n. 2) states that "in 1930 Griffith issued a new shortened sound version; he suppressed every mention of the Ku Klux Klan." See also Plaatje's objections to the film published in *Umteteli wa Bantu*, 18 July 1931.

5. Shaw embarked for South Africa in April 1916 (Gutsche 1972, 312).

6. *De Voortrekkers* has not generated anything like the debate, controversy, or scholarship elicited by Griffith's film. Considering the blatantly racist premises of the South African film, this is interesting in itself. There are also signs that the copy from the state film archives in Pretoria is less than pristine: sections have been badly spliced together, often repeating portions of sequences, titles appear on screen too briefly to be read, it is much shorter than the two hours indicated in the original advertisements (even allowing for some exaggeration for the sake of publicity) or by Gutsche (1972, 315) herself, who gives its length as ten thousand feet. This probably mutilated copy is compared here with the superbly restored version of *The Birth of a Nation* released by Kevin Brownlow and David Gill in 1993 (Connoisseur Video). For accounts of the difficulties involved in dealing with early silent films, see Usai 1988; Merritt 1990.

7. The former head of the South African National Film, Video and Sound Archives, Johan de Lange (1991), has produced a valuable catalogue of extant material, with an insightful introduction. See also Barnes 1992.

8. L. M. Thompson's *The Unification of South Africa, 1902–1910* (1960) remains one of the standard accounts of the complex process by which the

National Convention wrought a semblance of accommodation between English and Afrikaans South Africans.

9. The Afrikaans historian F. A. van Jaarsveld (1990, 13) makes explicit the comparison to George Washington.

10. In his psychological studies of racism in South Africa in the 1930s, I. D. MacCrone (1937) asked subjects to indicate which historical contacts between blacks and whites in South Africa they remembered learning about at school or elsewhere; at the top of this list was the "murder massacre of Piet Retief and his company" followed by significantly high figures for "Battle of Blood River" and "murders, massacres and treachery by Chaka [Shaka] and Dingaan" (267). See also Naidoo 1989, chaps. 4, 5).

11. Hall (1990, 12–13) makes a useful distinction between *overt* and *inferential* racism, the latter—somewhat more applicable to *De Voortrekkers*—being defined as "those apparently naturalised representations of events and situations relating to race, whether factual or fictional, which have racist premises and propositions inscribed in them as a set of unquestioned assumptions."

12. Just over half the film depicts the same incidents as in *De Voortrekkers*—a span of four of five years. This is remarkable in a film that sets out to present almost five hundred years of South African history! *They Built a Nation* (better known in South Africa by its Afrikaans title, *Die Bou van 'n Nasie*) (1938) was directed by Joseph Albrecht, a cameraman who had come to South Africa to work on *De Voortrekkers*.

13. See Dubow 1989, esp. chap. 1. He writes: "the first group of theorists to outline a systematic ideology of segregation were English- rather than Afrikaans-speaking, and . . . many of them were associated with the inter-war tradition of South African liberal thought. . . . The earliest examples of Afrikaner proto-apartheid theory date from the early 1930s, but although they bear the distinctive imprint of Christian-Nationalist thinking and embrace a purist view of total separation, in substance they are largely derivative of already extant segregation and trusteeship ideology" (22).

14. As the traders and Retief's party head for Dingaan's kraal, two American missionaries, Lindley and Venables, visit Owen on their way to meet the trekkers. This visit is entirely unmotivated, unexplained, and undeveloped in the film. Its function can hardly be to neutralize any taint of "Britishness" that may adhere to Owen in the film (as opposed to Preller's biography of Retief (1988 [1917])), as the narrative requires him to be a wholly good man who converts Sobuza to the paths of righteousness.

15. This is a point discussed at some length in Dubow 1989, 29–30.

16. The Afrikaans (still very "Dutch" at the time) reads in full as follows: "Moedeloos en ontevrede met a slegte regering het Piet Retief, 'n Kaapse Kommandant, hom opgemaak om 'n Grote Trek te lei naar die onbekende noorde, waar hul grond sou koop van die kaffers, om 'n Vrije Republiek te stig."

17. This concept, which has been influential in South African film theory, is

taken from Tomaselli (1980, 2): "film seen as a system of cultural indicators provides a symbolical insight into the ideological structures of society."

18. It is tempting to think that Preller may have done this to unsettle his audience and subliminally turn them against the British missionary, but this would fly in the face of the logic of the film, which hinges on Sobuza's authentic conversion by Owen (see n. 14 above). The racial addition is more likely to be simply a case of conventional piety from a missionary in Africa, with all its colonial patriarchal and patronizing overtones.

19. See, for example, the debates preceding Union in Thompson 1960. Dubow (1995, 17) writes: "the race paradigm as a whole often lacked specificity. This is nowhere more evident than in the case of the word 'race' itself which, until the 1920s, was often used a synonym for 'nation' (as in the British vs. Afrikaner 'race') rather than as a means of distinguishing between blacks and whites."

20. When Thomas Dixon was asked soon after the film's release whether he thought this was a practicable arrangement, "[h]e replied with great earnestness that he did, that it was possible to create public sentiment such that a beginning could be made in the near future, that a large faction of the Negroes themselves would cooperate in the enterprise and that within a century we could get rid of all the Negroes" (Silva 1971, 82–83).

21. Directed by Lesley Lawson (Afrovision, 1993). Part 1 is entitled *Roots of Struggle, 1912–1948*.

22. The ferocity with which the Bambata rebellion was quelled has often been noted. Bambata himself was beheaded and his head put on public display. For a detailed account of the growth of African nationalism in South Africa, see Walshe 1987.

23. After the Anglo-Boer War, Alfred Milner was appointed governor of the defeated Boer republics, now also British colonies. He brought with him a group of young men—sometimes referred to as "Milner's kindergarten"—to act as administrative officials.

24. Diawara (cited in Martin 1995, 405) adds that this had the effect of "overdetermining a new genre, produced exclusively for Black audiences, called race films." The response of black Americans to the film was immediate: they made films themselves specifically to counter the image of black people in *The Birth of a Nation*. See, for example, Snead 1995, 367–68 on the making of *The Birth of a Race* and Reid 1993, 12 on the significance of Oscar Micheaux in this respect. The increasing dispossession of black people in South Africa made such a development impossible in that country.

25. See Gutsche 1972, 315–16 for an account of the film's immense popularity. For a discussion of the later manifestations of Great Trek mythology, see Grundlingh and Sapire 1989.

26. This is not the "National Party" that came into power in 1948 and institutionalized apartheid; the latter party was a product of an ever-increasing

movement toward the right of the political spectrum, taking Preller along with it, incidentally, after General Botha's death in 1919.

27. In this respect Streble (1979) misrepresents *De Voortrekkers* as an expression of Afrikaner nationalism; strictly speaking the film was appropriated, rather than "produced," by Afrikaner nationalism. Hertzog won the "black peril" election only in 1929.

28. This is not simply a fanciful point. Okoye (1969, 230) makes it clear that the issue of weapons was crucial for Dingaan, whose political and military alliances with the trekkers, traders, and surrounding tribes were extremely complex. It was partly his fear of an invasion by the *Amabaro* (Boers), the power of whose weapons Dingaan was fully aware of, that led him to sanction the murder of Retief in 1838.

29. Davis (1996, 134) makes a similar point in stating that "the character of Sobuza, which is entirely fictitious, is not necessary in any way to the recounting of the exploits of the Voortrekkers. The only way it can be understood is as an attempt to integrate black South Africans into a benevolent hierarchy, where they could be fully accepted provided they knew their place."

30. Leab (1975, 20) notes that "significantly, few films of this period, not even comedies, portray black violence against white people or their property."

31. In Griffith's case the scale of the graphic values was partly also a matter of meeting the challenge of the Italian spectacles. But Frank Woods, who cowrote the script with Griffith, insisted in a lecture in 1929 that "every effort was made to have the picture authentic as an historical document" (cited in Geduld 1971, 85).

32. Sobchack (1990, 27) quotes a comment from Sande Cohen's critique of historiography: "There is no *primary* object or complex that warrants calling forth the signifier 'history.'"

4

"What Sort of Memorial?"
Cry, the Beloved Country on Film

Mark Beittel

At the U.S. premiere of the remake of *Cry, the Beloved Country* (1995), guest of honor President Nelson Mandela (1995) gave the film his endorsement, both applauding its evocation of "such strong emotions about the terrible past" and declaring it "a monument to the future." This moment was not without a degree of irony; some four decades earlier, D. F. Malan, then prime minister and one of the principal architects of apartheid, had been the guest of honor at the South African premiere of the 1951 version of the same film, shown in a whites-only Johannesburg theater.[1] On that occasion, Alan Paton (1988, 54–55), the author on whose 1948 novel both films were based, was there as well, and in his autobiography he reflected on whether he should have been present at the event in such company, but concluded: "It never occurred to me to refuse to attend. . . . After all, the production of *Cry, the Beloved Country* was a great event in South African film history." The 1995 remake was also hailed as a historic event: "the first major film to be made in the newly democratic South Africa," trumpeted both the *New York Times*'s review of the film and its advertisement.[2]

The timing of the novel's publication in 1948, the year the National Party came to power on a platform of apartheid policies, certainly helped make it an instant best-seller in the United States, but *Cry, the Beloved Country* has demonstrated staying power and continued international appeal: by the time of Paton's death in 1988, the novel had sold fifteen million copies in twenty languages, making it the best-selling South African literary work ever (Callan 1991, 17).

But *Cry* has not only been a literary success; it has also been an ongoing multimedia event, which has surely broadened its influence. Soon after its publication, the book was made into a musical by the well-known Broadway team of Maxwell Anderson and Kurt Weill (1949).

Although Paton (1988, 20–24) himself was not at all enthusiastic about this production (he saw it as projecting a vaguely atheistic worldview, very much at odds with his own profound Christianity), *Lost in the Stars* was an immediate hit; not only has it been revived repeatedly, it was made into a film in 1974. In the mid-1950s, a dramatic adaptation of *Cry* was published (Komai 1955), which has been staged on at least four continents. Forty years later, a hypertext version of Paton's story was created on the Internet as part of the marketing campaign for the film's remake (Open Book Systems 1995).

This advertising emphasized that, although South African producer Anant Singh had purchased the film rights to *Cry* about the time that Mandela was released from prison, he waited to make it until "South Africa attained democracy" (Videovision Entertainment 1995). The remake thus promised a "postapartheid" perspective on Paton's novel, presumably offering a different ideological stance than the original film adaptation, which was written and shot in 1950 after two years of Nationalist rule and just as major pillars of apartheid legislation were being enacted.

Curiously, both films were acclaimed for being "faithful" to Paton's novel. The *New York Times,* for example, praised the 1951 adaptation as "a faithful rendering of the novel to the screen" (Crowther 1952), and nearly forty-four years later, the same paper deemed the 1995 film "faithful to the hushed, semi-biblical tone of the book" (Holden 1995, B6). The films themselves make strong claims for their own fidelity to the novel. The opening credits of the 1951 adaptation not only introduce it as "a Zoltan Korda/Alan Paton Production," but also indicate that Paton wrote the screenplay; in his autobiography, Paton (1988, 19) describes his actual role as that of a "superior amanuensis," since Korda "construct[ed] the script." Nevertheless, Paton also makes it plain that he approved of virtually all aspects of the film, unlike the musical *Lost in the Stars,* except for the "miserable thousand pounds" (53–54) he was paid for the film rights. Similarly, the credits for the 1995 remake identify it as "based on the novel by Alan Paton," and several substantial sections of dialogue in it are taken directly from the novel with minimal alterations. Moreover, both adaptations underline their fidelity to Paton's text not only by opening with a voice-over of the novel's first sentences, but also by ending with a projection onto the screen of its final two sentences. This framing of the films is certainly significant.

Nevertheless, a narrow focus on fidelity to the novel obscures the similarities between the two films. They both restructure the novel by the visually dramatic device of continually cutting back and forth between the stories of Kumalo and Jarvis, in contrast to the novel's technique of first relating the story of Kumalo, then the story of Jarvis, and finally interweaving the two. Consequently, both films create additional episodes, which are crucial for understanding their respective ideological stances. Moreover, the two adaptations have been similarly compressed by the elimination of most of book 3, which shows the return of the protagonists to their rural homes and their efforts to improve conditions in the poverty-stricken village of Ndotsheni. Both films also reduce the role of or eliminate some characters, such as Jarvis's young grandson, who signals the future "new white man," and the black agricultural demonstrator who is sent by Jarvis to teach the villagers "modern" farming techniques. Consequently, both films tend to de-emphasize the prospects for change in rural areas and focus instead on the moral lessons to be learned from the tragic sojourns of the two fathers in Johannesburg. They also downplay the devastating collapse of African agriculture that occurred during the 1940s, a problem that is central to both the themes and the plot of the novel. (Indeed, surprisingly, the 1995 film virtually eliminates this aspect of the novel.)

Yet despite these similarities, the 1995 remake is not simply a colorized version of the 1951 film. Each film selects different episodes from the novel, creates scenes that have no corollaries in the text, and portrays the main characters differently. While these choices all provide important insights into the ideological stance of the respective films, the fundamental differences between the two lie in their narrative approaches to the story. A comparison is useful not so much to see how the films interpret the novel, but rather to understand how their interpretations function culturally in the two different political and historical contexts that produced them—and in this respect their rhetoric is of fundamental importance.

The 1951 adaptation is set in a "timeless present," avoiding references to specific dates, even when the text of an important letter and the front pages of two newspapers are projected on the screen. Consequently, this film treats the story in a symbolic mode as part of an indefinite present and emphasizes the struggle against evil and the hope for a better day. The 1995 adaptation, on the other hand, clearly establishes the date of the action near the beginning of the film by projecting the words "Natal, South Africa—1946" onto the screen, and in another scene a letter, including its date, is read aloud. The remake thus establishes itself as historical and promises to tell the audience what is important to remember about this specific moment of the past. While the 1951 film seeks to influence the present and the future, the 1995 remake is determined by the tragedy of the apartheid past—and this is why the hope of the first adaptation turns into tears in the second.

The Korda-Paton Adaptation (1951)

Although Paton himself and others at the time declared it a landmark in South African cinema, the 1951 film was actually a British production. It had an "international" cast, and both the black and white leads were played by non-South Africans: Canada Lee was a prominent black actor in the United States during the 1930s and 1940s whose career ended when he was blacklisted by Hollywood as a communist for his outspoken views on African Americans, and Charles Carson was a veteran British screen actor. Several of the other major roles were also played by actors of non-South African origin, and the film is certainly now best remembered for having Sidney Poitier in his second major screen role.[3] But some of the white and black secondary characters were played by South Africans, and the role of Absolom launched the film career of Lionel Ngakane.

Cry was directed and produced by Zoltan Korda, the youngest brother of Sir Alexander Korda, the prominent film magnate and financier. As young men, both brothers had been left-wing activists involved in the film industry in their native Hungary; after the First World War, they fled to make films in Austria, Germany, and the United States, and then settled in England, where Alexander founded London Films and directed or produced some of Britain's most successful films of the 1930s and 1940s. Following and working with his brother, Zoltan was also a successful director, best known for films set in "exotic" places with colonial themes, such as *Sanders of the River* (1935), which was based on Edgar Wallace's jingoistic novel (Wallace 1930 [1909]) and included footage shot in central and West Africa; *The Four Feathers* (1939), which has been described as "one of the grandest Empire films" (Katz 1994, 760); the original, nonanimated version of *Jungle Book* (1942); and the Humphrey Bogart vehicle, *Sahara* (1943).

During the 1930s, Zoltan often argued with his brother over their "empire" films. Although a left-wing sympathizer in his younger years, Alexander was by the 1930s a "confirmed Anglophile who saw the Empire builders as the embodiment of all the most noble traits in the English character and spirit" (Kulik 1975, 135). Zoltan remained more liberal and wanted their films to express some of the complexities of colonial rule. One of the specific issues they disagreed about was whether white men should shake the hands of "natives." Alexander thought not, but Zoltan insisted that under certain conditions they should—and he won on this point. Alexander, however, seems to have prevailed in the overall interpretations of these films, as is indicated by a scene near the end of *Sanders of the River*. Here the illegitimate African king Bosambo, who has been installed by the British under the policy of indirect rule, humbly and gratefully shakes the hand of his colonial master and says: "Lord Sandy, I've learned the secret of government from your lordship. It is this: a king ought not to be feared but loved by his people." While patently functioning as a tribute to the skills of the British commissioner, this scene comes across as ludicrously contrived, since "the main lesson created in the film is that Africans fear and respect the strong, harsh authority of their British protectors" (Dunn 1996, 160).

The symbolic device of the handshake is used more convincingly by Korda and Paton in the 1951 adaptation of *Cry*. The first handshake introduces the character of James Jarvis in a scene that was created for the film. Jarvis is watching his black farmhand plow when a neighbor approaches on horseback and hands Jarvis a Johannesburg newspaper. On the front page, there is a photo of Jarvis's son shaking the hand of a black man; the caption under the photo states that Arthur Jarvis is "Chairman of the Housing Committee." The dialogue makes it clear that the elder Jarvis does not approve of his son's liberal activism and introduces the connection between the housing crisis in urban areas and the shortage of labor on white farms. After the neighbor rides off, Jarvis mutters: "Houses. Well, I understand about the houses, but why does he have to shake hands?" The power of this photographed handshake to make Jarvis feel ashamed of his son's activities is pointedly underlined when he arrives home for lunch and his ailing wife asks to see the newspaper, having been alerted by the neighbor's wife. Jarvis admits that he has thrown the paper away in a field and sulks that the neighbor has probably already spread the shameful news. Jarvis's wife then changes the subject, asking him whether it is true that he was evicting an old black tenant who had worked for them for many years because the man's son had run away to Johannesburg and would not be available to fulfill the family's contract. Jarvis's attitude becomes evident when he explains that he must expel them because he is "running a farm, not a charity," and that while old Williams is all right, "his family are a whole lot of good-for-nothing scoundrels."

The second handshake in the film, also without precedent in the novel, has a contrasting significance to the first one. After receiving a letter from the Reverend Msimangu, the village priest, Stephen Kumalo sets off on his first trip ever to Johannesburg, which is portrayed as Sodom and Gomorrah both in the words of his traveling companions and in a series of accelerating images. Before his departure, a brief scene underlines his belief that blacks must stick together and help one another, but once he arrives in Johannesburg, he is easily cheated out of a pound of his meager savings by a smartly dressed young man, a scene vividly illustrating that in town blacks prey on other blacks, even if the victim happens to be a frightened, elderly man of the cloth. Finally, Kumalo arrives at Mission House in Sophiatown and is introduced to an integrated group of black and white missionaries, each of whom in turn warmly shakes his hand. Jarvis's attitude about white men shaking the hands of blacks is clearly contrasted to that of the missionaries. This scene not only shows that Mission House is an island of racial harmony, where white priests willingly extend their help to their black brothers, it also reflects the more general position occupied by religious people in the film: they are generous, humble, and untainted by bigotry. Of course Mission House is clearly under the direction of the white Father Vincent, who also provides Kumalo with religious guidance when Kumalo's faith is shaken by the many calamities he faces in Johannesburg.

After they are told of their son's murder, James Jarvis and his wife also make their way to Johannesburg. In the film, as in the novel, the Afrikaner police chief who delivers the bad news shakes hands when he greets Jarvis—the expected behavior of two white gentlemen. As Jarvis struggles to come to terms with his grief, he studies the Christian-inspired writings of his liberal-activist son and is profoundly moved by them. His son's enlightened stance and prominent position in Johannesburg are visually highlighted by the large racially and ethnically diverse crowd of mourners at the funeral. After the funeral, the widowed wife of Arthur shakes the hands of the other mourners, including those of the black women who approach her. When a black man approaches the elder Jarvis with his hand extended, the elder Jarvis at first hesitates, then shakes his hand and the hands of other blacks who approach him—the precise gesture that had been such a source of shame when his son was still alive. His wife looks on angelically, indicating her approval. This scene signals the beginnings of Jarvis's profound spiritual transformation.

Later—after the trial of Kumalo's son, who is found guilty and sentenced to hang for the murder of Jarvis's son—there are several loose ends to tie up before the two men can return to their rural homes. As Jarvis prepares to leave, he is escorted to the train by the father of Arthur's widow, who has a conservative, law-and-order attitude, and by her brother, who shares the liberal views of Jarvis's son and is the cofounder with him of a boys' club for Africans. As he boards the train, Jarvis solemnly shakes hands with the father and then with the son, to whom he also hands an envelope that he says is not to be opened until his departure. When the train moves away from the platform, the young Harrison tears open the envelope and discovers to his astonishment that Jarvis has donated a thousand pounds to the boys' club. This act marks another stage in Jarvis's transformation, since he begins to take concrete actions based on his newfound beliefs. His new role as a liberal benefactor contrasts sharply with his earlier behavior, when he spoke contemptuously of charity and callously referred to the family of black tenants that he was about to throw off his land as "good-for-nothing scoundrels."

While the film vividly shows the spiritual transformation of a white farmer, it also implacably isolates the enemy of the Christian liberal ideology that it promotes throughout. This is evident in the handshake that occurs right after the trial of Stephen Kumalo's son. This scene, which again has no equivalent in the novel, shows Msimangu (in what possibly was a career-making moment for Poitier) confronting Stephen's brother John. His son had participated along with Stephen's son in the attempted burglary during which Jarvis's son was killed; unlike Stephen's son, John's did not confess and has been set free by the court. After the court has adjourned, we see John Kumalo busily shaking the hands of all the black men around him, when Msimangu approaches. Just as their hands come into contact, John declares to the gathered crowd that the court's decision was "justice," and Msimangu reacts in anger: "Justice? Is that what I heard you say?" When John lamely tries to defend his words, Msimangu angrily declares: "Keep your word in your mouth, and when you open it again in your great meetings, with your great bull voice, spare us your talk of truth and justice." In a highly charged dramatic moment, Msimangu turns from John and asks the assembled men, "Where can I wash my hand?" He wipes his hand on his cassock and, along with Stephen, walks away.

In an article about Poitier for *Look* magazine, James Baldwin (1968, 52), who did not like the film, wrote that he thought this particular scene was a "moving miracle of indignation." Viewed in isolation from the larger plot, Msimangu's angry gesture and verbal outburst seem to be the laudable rejection of a reprehensible act by an individual: John's son has gotten off because a witness perjured herself and provided him with an alibi. The full significance of this scene, however, becomes clear only when one focuses on who John is and what he represents.

Earlier in the film we learn that John is a carpenter and a prominent political figure in Sophiatown. But even before we first encounter him, John is portrayed negatively by his sister Gertrude, who informs Stephen that when she went to John for help, he told her that her trade as a liquor seller and prostitute was as good as his. Later, when Stephen and Msimangu visit him during their search for Stephen's son, John blithely states that his wife has left him and that he now lives with a woman to whom he is not married. Moreover, he has allowed their two sons to go off on their own in Johannesburg. When he is put on the defensive by his brother and Msimangu, John starts to lecture the two men about the poor material conditions in the township and the church's lack of leadership in resolving these problems. He is particularly critical of the hypocrisy of the church and of what he perceives as his brother's mission to get him, their sister, and their sons to return to Ndotsheni. "There is a new thing growing here," he declares, "stronger than any church or any chief." Wearing his overalls, standing in his workshop, speaking about the working-class issues of housing, wages, and poverty, and defying and challenging the moral teaching and leadership of the church, John is obviously symbolic of anticlerical black political leadership: he does not even need to be identified as a communist. And the critique of what he stands for is that he has become immoral, irresponsible, arrogant, hypocritical, and ultimately corrupt during the years he has spent in Johannesburg. As such, he is starkly juxtaposed to Msimangu.

As Ezekiel Mphahlele (1974, 160) has observed with regard to the novel, "human nature is falsified because there are bad characters as against good ones—in two distinct groups." The critic Patrick Colm Hogan (1992–93: 208) argues that *Cry* posits a simple but clear distinction between good leaders, who are either white people who help blacks or black folks who devote their lives to Christ and accept white leadership, and bad leaders, who are invariably secular blacks. In the book, John Kumalo is the main, but not only, example of the latter, since the chief of Kumalo's village is clearly presented as incompetent and the school headmaster as ineffective. Though the novel does provide a possible positive model for a secular black leader in Dubula, the patient organizer of the bus boycott, Msimangu insists that Dubula was originally a church person (Paton 1987 [1948]). But even this degree of complexity has been eliminated from the 1951 film: the immoral and corrupt John is *the* model of secular black leadership, and there is a stark contrast between him and the devout Msimangu. Msimangu's powerful "Where can I wash my hand?" is followed by the symbolic wiping of his hand on his cassock; then he and Stephen walk away, leaving John standing there foolishly.

One South African critic suggested that the portrayal of John in the film was designed to cater to the U.S. audience (Sachs 1951). However, the late 1940s was a period of spreading and deepening influence by the Communist Party of South Africa (Bonner, Delius, and Posel 1993, 16–17). Part of the National Party's reaction to this development was to pass the Suppression of Communism Act in 1950, which drove the party underground, but certainly did not eliminate its influence. The government extensively used the provisions of the act to ban opponents whether or not they were communists, and in his autobiography Paton (1988, 37–39) emphasizes that he was strongly opposed to this piece of legislation. Nevertheless, Paton was staunchly anticommunist, and on this point he and the exiled Hungarian Korda were in complete accord (Alexander 1994, 274–75).

In the novel and the film, Kumalo's sister Gertrude comes to town and sinks into liquor selling and prostitution, his son Absolom falls into a life of thievery and murder, and his brother John becomes a godless and corrupt politician. The film goes beyond the novel, however: it not only dramatically demonizes John's politics as communist and indicates how good black leaders like Msimangu counteract the evil embodied in John, it also shows that innocent blacks like Stephen Kumalo must walk away from the menace of communism—even if this means turning their backs on their own brothers. Thus, in far starker and more strident terms than the novel, the film poses a clear-cut polarized vision of evil communist against good Christian leadership in the black community. It was a message that fit the temper of the times—and also one that Prime Minister Malan would have found agreeable when he attended the film's opening night in Johannesburg.

Yet what might have pleased Malan even more is the film's unquestionable endorsement of the message that the "real" home of Africans was rural places like Ndotsheni, and that in urban areas they would inevitably be tempted into lives of immorality, corruption, and crime. This is clearly illustrated not only in the degeneration of Kumalo's family, but also in Absolom's futile wish, expressed during his father's final visit in prison: "If I were back in Ndotsheni, I should not leave again." These words are uttered at a point in the film when it is absolutely clear that

Absolom acted out of fear rather than evil; therefore his explicit analysis that nothing bad would have happened had he never left his rural home carries great weight.

As compatible as this message may be with the basic tenets of apartheid,[4] it should by no means obscure Paton's dedicated opposition to the National Party and its racially divisive policies. Both the book and the film are indisputable pleas for whites to act charitably toward their black neighbors, and the exemplary model for this appeal is Arthur Jarvis. It is through his leadership and sacrifice that even misguided white men like his own father can be redeemed and learn to express the spirit of liberal Christianity that Arthur personifies. The presence of other white characters such as Father Vincent, the head of Mission House, and Martens, the dedicated if at times hotheaded caseworker of the reform school, reinforces the positive image of liberal activism. And in this sense, the film is political in that it presents the hopes and the fears of the white liberalism that Paton championed throughout his life. In so doing, the film reflects also the limits of liberal ideology: not only was communism to be opposed, but the existing social order was to be left intact.

This becomes clear at the end of the film, when Jarvis's ailing wife dies and Kumalo grieves deeply. He wishes to join the other mourners standing around Jarvis's house, but angrily realizes that the local whites would never tolerate this. A friend of his who works for Jarvis arrives and tells Kumalo: "You could write a letter. You could make flowers. You could do what the white people do." Of course, the white people can stand around the house, which Kumalo, who lives as close to the Jarvis farm as they, cannot: all he can do is imitate from a distance "what the white people do."

Later, as he is climbing a mountain to pray at the scheduled moment of his son's execution, Kumalo meets Jarvis, who tells him: "Your flowers were of great beauty." Jarvis then says that he has spoken to the bishop so that Kumalo will not be sent away from the village. "How could you?" asks Jarvis. "For what did my son die if you were to go away?" For Jarvis, the execution of Kumalo's son means that "one thing is about to be finished, but here [in Jarvis's charity] is something that has only begun. And while I live it will continue." This episode marks the completion of Jarvis's spiritual transformation, as the dialogue between the two men underlines:

Kumalo: Do not go before I have thanked you for all the things you have done, for . . .

Jarvis: I knew a man who was in darkness until you found him . . .

Kumalo: Of all the white men I have ever known . . .

Jarvis: I am not a saintly man . . .

Kumalo: Of that I cannot speak, but God put his hands on you . . .

Jarvis: That may be, that may be.

I have suggested that the ideology of much of the 1951 film is re-flected symbolically through handshakes, and during this last encounter between the two protagonists the viewers' expectation is that Jarvis will shake Kumalo's hand. On the contrary, he makes no such attempt—he does not even get off his horse. For while he may shake the offered hands of the black men at his son's funeral in Johannesburg, he can bestow gifts on Kumalo and the villagers precisely because of his status as an influential and wealthy white farmer, and symbolically he belongs up on his horse as he dispenses them.

In ways that take good advantage of a visual medium, the 1951 adaptation vividly and faithfully follows the novel by portraying black South Africans as innocent but corruptible peasants and white South Africans as misguided but redeemable tyrants. Though the film opens, concludes, and indeed mainly focuses on the figure of Kumalo, his function is simply to endure stoically the troubles that rain down on him. It is Jarvis who is transformed by events, Jarvis who, following in the footsteps of his dead and saintly son, is a living monument to the human capacity for spiritual renewal.

The film received mixed reviews in the South African press, with the liberal English papers generally favorable, and was very positively reviewed in the United States and Britain; it also won several prizes, including the 1952 Golden Laurel from the Museum of Modern Art for its "contribution to mutual understanding and goodwill." Nevertheless, the film was not a commercial success, which in the United States may have been because one of its stars was blacklisted and because the distributor initially released it under the glaringly inappropriate title of *African Fury* (Davis 1996, 44–7).

The Roodt-Singh Adaptation (1995)

The 1995 production of *Cry* was made by the team of Darrell Roodt, a prolific director and the self-defined bad boy of South African cinema, and Anant Singh, one of the first and most successful black film produc-ers in South Africa. They had worked together for years on films such as *City of Blood* (1983), a B-grade thriller shot in Johannesburg; *Place of Weeping* (1986), which they marketed as the "first anti-apartheid feature film made in South Africa" (Videovision Entertainment 1995); and *The Stick* (1987), a controversial war film. They also successfully brought Mbongeni Ngema's *Sarafina* (1992) to the screen and made a bad road comedy set in the United States called *Father Hood* (1993). It would be fair to describe their artistic record as mixed.

Although the production and direction of the 1995 film were in the hands of South Africans, some things had not changed: as in the 1951 production, the leading roles in the new film were played by an American actor—James Earl Jones, the voice of "This is CNN" and of the father in *The Lion King,* but also an award-winning stage and screen actor—and by a British actor—Richard Harris, whose voice was less famous but whose acting had also won awards. Both men had acted before in films that were at least partly made in South Africa: Jones in *Allan Quatermain and the Lost City of Gold* (1987) and Harris in the mercenary films *The Wild Geese* (1978) and *Game for Vultures* (1979). Such casting decisions also conformed to the minigenre of the Hollywood antiapartheid film, in which non–South Africans usually have the leading roles. Consider, for example, Kevin Kline and Denzel Washington in *Cry Freedom* (1987), Donald Sutherland in *A Dry, White Season* (1989), and Danny Glover in *Bopha!* (1993). All of these films, of course, also have South African actors; in *Cry,* indeed, all the parts but Stephen Kumalo, his brother John (Charles Dutton), and James Jarvis are played by South Africans.

Singh and Roodt clearly hoped that *Cry* would be their break-through "serious" film, and they went to great lengths to promote their remake as more than just a commercial venture, to capitalize on the current international interest in South Africa and on the continuing popularity of Paton's novel. One obstacle Singh faced was convincing his potential collaborators that the 1946 story was of continuing relevance to 1990s South Africa. When Singh first approached Jones to play the part of Kumalo, for example, Jones reportedly responded: "Isn't that a museum piece?" (Videovision Entertainment 1995). To counter this image, Singh hired the British screenwriter Ronald Harwood, who had been born in South Africa and had written several novels and plays about the country, to adapt Paton's novel. Like both Jones (for his role in *The Great White Hope*) and Harris (for his in *This Sporting life*), Harwood had been nominated for an Academy Award (for the script of *The Dresser*), and Singh clearly hoped that his *Cry* might also be honored by the Academy of Motion Picture Arts and Sciences. Though the film received generally good, and even some excellent, reviews in South Africa, Europe, and the United States, it did not win any major international awards, though in 1996 it was honored as the best film at the Southern African Film Festival in Harare. Like its predecessor, the film was not a commercial success.

As the director of a remake, Roodt insisted that his goal was to achieve something quite different from the 1951 adaptation. "The original film was colonial," he said in an on-set interview, "the characters one-dimensional, divided between good old British upper-class guys and noble peasants, a bit too rah-rah. I'm making it more human" (Pretorius 1994). Elsewhere (Videovision Entertainment 1995) Roodt emphasized that this humanity would be not only more complex but also more historical: "I was able to approach the film with massive hindsight, to look back and shake my head. . . . It is the pain of remembrance with which I have imbued the picture. . . . We are trying to understand the past, and for me, the new direction of films in South Africa will be about retelling history." Thus Roodt established a standard for evaluating his adaptation of Paton's Christian parable of a good spiritual man in an evil material world.

Roodt presents Kumalo as something more than a "noble peasant" by the seemingly odd device of having the same actor do the voice-over of the omniscient narrator and play the character of Kumalo. The film begins with Jones's well-known voice narrating the story. After the arrival of the letter that sends Kumalo on his way to Johannesburg, Jones as Kumalo expresses in voice-over his fears about his upcoming trip and his reflections on why the young people of his village are leaving for the mines and the cities. He then observes: "For who can enjoy the lovely land and the sun that pours down there when white will not live equally with black, a land where the white man has everything and the black man nothing." Unlike the novel, the film imposes Kumalo as the narrator and thus suggests that he possesses far more consciousness and knowledge than the other characters, a position that contrasts oddly with his subaltern role.

Jarvis is presented in a scene created for the film as espousing the principles of racial segregation. Talking with his daughter-in-law about why his son has opened a boys' club for Africans in Johannesburg, he expresses his inability to understand his son's activities: "I wish he'd leave things as they are. . . . Blacks have their place, we have our place; blacks have their lives, we have our lives—but separately." Later, in another scene created for the film, Jarvis goes with the police to identify the body of his son. After he sees it, he declares: "Bloody Kaffirs!

Whoever did this, find them, hang them. Bastards!" The point of these scenes is to show that Jarvis does indeed have the attitudes of a white South African farmer and is not one of the "good old British upper-class guys" that Roodt felt were portrayed in the 1951 film.

As in the earlier film, Roodt also uses the device of the handshake to depict racial interaction. The first instance occurs when Kumalo arrives at Mission House and is greeted by Msimangu (Vusi Kunene). Kumalo's hand, warmly held by Msimangu's, fills the entire frame, underlining, with the help of the greeting in Zulu, a feeling of black brotherhood within the clergy. This gesture contrasts with the earlier film, when Kumalo's hand is conspicuously shaken by a racially mixed group of missionaries.

The second scene is one of a refused handshake. In the midst of Arthur's funeral, the camera cuts directly from Jarvis to a realistic documentary-like episode of a police raid, which shows black men and women being beaten up by policemen. During this scene, Jones's voice again assumes the function of the omniscient narrator:

> There is fear in the land, and fear in the hearts of all who live there. And fear puts an end to understanding, and the need to understand. . . . Cry, the beloved country, for the unborn child that is the inheritor of our fear. Let him not love the earth too deeply. Let him not be too moved when the birds of his land are singing, nor give too much of his heart to a mountain or a valley. For fear will rob him of all, if he gives too much. Yes, cry, cry, the beloved country.

As the narration unfolds, the camera first fades into a tight close-up of Jarvis's face, then pulls back to show us Jarvis standing in front of a line of greeting mourners. He shakes each person's hand until a young black man cautiously offers his, which Jarvis pointedly refuses; Jarvis then shakes the hand of the next white person. The interlacing of these two scenes serves the function of justifying Jarvis's refusal to shake the black man's hand: it is realistic that the racist Jarvis acts in this way. But it is important to see how this scene affects the structure of the narrative: unlike the 1951 film, the later version does not initially dramatize Jarvis's metamorphosis at the funeral through the symbolic language of the handshake; it occurs only later, when it is literally announced by Jarvis himself. This delay does not mean, however, that the change is treated in greater depth. Rather, in the name of realism, the second adaptation suffers from a lack of the psychological complexity of character rendered through symbolic language in the first.

In the 1995 film, Jarvis's metamorphosis occurs abruptly during one of the grand coincidences in the story, when the two protagonists encounter each other for the first time. Kumalo recognizes who Jarvis is first, and he is afraid. Kumalo eventually reveals that his son is the man who killed Jarvis's son, and, after a dramatic pause of reflection, Jarvis declares: "I understand what I did not understand. There is no anger in me." In both the novel and the two films, Jarvis's conversion results from reading his own son's writings, starting with the final words that Arthur penned before going downstairs to his death. The 1951 film shows this process literally, with the result that the pieces of projected text are excessive and dull; the 1995 film overcomes this technical problem by reducing Arthur's quoted words to a few fragments, read aloud by his father. Significantly, one of these begins with the dramatic interrogation: "What sort of memorial do we want? What sort of memorial do we deserve?" The "we" here clearly refers to white South Africans.

In the 1995 film, this episode is soon followed by an added scene that introduces the black teacher who is the secretary of the Claremont Boys' Club founded by Arthur, which Jarvis visits in his quest to understand his son. Identifying Jarvis as "a friend," the teacher consoles him and gives him a didactic explanation of the significance of his son's life for South Africa, declaring that Arthur "is the only man I have ever met, black or white, who saw me for what I am, what I really am." Jarvis says: "He was on your side, which makes what happened . . ." The teacher interjects: "He was on no one's side, sir, except for ours—yours and mine." The teacher's words end with the exhortation: "You must be proud of him; he is a tribute to you."

These two episodes foreground the focus of the film as it has been explicitly declared by Roodt—retelling history. The intention to historicize Paton's parable of good versus evil is made clear early in the film with the caption: "Natal, South Africa—1946" and by the fact that Jarvis's metamorphosis is centered on such key words as "memorials" and "tributes." The issue of what conception of history informs this narrative thus becomes imperative, and its articulation is related to questioning why the historical rendering of Paton's story does not lift it from its fable frame. Noting that Arthur's thinking is reduced to a preoccupation with memorials and his life is translated into a tribute to his father, we clearly see that this film is dominated by a conception of history that is monumental—it freezes the process of the present continuous reinterpretation of the past into a series of neatly connected "facts" and magnified, isolated "events." Within this frame, memory is reduced to memorial and the vital process of theoretical reelaboration of the past into the present is limited to a series of "museum pieces" held together by a linear cause-consequential reconstruction of a past, whose main purpose appears to be that of erasing what Herman Melville has called "its ragged edges." Monumental history involves a remembering of the past that reduces and eliminates even as it magnifies and invents, in order to create a consistent—ultimately, a black and white—tale.

The figure of John, Stephen Kumalo's brother corrupted by the city, is instrumental to this operation: he is indeed the appropriate evil counterpart to the personification of good white liberals and black clergy that the film promotes. He is the "other" in the morality play in which Jarvis and Kumalo are exemplary. We first encounter him at a public meeting, where he unquestionably appears as a demagogical politician. John is more surprised than pleased to find that his brother is in Johannesburg and in the company of Msimangu, whom he clearly detests. Stephen asks John why he has not written, and his brother responds disdainfully: "You people in Ndotsheni do not understand the way of life in Johannesburg. I thought it better not to write: trouble, unnecessary trouble." Before Stephen can ask about his son, John immediately jumps to the conclusion that he has searched him out only to ask for money for the church. John's undisguised contempt not only for the church but also for the capacity of the people of Ndotsheni to understand the city—equated in the film with understanding South African politics—emphasizes that he stands for his brother's "other"; obviously, he is also "the other" of the still unreformed Jarvis. While in the 1951 film John carries the flag of the liberal fear of communism but is clearly a representative of the politicized urban working class, in this film he is simply a caricature of a transcendental evil. Dressing and speaking like an American movie gangster and inexplicably wealthy for a carpenter, he is deprived of any social referent—he is only himself, and a camera movement that rotates around him underlines his isolation as he talks to the crowd.

The moralistic message dramatized by John is amplified by a pervasive sentimentalizing of the story. In scene after scene, Kumalo responds with tears to acts of humanity by whites. When Jarvis announces that he has no grudge against Kumalo for the murder of his son, Kumalo's initial fear of Jarvis dissolves in tears; when Kumalo learns that the liberal white lawyer will not only represent his son by telling the truth but will do it pro bono, he cries again—an action that is underlined by his observation that "I cry too easily. I wish I did not so easily." Kumalo's tearful response to the overwhelming goodness of the white men he encounters is further intensified by a scene in which Msimangu's function as a sophisticated and worldly guide to black Johannesburg is

85

dramatically undercut by his decision to give up all worldly activities for full-time prayer. His motivation for doing so serves to further aggrandize the position of whites: "I have this great fear in my heart that one day when the white man turns to loving he will find that we have turned to hating."

It is thus not surprising that the film adds a crucial piece of dialogue to the final encounter between Kumalo and Jarvis. As in the novel and the earlier film, Jarvis offers to rebuild the rundown church; in this film, however, he also asks that a stone with his son's name be placed there. Like the handshakes in the 1951 adaptation, this stone is a device that functions at an independent symbolic level: it reinforces precisely the idea of a history frozen into a construction of history. The stone that Jarvis literally "buys" from Kumalo by making his donation underlines the conception of history that has provided the foundational material for this film and that, I suggest, constitutes a major problem. This symbol is added to a scene already heavy with mythical tones: when Jarvis, high on his horse, encounters Kumalo struggling up the mountain on the day of his son's execution, he appears framed like God waiting for Moses. Jarvis shows his omniscience when he welcomes Kumalo, saying that he "knew" Kumalo would come up the mountain on the fifteenth day, and then proceeds to determine not only the future of the church—which in this adaptation is literally all there is of the black rural community—by making his donation, but also of historical memory by deciding what posterity must remember of "Natal, South Africa—1946." Apparently, all there is to remember of this piece of history is the name of his son.

This final symbolism bears heavily on the political significance of the contemporary rendering of Paton's fable, a rendering that silences Absolom's death in order to celebrate the triumph of Arthur's life. In the film, Absolom indeed must die—hanged—before his own child, supposedly a harbinger of a new South Africa, is born. When Jarvis asks Kumalo to put a stone in his church with the name of his son on it, he emphasizes that it is for a boy "who had brightness in him." Clearly Roodt's intention to "retell history" is guided by the project to tell only its bright side. To borrow from Toni Morrison (1992), we are left with the task of "playing in the dark" in order to find out how much darkness so much brightness covers up.

Determined to memorialize Paton's Christian liberal ethos, Roodt not only reproduces the excesses of the original novel but even exaggerates them. As Justin Pearce (1995) observes, the film both uncritically embraces the novel's implication that South Africa's social problems can be resolved by a return to a prelapsarian rural past and systematically vilifies John to the point of reducing him to a caricature. I would add that Roodt's reductive approach even extends to the religious figures. Consider, for instance, Msimangu: while the 1951 film eliminates this part of the original story, the 1995 adaptation dwells on his decision to abandon social commitment for a monastic life of prayer, thereby obliterating the significant role that black religious activists played in the struggle against the racist regime. And even the figure of Stephen Kumalo, by seemingly being endowed with the consciousness of the omniscient narrator and yet responding sentimentally with tears to every trial that befalls him, is deprived of the stoic dignity with which this character is portrayed in the 1951 film.

The final evidence of Roodt's failure to "retell history" is that his film, just like Korda's, ends by projecting on the screen the last two sentences of the novel, which read like an epigraph on a memorial: "For it is the dawn that has come, as it has for a thousand centuries, never failing. But when that dawn will come, of our emancipation, from the fear of bondage and the bondage of fear, why, that is a secret." Both films are indeed faithful to the novel when they superimpose these words over the image of the humble Kumalo down on his knees praying. In turn, superimposed over that image in our imaginations is one of an ennobled Jarvis high on his horse, the reins of power firmly in hand.

Notes

1. According to Davis (1996, 46), not even the black actors who appeared in the film attended the opening. For newsreel footage of this event, see *In Darkest Hollywood* (1993).

2. The quotation is from the first sentence of the review by Stephen Holden (1995); the full-page advertisement for the New York premiere two months earlier (*New York Times,* 18 October 1995, B5) differs only by the substitution of "motion picture" for "film."

3. Poitier (1980) had, in fact, turned down an offer to appear in *Lost in the Stars* to work on this film.

4. "In the end," Davis (1996, 46) observes, "the South African world depicted on the screen in *Cry, the Beloved Country* is not so far removed from the self-delusory world of apartheid. In the film, evil does not flow from the racist state, but from the social ills of massive and uncontrolled migration to the cities—precisely the *swart gevaar,* the fear of competition from black labour, that lay behind the creation of the apartheid state."

5

Come Back, Africa
Black Claims on "White" Cities

Isabel Balseiro

Introduction

Filmed clandestinely in Johannesburg and Sophiatown in 1958, Lionel
Rogosin's *Come Back, Africa* won the critics' award at the Venice Film
Festival in 1959 and was widely reviewed following its international premiere. However, the film was not shown publicly in South Africa until
1988. *Come Back, Africa* revolves around the experiences of Zacharia,
a rural migrant to Johannesburg, whose life tragically crosses paths with
a local Sophiatown *tsotsi*,[1] Marumu. This chapter juxtaposes Rogosin's
pioneering feature, made with the cooperation of a number of Sophiatown intellectuals, with Alan Paton's novel *Cry, the Beloved Country*
(1987 [1948]) and, in less detail, with Bloke Modisane's autobiography, *Blame Me on History* (1990 [1963]).
     Sophiatown in the 1950s was not only a multiethnic neighbor-
hood, but one in which the majority black population was crosscut by
divisions of social class, with doctors, writers, *tsotsis,* and members of
the lumpen proletariat all vying for a place in a fledgling black urban
South Africa. Rogosin's film is intriguing, not merely because it has been
largely forgotten or because it is one of the few visual records of Sophiatown life,[2] but because it treats the differential impact of apartheid on
both the rural migrants to the cities and the urban black intelligentsia.
A scathing critique of white liberal expectations is filtered into the film
through a scene where black intellectuals tear apart the illusory perception of Africans as innocent, tribal "Natives" (the stuff of Paton's *Cry,
the Beloved Country*) lost in the "city of gold," Johannesburg. *Come
Back, Africa* offers a glimpse at the formation, and affirmation, of a
new African urban identity irrevocably severed from its rural origins.

Zacharia

Opening shot: a long slow pan of a dark, clouded, moody sky suddenly panning to or cutting to a stark black outline—steel girders of new construction indirectly suggesting a crucifixion.

   From the screenplay to *Come Back, Africa*

On the surface, the story of *Come Back, Africa* is a simple one and emblematic of the fate shared by many African migrant workers. Driven from Zululand by great need, Zacharia arrives in Johannesburg in search of work. Rogosin's camera follows him around the "golden city" as he goes from one exploitative job to the next. His wife (Vinah) and children join him in Sophiatown and together they struggle to overcome the hurdles placed in their path: pass regulations, permit raids, township violence, and the like. While Zacharia is in jail for a pass offense, Vinah is killed by a local *tsotsi*, Marumu. The film ends with a harrowing image of Zacharia pounding on a table, desperate at the loss of his wife. What makes Zacharia's particular story not so simple and Rogosin's pioneering feature worth revisiting is the sheer power with which it records the interactions between personal and communal narratives, rural and urban crossings, intellectual and political aspirations. As its title suggests, *Come Back, Africa* documents social history in the making.[3]

   Visually striking, the opening image of *Come Back, Africa* forebodes a sacrifice. One after another, panning shots over the tops of buildings present a ghostly picture of the city at night. Devoid of people and completely silent, Johannesburg appears inhuman in its desolation. The camera slowly moves in a horizontal plane across the backs of buildings until the sound of a violently ringing bell shifts the focus abruptly to an abysslike bird's-eye view of the streets below. With this sudden shift, a sense of falling that will recur throughout the film grips the viewer. Progressively, the shots recede to a dilapidated part of the city and finally rest on a doorway. Insistent pounding on a door is heard as the image fades out.

   An early morning scene of Johannesburg follows: traffic noise, crowds of people going about their business, bicycles snaking between cars, and newspaper sellers. Throngs of workers file along the sidewalk looking somewhat bewildered. Among them we find Zacharia, clutching a suitcase. We first see him from a low angle shot, the camera looking up at him in a medium close-up. Then we watch him gaze at the towering buildings above as the camera takes his vantage point. We begin to see the city through his eyes, noticing a dizzying mass of bodies moving forward ahead of him. Superimposed on the marching figures we read the caption: "This film was made secretly in order to portray the true conditions of life in South Africa. There are no professional actors in this drama of the fate of a man and his country. This is the story of Zacharia—one of the thousands of Africans forced off the land by the regime and into the gold mines."[4]

The film visually captures the interplay between collective and individual consciousness through the transition from one scene to the next. Transitions are marked by the repeated image of hundreds of blacks marching into and out of packed trains and buses. On their way to and from work, crowds rush through train platforms and streets while a background noise of approaching drums increases, inciting the passersby to hasten the tempo of their mechanical movements. No respite is allowed them, as a constant flow of human beings devoid of individuality moves relentlessly forward.

When we catch our first glimpse of Zacharia he is among the mass of people in the streets of Johannesburg. His torn jacket, shabby hat, and awkward walk give him away as one caught somewhere between the stylish blacks bustling by in smart suits and those covered in blankets, their wide eyes nervously scanning the streets for a familiar sight. Although sharing his lot as "native" with these two diametrically opposed types, the urbanite and the tribal African, Zacharia somehow remains his own man throughout the film. By allowing the viewer to follow Zacharia's steps closely—seeing passing shots of the city, the mine compound, the European house, the hotel kitchen, the car garage, and Sophiatown from Zacharia's own vantage point—Rogosin creates an immediate identification with the character, placing him in a pivotal position that will mediate our understanding of the formation of an urban identity.

In this regard, the repeated transitional images of thousands of blacks rushing forward into the city powerfully suggest the inevitability of a historical process. Despite the ambitions of the architects of grand apartheid, Rogosin suggests in his script directions, history cannot be stopped: "Every time they march in, they change slightly. First they walk by with the ragged suit, gradually improving in appearance and awareness until they have a political identity. Throughout the film this marching in and out will . . . [show] the gradual yet continual change and historical process which in itself will become history" (Rogosin, Nkosi, and Modisane 1958, scene 20). This marching forward of history necessitates Zacharia's participation as it does the participation of those around him. But in order to make his story significant, the film inserts it into the larger struggle black people waged to attain an urban identity

90

apartheid denied them. The interplay between Zacharia and Marumu, their respective stories, and the *Drum* journalists Lewis Nkosi, Bloke Modisane, and Can Themba also form part of the history of Sophiatown, a history to which the film pays homage.

As a symbol of cosmopolitan black urban life, Sophiatown was more than just a place:

> It came to name an era and a departed style of life. . . . Sophia, or Kofifi as the locals knew it, lingers in South African argot as a short-hand for 50s cultural brio—for the journalists and fiction writers, the shebeen queens presiding over speakeasies, and the jazz artists and gangsters who revered style. . . . The legacy of Sophia defies simple resolution. It is a sign of apartheid at its most calamitous, yet also a guiding memory of possibility—a gravestone that doubles as a beacon.
>
> (NIXON 1994, 12)

By the time Rogosin made his film, Sophiatown had become one more casualty of the Group Areas Act of 1950, and its destruction was well under way. In the film, the forced removal is alluded to by the slogan "Hands off the Western Areas" prominently visible on a wall as Zacharia and Vinah cross the township in search of housing. Although Sophiatown culture has since been well documented, *Come Back, Africa* stands out as a unique testimony in that the film was made as the demolition was taking place.[5] Its creation was the result of close collaboration between Rogosin and Lewis Nkosi, Bloke Modisane, and Can Themba, three of the most talented writers of the magazine *Drum*.[6] A particularly significant aspect of the film, one that cannot be overemphasized, is the fact that Rogosin's homage to Sophiatown is filtered through the eyes of one of its least celebrated inhabitants: the migrant worker. Awarding Zacharia the status of protagonist puts migrant workers' participation in the formative cultural process involving the articulation of an urbanized African identity firmly on the map. In such a process class analysis cannot be absent, something *Come Back, Africa* hints at through the constant dynamics of individual versus collective consciousness.

The tension between collectivity and individuality is mirrored by the ambivalent cinematic position of this work. Some critics have called *Come Back, Africa* a documentary, while others fit it squarely into the fiction film category.[7] Even though it has many of the features of a documentary (the use of only two handheld cameras, grainy texture, nonprofessional actors, an explanatory caption at the beginning claiming neutrality, and improvised dialogue), *Come Back, Africa* grapples with and strives to convey an individual story, that of Zacharia. Indeed, a concern with the personal story is crucial to Rogosin's exposé of apartheid. According to the director,

> My aim was to express realism in a dramatic and poetic manner, to abstract and then humanize, or better still, synthesize. This is how the film evolved. The plot was neither purely factual nor really fictional. . . . The characters, of course, were found in and came out of the place itself. But they were molded, according to their dramatic, humorous and symbolic significance, to what the system of repression was doing to them. Since they were all its victims, I let them express and bring to the surface the deep emotional effect of *apartheid*.
> (ROGOSIN 1960, 26–27)

Rogosin's camera follows the workers in the opening scenes until they arrive at a mine compound. The new recruits are rounded up and given a cognitive test using square blocks of wood that they have to arrange as quickly as possible. Isolated in their cubicles, partitions erected between the small desks, hundreds of workers are put to the task of making miniature models. This image of black men mechanically assembling make-believe buildings recalls the symmetrical, towering skyscrapers in the opening sequences. On the labor of these men rests the foundations of the modern city they are barred from inhabiting.

The script (Rogosin, Nkosi, and Modisane 1958, scene 2) describes how, at different points throughout the film, the camera pans over new structures, "naked steel girders suggestive of bayonets, death, war. The twisted steel rods imply . . . concentration camps . . . the open pits and twisted steel inside the floor of the new buildings suggest bomb craters." At first, daytime sequences of Johannesburg show mine dumps "mysteriously peeping through the buildings" before the camera allows us to recognize what they are; later they are set impressively against the city in long shots. These takes often dissolve into one another, "finally ending on an image of the mine derrick next to a golden mine dump."

Amid the ubiquitous mine dumps and overpowering edifices of apartheid's industrial society, Zacharia's human drama unfolds. In a metaphorical sense, it is the crucifixion of hundreds of thousands of men like him, those who build the structures and work the mines, that the opening shot suggests: black men sacrificed at the altar of a capitalist labor system that shifts populations at will. When Vinah is killed by Marumu, Zacharia's desperate pounding against the table in the final scene recalls the banging on a door at the beginning of the film. A close-up of Zacharia's ravaged face is intercut by a series of flashbacks to the gang laborers striking the rocks and to the repetitive thumping of feet on the pavement as workers march off of the trains and into the bowels of the mines.

Johannesburg, Rogosin suggests, is a place where ideology displaces people. This displacement is in shocking contrast to the personal images of black life the film also offers. On the one hand, Rogosin captures the small events of everyday life with a keen neorealist eye (the joyful reunion between Zacharia and his wife, the intimacy of the family's shared meal); on the other, shots of a slick, modern city are juxtaposed to the ragged landscape of the townships, where donkeys, chickens, open sewers, and half-naked little children are reminiscent of an almost preindustrial era. The opening images spell modernity, and yet the buildings Rogosin shows us are empty because they cannot be occupied by those who build them, those who march into the city in the early hours of the morning but are forced to leave at dusk. In 1959 Johannesburg, workers are shown to occupy a borrowed urban space. But it is a space they are gradually laying claim to and making their own. After all, it is the African presence that injects life into the desolate city every working day and even during weekends, when the downtown is taken over by street performers in an extraordinary display of artistic talent—pennywhistle bands, gum boot dancers, puppet masters, and municipal orchestras vying for the attention of mostly black passersby. The emergence of a vibrantly urban black cultural life is further emphasized through the participation of Modisane, Nkosi, and Themba, who give the film much of its intellectual backbone.

The White Liberals

> Well, I'm telling you, the liberal just doesn't want a grown-up African. He wants the African he can sort of patronize, pat on his head and tell him that "with just a little bit of luck, someday you'll be a grown-up man, fully civilized." He wants the African from the country, from his natural environment, unspoilt.
>
> Lewis Nkosi, in *Come Back, Africa*

Zacharia is a liberal's dream. One of the thousands of "innocent" rural blacks who migrate to Johannesburg in search of work, he is a stranger both to the cosmopolitan wisdom of the "grown-up African" and to the ruthlessness of city cunning. Marumu, on the other hand, is the liberal's dilemma. Part and parcel of the urban landscape through which Zacharia must cautiously tread, Marumu symbolizes an unavoidable fixture of township life: the "spoilt" African, the gangster. Unlike Zacharia, who hails from Zululand, Marumu grew up in Sophiatown and learned the hard way, from his early years, to fend for himself. After losing his father to crime, he turned to violent ways and eventually became a *tsotsi*.[8]

These two characters, the gangster and the naive rural migrant, staples of South Africa's film and literary language during the first half of the twentieth century, play opposite each other in *Come Back, Africa*. Rogosin, however, creatively makes use of each for his own purposes: to expose the structural damage wrought by apartheid policies on the black population, urban and rural, and to make a frontal attack on liberalism, the ideals of which are mocked in the film by a very young Lewis Nkosi. As suggested by the quotation that heads this section, words uttered during the film's improvised shebeen scene, Nkosi's critique of white liberals underlies Rogosin's project in *Come Back, Africa*.[9] Given the liberals' unabashed longing for "unspoilt" Africans and apartheid's inevitable dependence on black labor in the cities, viewers are left wondering whether Marumu's trajectory in Johannesburg, one referred to but not seen in the film, is not destined to be replicated by Zacharia. This section explores the image of urban blacks in the 1950s as fatalistically wavering between these two staple characters and ultimately questions the supposed downward spiral from country bumpkin to cold-blooded hoodlum, from Zacharia to Marumu.

Journeys into the "city of gold" are a recurrent motif of South African literature and film in the first half of the twentieth century. While the theme is recorded in full-length features like *African Jim* (1949)[10] as well as in documentaries such as *Pondo Story* (1948), perhaps the prototypical characters who symbolize that journey in literature are the Reverend Stephen Kumalo and his son Absolom in *Cry, the Beloved Country* (Paton 1987 [1948]). In *Come Back, Africa*, Zacharia functions in much the same way as does Absolom Kumalo in *Cry, the Beloved Country*. But unlike Absolom, Zacharia does not rely on a figure such as the Reverend Stephen Kumalo for moral guidance. *Come Back, Africa*, in fact, summarily rejects such misguided morality. Paton's novel was first published in 1948, more than ten years before Rogosin made his film. In the intervening decade, drastic political and social changes took place in South Africa, changes that by the late 1950s no longer allowed for the type of liberal melodrama depicted in Paton's text. While it is clear that South Africa had a long history of racial discrimination and legislation before 1948, it was not until the National Party's electoral victory in that year that the official policy of apartheid was systematically set in place. Of course, it can be argued that regardless of the date of publication, Paton's renowned first novel is very much a product of the type of liberal ideology that preached Christian reconciliation instead of advocating political activism—an issue brought up in *Come Back, Africa* by the Sophiatown intellectuals.[11] And, as Rob Nixon (1994, 26) succinctly puts it, *Cry, the Beloved Country* "was the book they wrote against."

In *Cry, the Beloved Country,* Paton exposes what many white South African liberals considered the paramount problem of South African society in the 1940s, namely the destruction of the tribal system by Europeans. It is precisely the pastoral yearning inherent to what Paton calls the "broken tribe" in *Cry, the Beloved Country* that *Come Back, Africa* rejects. The epigraph that opens this section points to the inadequacy of the type of liberal approach taken by Paton to provide satisfactory answers to South Africa's black population in the middle of the twentieth century.

Like Absolom, Zacharia arrives in the "city of gold" from Zululand ill equipped to face the challenges of urban life. Both find inauspicious receptions. Absolom, who ostensibly goes to Johannesburg in search of his Aunt Gertrude, soon "falls" into bad company and eventually murders a white man, although he has become the object of a rescue mission by his father, Stephen Kumalo, well before then. Despite his turn to violence, Absolom is clearly presented as overwhelmed by the fast pace of the township, a lack of direction, and his impressionable youth. It is his incursion into the city, the reader must infer, that precipitates his downfall. None of the structural imbalances circumscribing the dismal conditions Absolom is made to confront in the city inform the novel the way they do Rogosin's characterization of Zacharia. In a documentary tracing the representation of South Africa through film, Lewis Nkosi argues:

> When you look at *Cry, the Beloved Country* [Zoltan Korda's 1951 film version], it portrays the system of justice in South Africa as dispassionate, very calm, obviously politically uninvolved. But from the point of view of the black community the main defect of the film was in ascribing criminality to the character of Absolom, the murderer, without assigning proper responsibility to the system itself.
> (*In Darkest Hollywood* 1993)

Rogosin is careful to show that although Zacharia's experiences, especially the loss of his wife at the hands of a Sophiatown *tsotsi,* may eventually steer him down Absolom's violent path, Zacharia is affected by historical forces—the same historical forces ignored in *Cry, the Beloved Country.*[12] An early scene in *Come Back, Africa* depicts Zacharia entering a mining compound housing facility where he greets a group of fellow migrant workers. The bunkhouse sequence provides a concrete visual reminder of the vast rural migrations to the cities. Subsequent mine shots impress on us the robotlike training of the new recruits followed by the workers' descent with lanterns in the night through subterranean corridors. Rogosin "opens [*Come Back, Africa*] on the question of labor and capital. It is the dialectic between the two which determines the structural workings of the film" (Masilela 1991, 64).

The bunkhouse scene also introduces the audience to the dire living conditions in the mines and, indirectly, to similar conditions in the rural areas from which the workers hail. Row upon row of bunk beds barely covered by thin blankets offer the only comfort to these men nostalgic for faraway homes. A conversation starts in Zulu, as the workers ask each other their origin and the circumstances that bring them to Johannesburg. Zacharia explains that he has sought work in the mine because the recruiting officer told him that was the only way he could come. Among the reasons the men give for their journey into the city are the poverty of the land, soil erosion, overcrowding, and the difficulty of earning a living back home—all effects of a long history of policies stripping Africans of their rights that culminated in the institutionalization of apartheid laws after the election of the National Party in 1948.

Through the miners' exchange, Rogosin also makes an important commentary on how apartheid labor policies affected black women and families. As men were forced to migrate to seek employment in urban areas, they often had to leave their wives soon after marriage. Apartheid allowed only the man to seek work in the cities, confining his wife and children to the rural areas. In addition to the economic advantages of hiring a "single" man (salaries did not have to account for supporting a household), this practice also served apartheid's influx control objective of keeping black populations in "white" cities to a minimum—a dubious aim achieved in great part through forced removals.[13] The breaking up of black families was thus actively pursued and frequently achieved.[14] Indeed, "[t]he migrant labor policy was at heart a policy about the family, and about controlling the reproduction and division of labor within the family" (McClintock 1990, 213).

Apartheid labor policies, applied indiscriminately to millions of Africans, are portrayed in the film as they affect specific individuals. In an article entitled "*Come Back, Africa*: On Making a Film," Lewis Nkosi comments on how Rogosin managed to capture visually the human toll of deceptively impersonal legislation and praises the director's ability to go beyond the legalese and into the flesh through which those regulations cut:

> Before he could even collate a mass of confusing facts in which any stranger coming to South Africa immediately becomes bogged down, Lionel [Rogosin] had to try and relate these facts to concrete life situations. That was precisely the problem: this effort to try and find a "seeable" relationship between a mass of statistics and the real life situations which they purport to interpret. How does one translate into visual terms the heinous effects of [apartheid]?
>
> (NKOSI 1960, 12)

One of the ways in which *Come Back, Africa* succeeds in matching the statistics to real life situations is precisely in its treatment of the family, an issue broached initially in the bunkhouse scene. Since, according to apartheid labor policies, Zacharia and his bunkmates will have to work in Johannesburg for a year or two before they are given permission to return home, it should come as no surprise to the viewer that in many instances the women left behind would feel a great deal of frustration. Curiously, while the consequences of that frustration do not manifest themselves in the migrant workers' conversation in the film, they do in the original script. In the 1958 script, one of the workers recounts the story of a doctor called out at night to investigate a case of infanticide. The incident involved a woman suspected of strangling her newborn child, when in fact there was no child; she had had a false pregnancy. In the script, the group of workers also comments on the desire of young girls not to marry, for if they do, they have to work for the mother-in-law when the husband leaves to go to the city. In short, what is the point of marrying when couples cannot find a viable way of life together, given the insidious conditions imposed by apartheid policies that undermine the stability of black families? While one can only speculate as to why Rogosin ultimately left out these interesting exchanges, it is significant that his original intention was to deal with the women's issue at greater length. As will be discussed later, Zacharia's own family is broken beyond repair by the hostile urban environment engendered by discriminatory policies.

In a subsequent bunkhouse scene, the men exit the room, leaving Zacharia alone. He takes advantage of his momentary privacy to write a letter to his wife, Vinah. He reads out loud what he writes, which is, surprisingly, in English. For all his unsophisticated country ways, it is established within minutes of the film's opening that Zacharia is multilingual: he speaks mostly in Zulu with his fellow workers but understands when they respond in Sotho, and the mine supervisor gives orders in Fanakalo (a lingua franca used in the mines based on a variety of southern African languages).[15] And language is the medium through which the migrant's dream is revealed, a dream that his passage through the city will not only transform but truncate. He writes:

> My dear Vinah: I'm pleased when I'm writing this letter for you. I think you'll also be pleased if you can get it. But the only thing . . . my contract. I did not know that it'd be too long and I'm [sic] really want to be at home. Can you be pleased? . . . I want to come back home. Really, I'm really lonely for you. Pass my regards to my sister Josephine and to my children. I'll try my best to be with you [as soon] as possible. It's me, Zacharia Mgabi.
> (COME BACK, AFRICA 1959, SCENE 2; MY TRANSCRIPT)

In *Cry, the Beloved Country*, Absolom Kumalo, of course, does not make it back to Natal either, but for very different reasons. Paton's novel unequivocally attributes Absolom's tragic end (he is sentenced to death by hanging) to the curse of the city, portraying Johannesburg as a cesspool eager to swallow up unknowing, detribalized "natives." In Rogosin's film, the tribe no longer plays a major role. As the viewer catches the first glimpse of Zacharia, he is already combing the metropolitan landscape, alert to the rush of people and traffic. Through the course of the film he progressively negotiates his way around that landscape. The city effects significant changes in his personality but, although Rogosin spares him no obstacles, he ultimately manages to get a foothold in the urban setting.

Paton's novel finds resolution in the idyllic hills of Natal and the illusory tribal integrity of precolonial South Africa, clinging to a nostalgic image of African identity firmly entrenched in a rural past. Reading *Cry, the Beloved Country* from the vantage point of 1959, Paton's pastoral tone is alarmingly prescient of the Afrikaner political project of stubbornly forging the "unspoilt" African. In fact, Paton's insistence on a return to the ancestral land is dangerously in tune with the National Party's development of the homeland policy.[16]

Against Paton's evocation "of a missionary ethos of white trustee-ship" (Nixon 1994, 26), Rogosin juxtaposes the fierce independence of the Sophiatown intellectuals, whose goal was to firmly root the cosmopolitanism of the new African identity. Their profound distaste for Paton's novel is powerfully voiced in the shebeen scene, where Modisane, Nkosi, and Themba tear to shreds Paton's antagonistic account of urban life and his concomitant embrace of tribalism. After

Zacharia has a confrontation in the street with the *tsotsi* Marumu, he joins a friend, Stephen, and they go to a shebeen. Inside they find a lively group of people smoking, drinking, and talking. Among them are Bloke Modisane and Lewis Nkosi, the *Drum* journalists who cowrote the script with Rogosin, and also Can Themba; all three play themselves in the film. Once Zacharia describes what just happened to him in the street, a conversation ensues about the violence and despair that bring forth such behavior in people like Marumu. Blame is assigned to the appalling conditions of apartheid and to state violence, which breeds individual violence in the likes of Marumu (an issue I take up in the next section). Bitterness against white society becomes the topic of their argument, but Morris, another drinker in the shebeen, defends Europeans, saying: "But the liberals are trying to meet us halfway." At this comment many burst into laughter and jeers. Someone beats his arms on an imaginary drum and makes fake tribal noises. That's when Nkosi launches his attack on liberalism:

> What liberals? Do you know who are the liberals in this country? The exquisite young lady who gets to the party and wants to insist that you must drink that cup of tea. And don't be afraid, don't be afraid to drink that cup of tea. Do you? Are you afraid? Just have tea. Don't be afraid of whites.
>
> *Morris*: But what's wrong with drinking tea?
>
> [Background noise. Someone shouts: "You're a native!"]
>
> *Modisane*: You want to sell your humanity over a cup of tea? Do you think all our problems would be wiped out over a cup of tea? As far as they are concerned, all our problems would be wiped out over a cup of tea.
>
> *Morris*: I don't quite understand. You people don't seem to appreciate the liberal point of view. It was embodied in Alan Paton's book.
>
> *Modisane*: Ja, that sickly Reverend Kumalo came to town and said "yes, baas" to every white.
>
> [Modisane bends his head, mimicking Kumalo's gesture. He cups his hands together in a praying motion.]
>
> *Nkosi*: Never grew up. [He points to Morris.] You want to be . . . the old reverend gentleman who thinks the world of whites. He still boss and what does he do when he gets back to the country?
> (COME BACK, AFRICA 1959, SHEBEEN SCENE; MY TRANSCRIPT)

The exchange continues and eventually leads to the statement by Nkosi that opens this section.

For Modisane, Nkosi, and Themba, the Reverend Stephen Kumalo symbolized the "anti-hero who incarnated the unctuous religiosity, the deference, and the urban incompetence that were antithetical to all they professed" (Nixon 1994, 27). The unbreachable division set up in *Cry, the Beloved Country* between urban degeneration and rural regeneration clashes against the type of life black intellectuals were engaged in creating in Sophiatown. The *Drum* writers rightly understood that Paton's antiracism colluded with the National Party's policies against urban Africans, whose detribalization was deemed "unnatural." While urbanization came at a high price for many Africans—and Zacharia is a case in point—it also offered economic incentives. Moreover, urbanization provided peasant Africans a chance to insert themselves into the fabric of twentieth-century South African modernity—a reality the Sophiatown intellectuals recognized and the film explores.[17]

Zacharia and others like him (those who share his predicament in the mine compound, in the European houses, in hotel kitchens, as laborers) must carve a place for themselves in Johannesburg—a place Modisane fiercely defends in his autobiography, *Blame Me on History* (1990 [1963]).[18] While Paton freezes Absolom and Stephen Kumalo in the countryside, Rogosin positions Zacharia within the space between the hills of Natal and the sharp outlines of the Johannesburg landscape visually symbolized by the steel girders of the opening scene. No longer an integral part of the world he left behind in Zululand and not yet fully integrated into the city ways of Marumu or those of Themba, Nkosi, and Modisane, Zacharia occupies an interim space filled with possibilities and risks, a space in the making, as the film graphically depicts.

In the shebeen scene where Modisane, Nkosi, and Themba expound on the misguided morality of Paton's novel, Zacharia's role is primarily that of listener. He sits and drinks along but seldom participates in the conversation beyond his initial relation of his altercation with Marumu. While still a stranger to their intellectual exchange, he is nonetheless much more at home in the shebeen now than he was previously. The first time his friend Stephen takes Zacharia to a shebeen he is bewildered by a woman's sexual advances. Not knowing how to handle the situation, Zacharia angrily pushes her away and storms out of the room. Once outside, he falters, unfamiliar with the deserted streets of Sophiatown. When he next goes back with Stephen, Zacharia recognizes Martha, the shebeen queen, and finds himself at ease among the drinking men and women.

Zacharia further negotiates his claims on the urban landscape through his encounter with a white Madam who hires him as a domestic helper. After having a few drinks from a bottle he finds while cleaning the bedroom, Zacharia starts admiring himself in front of a mirror, donning one of the Madam's scarves. Slightly drunk, he turns on the phonograph and starts dancing. The white Madam catches him in this performance and screams at him. At first submissive, he then retaliates with the humorously impudent remark, "the room too much filthy." When she threatens to fire him, he dares her to call the police. His reaction here is in stark contrast to his demeanor when initially hired. In an earlier kitchen scene, the Madam berates him for spoiling a mushroom soup; Zacharia grumbles but puts up with the humiliation. One of his first experiences inside the white home involves the discovery of a mirror. Upon seeing his reflection in the glass, Zacharia is startled and retreats. Here Rogosin uses Zacharia's surprise to signal his country ways; by the second scene involving a mirror (when he dances uninhibitedly in front of it), we observe how far he has come in appropriating what was once for him a foreign object.

Many forces impinge upon Zacharia's rightful appropriation of the urban space—the constant harassment to produce work permits, the abuse he suffers at the hands of the police when they raid his wife's room and find him there without a pass, his unfair firing as a waiter when a European woman falsely accuses him of attempting to rape her in a hotel room—but it takes a tragedy to finally make the viewer realize the rootedness of Zacharia in Johannesburg—a rootedness, the film suggests, to which all migrant workers seem destined. After Vinah's death, what kind of future could possibly await him in Zululand? She was quick to join him in Johannesburg, bringing their children along in search of a better life, her greatest hope being that they could get access to formal education.

Undoubtedly the city changes Zacharia, as it does others, but not all change involving "natives" is for the worse, as *Cry, the Beloved Country* would have one believe. To avoid fulfilling the ominous prophecy inherent to Paton's novel (all "tribal natives" are condemned to a life of crime in the cities), Zacharia must anchor himself in a reality that at first repels him. Struggling against a white liberal ethos that would have rural blacks living under "benign" white trusteeship as far away as possible from the urban centers, Zacharia strives to keep pace with the changes demanded of him in order to become a modern, new African—turning into one, as a matter of fact, not by choice, but by force of circumstances. Out of necessity, Zacharia becomes enmeshed in the whirlpool of market forces that requires the exploitation of peasant labor while obstinately denying blacks an autonomous role in an industrialized South Africa.

Marumu

> No, no, no, no, no, no . . . let me explain Marumu. I lived with him when he was young and I saw him grow up. He grew up with me. But I think it is important for you to understand. When we are young, we had our little fun. In the first place it was just fun. . . . He wanted to, to grapple with things that were bigger, and the only way he could get those things was through force and . . . so he saw things in terms of force. It happened to all of us. We wanted some kind of force. But we weren't prepared to go to the extent that he was. . . . He wanted bigger things, he wanted a bigger, better way of life and he had to use force for it, and the result of it was the only way he could get the things he wanted was to kick in people, to bully people. . . . Look what's happened to him. Now he has become a man who thinks the only way he can do things is to get them from force. And sometimes he forgets the things that he wants and he only remembers the force.
>
> Can Themba, in *Come Back, Africa*

If Zacharia is the "uncontaminated" rural migrant worker painstakingly trying to find his way around unfamiliar territory, Marumu embodies all the city cunning of an archetypal hard-boiled *tsotsi* who no longer abides by the rules of apartheid, let alone tribal custom. Rather than allowing Marumu to disappear behind the anonymity of "native" crime statistics, Rogosin situates him in the context of a violent environment. The film thus focuses the viewer's attention on the overarching effects of apartheid legislation on township life. Instead of demonizing the city as the source of evil, Rogosin portrays a brutalized (and brutalizing) Marumu at odds with a police state that provides both the conditions and provocations for Africans to break the law.

While the essential elements of community were present in Sophiatown in a way that distinguished it from the drabness of other townships, as pictured in the vivid images of pennywhistlers, religious ceremonies, traditional dances, cinema queues, and political discussions in *Come Back, Africa*, living conditions were no less harsh. As in most townships at the time, municipal services failed to keep pace with the growing population; electricity and running water were widely unavailable, and the majority of the inhabitants belonged to a working class "whose reality was illiteracy or semi-literacy, grinding poverty, rackrenting landlords and harsh police action" (Chapman 1994a, 192). Alongside this majority stood the newly urbanized Africans: schoolteachers, clerks, journalists, and nurses. They constituted the barely emergent professional elite. At the fringes were the *tsotsis,* ready to wreak havoc at the drop of a hat.

Against the onslaught of apartheid legislation aimed at controlling the black population's every move, the *tsotsis* opted to redefine themselves as outsiders—outlaw agents defying the laws of a repressive state. As such, the *tsotsis* had admirers among the *Drum* writers. In his autobiography, Modisane goes as far as arguing that outlawry is justified as a response to white authority:

> The white man fears the tsotsis who are perhaps among the only Africans who have personal dignity; they answer white arrogance with black arrogance, they take their just desserts from a discriminating economy by robbery and pillage. The educated African is confined by academic rationalizations, the tsotsi is a practical realist; he is sensitive and responds to the denials and the prejudice with the only kind of logic Western man understands and respects.
>
> (MODISANE 1990 [1963], 227–28)

Given the powerlessness blacks were made to feel, one can see the appeal *tsotsis* would have for Modisane. In a symbolic sense, the brutality of police raids could somehow be countered by the *tsotsis'* reckless violence. The *tsotsi's* spirit of male competitiveness, his inborn rage, physical prowess, street savvy, and fierce territoriality in a congested Sophiatown are qualities *Blame Me on History* celebrates.[19] And Modisane is not alone. Can Themba and Casey Motsisi, for example, were also "inclined to glamorize the tsotsi as the superior villain: one who had made the city yield its pleasures of flashy clothes and V-8 motors" (Chapman 1994a, 193).

Drum featured crime side by side with the thrills of city life.[20] The journalists' partiality to *tsotsis* and crime stories can best be understood in the context of the former's infatuation with cinematic images. The writers fell under the spell of 1950s Hollywood movies; consequently, celluloid gangsters play an important role in Sophiatown culture (see Nixon 1994, 31–36). The *tsotsis,* who shared cinema halls and illegal shebeens with the black intellectuals, also turned to Hollywood for their style of dressing and what Rob Nixon aptly describes as their "criminal chic." Some of the journalists proudly boasted: "we [at *Drum*] created a new class of black person who simultaneously earned the admiration of tsotsis and respectable people. We could talk to them [the *tsotsis*] on their level. We were nearer to them than the average black professional person" (cited in Nixon 1994, 259). And, although such idealized closeness has not gone unquestioned, it is undeniable that these two types of players often crossed paths.[21] The incongruous crossover appeal between *tsotsis* and intellectuals owes much to their mutual, albeit divergent, claims on an intrinsically urban landscape. Territoriality over the Sophiatown streets binds the *tsotsi* to the intellectual vanguard's unmitigated defense of a new urban African identity. Hence Themba's passionate intervention in the shebeen scene where he attempts to explain the social, political, and economic circumstances that produce the likes of Marumu.

Zacharia sees Marumu for the first time in an Indian shop, where the latter ignores the queue and pushes his way to the front. Shortly thereafter, Marumu provokes Zacharia into a fight in the street when Zacharia refuses to hand over his cigarettes. Shaken by the confrontation, Zacharia relates the incident to Martha and the others when he and Stephen enter the shebeen. Protests arise against Marumu and there's talk of the need for "eliminating rotten elements" like him. At this point, Themba interjects with his persuasive "No, no, no, no, no, no . . . let me explain Marumu" pitch, quoted at the beginning of this section. It is from this angle that Rogosin records a firsthand account of the intricate relationship between gangsters and intellectuals.

Themba views Marumu's aggression as self-preservation in an environment that excludes him from full economic and political participation. Angry at the dismal conditions created by pervasive discrimination, Themba maintains that the wasteland brought forth by white laws, not Marumu, ought to be blamed for the senseless violence. In a society that does not care, Themba realizes (and is at pains to have others realize) that it is the intellectual's responsibility to make the necessary connections between Marumu's alienation and the structural forces that produce it. While some speak of the need to rid Sophiatown of "rotten elements," Themba draws attention to Marumu's background: his father "got brutally butchered by some *tsotsi*," his mother "repressed him," schoolboys derided him, and girls were afraid of him. Cornered, Marumu sought and found a niche for himself with those who used force to get their way.

The contrast Modisane sets up between *tsotsis* and educated Africans in *Blame Me on History* is worth exploring in light of this scene. If the educated African's "academic rationalizations" have made him wary of standing up to white authority, could the *tsotsi*'s uninhibited contempt and rampant aggression be a legitimate means of resistance? Could *tsotsis*' survival tactics, their visceral repudiation of law and order, their disdain for Christian values, and their rejection of a work ethic offer a way out of the self-effacement inflicted by apartheid? Although Modisane toys with these ideas, his autobiography answers in the negative. After relating an incident in which as a youngster he and a group of friends severely beat up a member of a gang in retaliation for his having stabbed a friend, he asks:

> What if he had died? What possible justification could there have been for it? That he stole a watch and a wallet? Was that the equivalent of a life? I was horrified by the inhumanity, shutting my eyes and blacking from my mind memories of my father; the equation was obvious, I could not pretend to hate violence and yet allow myself to be manoeuvred by it in claiming death. We were not the police, we were not the tsotsis, and yet we had come close to becoming the harbingers of death.
> (MODISANE 1990 [1963], 69)

He relentlessly shows that a primary force in the lives of urban blacks during the 1950s was violence: the political violence unleashed by apartheid legislation as well as the resulting criminal violence that exploded within the congested quarters of the townships—and he does not hesitate to place the heavier burden on the first. In a powerful moment of bitter realization Modisane (1990 [1963], 153) laments:

> My young mind was unable to understand the apathy of the white South Africans, the intensification of oppressive legislation against the Africans, the brutality of the police, all the injustice committed in the name of apartheid did not seem to concern them or violate their sense of justice and right. I was staggered by the complacent ignorance about the condition of my life in the slum yards which smelled of urine, by the fact that my human rights were disregarded by the body politic. . . . There had been a time when they had been incensed into silent indignation; and yet now, because they had been educated into an acceptance of the primacy of law and order, they did not—as their reflections in the Southern States of America—mob themselves into a lynching pack; perhaps it was that they held a dependable reliance on the banditry of the law to adequately approximate their murderous anger.

Themba is an eager mediator between the paralyzing frustration expressed by Modisane's intellectualizing and the quick-paced, knife-happy spontaneity of the *tsotsis*. Nkosi (cited in Nixon 1994, 33) once called Themba "the supreme intellectual *tsotsi*," and as such he is in an ideal position to bridge the gap between Marumu's abuse of force and Modisane's "banditry of the law." In his defense of Marumu, Themba begins to make a connection between *tsotsi* violence and social consciousness, between exclusion, poverty, and alienation on one hand and

105

antisocial behavior on the other. Unless it is recognized that Marumu is as much social victim as he is victimizer, the spiraling township violence will be perpetuated. Rogosin illustrates just how easy it can be to slip into an underworld of lawlessness when he shows Zacharia ruthlessly pounding Marumu during the street fight. Themba tries to persuade his drinking partners that while it may be too late for Marumu, there is still a chance for Zacharia. When Modisane tauntingly asks, "Why don't you try talking and understanding Marumu?" Themba responds:

> Because we left it too late. We left it too long. If we had talked to Marumu thirty years ago, we might have made him part of us, part of our life, we might have made him feel that he belongs to us. Like our dear friend here [pointing to Zacharia]. If we had accepted him [Marumu] as soon as we could, we could have found this place in our lives. On the one hand, we have him [Zacharia] trying to enter our life; on the other, we have the other guy [Marumu] going out of our lives, resisting us, feeling that he is an enemy to this life, but if we had tried hard enough for all sorts of people to get together, to belong together, to feel that they belong . . . And what's wrong with all different kinds of people getting together?
>
> (*Come Back, Africa* 1959; my transcript)

Finding common ground where such apparently disparate characters could interact augurs the beginning of a breaking down of barriers. It is at this juncture in the film that class boundaries start to fade and political aspirations filter in. While it may be too late to reintegrate hardened criminals into a classless community of socially aware Sophiatown constituents, Themba's call for "belonging together" addresses the need to consider the position outcasts like Marumu might have been prepared to occupy if only given a chance. In other words, through Themba's rationalization of Marumu's actions, Rogosin brings to the fore compelling reasons to start looking at the politicization of crime. Perhaps together, one is tempted to speculate, *tsotsis,* migrant workers, and intellectuals might have been able to effectively defend a space in which all were significant players.[22]

Conclusion

Through a comparative approach to the figures of the migrant worker and the *tsotsi,* Rogosin forces us to see them as integral components of an urban political economy. While Zacharia's "assumed" innocence makes him fall prey to unavoidably exploitative situations in the city, Marumu's streetwise ways spare him the drudgery of daily subjugation to a system of life in which Africans are amorphously positioned as "natives." The price Marumu pays for his detachment from the oppressive system is alienation from those it represses most, and hence dehumanization. The ultimate manifestation of such dehumanization is the murder of Zacharia's wife, when Marumu mercilessly asphyxiates her as she resists his advances.

After the senseless murder, then, how can Zacharia escape his "fate," Paton's liberal prophecy of widespread crime among urbanized peasants? As I argued earlier, the gap between migrant workers and black intellectuals, much like the enormous rift between whites and blacks under apartheid, might have been bridged through what Can Themba in the film ingeniously calls "getting at each other": "I'd like to get people to get at each other. If I could get my worst enemy over a bottle of beer, maybe we could get at each other. It's not just a question of talking to each other but a question of understanding each other. Living in the same world."[23] If Zacharia can "get at" the city ways, if his path is smoothed over by an understanding of his condition, he may just succeed in escaping Absolom Kumalo's tragic end and Marumu's dehumanization. What of the role of the underclass in the articulation of an urban African identity? If, as eloquently argued by Themba, there is still a chance for Zacharia to avoid adopting the lifestyle of Marumu despite the enormous obstacles he must surmount, the question that remains is: what will he become? Once he rejects indiscriminate violence, will he be on his way to becoming what Modisane calls a "Situation," "an eternal alien between two worlds"?

> There is a resentment . . . against the educated African, not so much because he is allegedly cheeky, but because he fails to conform to the stereotype image of the black man sanctified and cherished with jealous intensity by the white man; such a native must—as a desperate necessity—be humiliated into submission. The educated African is equally resented by blacks because he speaks English, which is one of the symbols of white supremacy, he is resentfully called a *Situation,* something not belonging to either but tactfully *situated* between white oppression and black rebellion.
>
> (MODISANE 1990 [1963], 94)

After all, if he listens too closely to them, Zacharia would need to give up his rural identity, not only because of economic pressures, but also because of the *Drum* journalists' own biases against anything tribal. In their defense of a new urbanized African, as was noted earlier, many black intellectuals expressed profound aversion to a tribalism that they associated with rural life.[24] And yet *Come Back, Africa* strikes a balance between the old and the new African, the urbanite and the ruralist, documenting as it does Pedi dances alongside pennywhistlers, African languages as well as English and Afrikaans, each with its particular register of meaning (Masilela 1991, 64), black men covered in blankets and those dressed in European suits. Will Zacharia be turned into a shadow of the Sophiatown intellectuals—not his own man, but their creation?

Far from giving any clear answers, *Come Back, Africa* offers an ending that enables us, decades later, to extend the discussion opened by the film. While it is unlikely that Zacharia would ever become the "Situation" Modisane so poignantly describes, it is also hardly realistic to imagine that the role of the rural migrants (who make up the new urban underclass) in the articulation of an urban African identity would be championed by a group of intellectuals so dismissive of the rural "past." As Rob Nixon observes, "their distaste for state-imposed rural identities led many of the Sophiatown set to overreact with an often uninformed disparagement of rural experience per se. Thus their syntheses brought about new exclusions, their innovative eloquence fresh silences" (Nixon 1994, 40).

Come Back, Africa is a visual response to such silences, highlighting the interlocking spheres of rural and urban identities. Ironically, the front cover of *Drum* magazine's first issue vividly depicts the type of exclusion Rogosin interrogates in his film. "In counterposing silhouetted figures of a tribesman and a city-dweller, [the editors of *Drum*] showed some alertness to the transitional nature of black life in the city" (Chapman 1994a, 187), but they left out the intermediate figure of Zacharia. In *Come Back, Africa*, Rogosin offers one more piece to fit into the puzzle that might help us grasp the urbanizing process during the 1950s and its effects on the development of a new African identity.

Notes

1. *Tsotsi* is used in South Africa to denote "gangster." In this chapter I will be using *tsotsi* and "gangster" interchangeably. According to Rob Nixon (1994, 33), the term "entered local parlance in the 40s as a corruption of the American idiom 'zoot suit.' The gangsters were thus named because they favored narrow trousers; so narrow, in fact, that they sometimes resorted to vaselining their legs in order to ease on the trousers."

2. Since the 1980s a renewed interest in Sophiatown has yielded a musical, the Junction Avenue Theater's 1986 *Sophiatown* (Purkey 1996) and two documentaries, William Kentridge and Angus Gibson's *Freedom Square and Back*

of the Moon (1987), and Jürgen Schadeberg's *Have You Seen Drum Recently?* (1995). In a more recent production, Daniel Riesenfeld and Peter Davis also deal with the Sophiatown Renaissance at some length in part 1 of their documentary *In Darkest Hollywood* (1993).

3. "Come Back, Africa" is the English translation of *Mayibuye i-Afrika,* a rallying call of the African National Congress dating back to the 1940s.

4. This disclaimer is not entirely true. Miriam Makeba, who has a small role in the film, starred in the hugely successful jazz musical *King Kong* (Venice Film Festival Caption 1959). Two other female characters had, I suspect, some previous acting experience: Hazel, the sophisticated city woman who, according to script directions, tries to "fleece" Zacharia in the first shebeen scene, and Vinah, the wife, whose smart European dress and fluent English render her characterization of a rural woman straight out of Zululand hardly believable.

5. Firsthand chroniclers of Sophiatown culture include Bloke Modisane (1990 [1963]), Can Themba (1983 [1972]), Nat Nakasa (1985 [1975]), Lewis Nkosi (1965), Todd Matshikiza (1985 [1961]), Ezekiel Mphahlele (1989 [1959]), and Don Mattera (1987). Scholarly work on the topic includes Chapman 1994b; Nicol 1991; Stein and Jacobson 1986; and Coplan 1985.

According to Peter Davis (1996, 55), "Rogosin was the last to film Sophiatown before it disappeared completely, and he was the only one to offer a glimpse of a rich culture that was ruthlessly expunged." He further credits *Come Back, Africa* as the first film made in South Africa to feature two black scriptwriters and to use indigenous African languages (51).

6. Founded in 1951 by Oxford-educated Jim Bailey, *Drum* was originally intended to represent the rural traditions of Africans in urban areas. By 1955, however, "the Sophiatown 'set' virtually wrote the entire magazine, and the content . . . changed to include crime, jazz, gangs, speak-easies, pin-ups, and celebrities; which vied for space with human interest stories and exposures of the injustices of apartheid. . . . *Drum* became a symbol of a new urban South Africa, centered on and epitomized by, Sophiatown. It was assumed that for the journalists to deal with African urban life they had to descend to its very depths as well as climb to its heights; many achieved both extremes with some aplomb" (Gready 1990, 144).

7. Among those who consider it a fiction film are Ntongela Masilela (1991), Keyan Tomaselli (1989), and Rob Nixon (1994); those who classify it as a documentary film are Paul Rotha (1960), and Roger Sandall and Cecille Starr (1960); yet others refer to *Come Back, Africa* as "cinema journalism" and "fictional documentary" (Come Back, Africa 1960).

8. In this regard, an interesting parallel can be observed between Marumu and Bloke Modisane. The latter's father was also brutally murdered in the streets of Sophiatown—a fact that provides a powerful driving force to Modisane's autobiography.

9. It should be noted that the film takes issue with a specific manifestation of white liberal ideology, namely the paternalism expressed by Alan Paton's *Cry, the*

Beloved Country. This, of course, does not preclude myriad other manifestations of liberalism or the fact that some of the *Drum* writers themselves at times fell prey to the very liberalism they inveighed against.

10. It would at first glance appear that Zacharia has something in common with the protagonist of Donald Swanson's *African Jim* (1949) (also known as *Jim Comes to Jo'burg*), who also seeks work in Johannesburg in order to return with money to his kraal. However, all purported similarity is quickly diffused when the patronizing voice-over that opens that film claims: "This is the story of a native boy in Africa. This is the story of one of my African brothers. His name is Jim Namahiston [?], but we will simply call him Jimmy. This is the country where he was born and grew to manhood. This is where he lived in the freedom of the wide hills, tending the crops, and herding the cattle. It was a simple life, and a good life, and Jim was happy. But to many of us there comes a time when we leave, [when] we feel the urge to leave the country and travel to the cities. Often the young men go for a year, sometimes two, or even more so that they may earn money and then return to their people and buy cattle and marry. Sometimes it is just a spirit of restlessness and adventure that sends them traveling. So, then [one day] changing into town clothes, which are among his proudest possessions, Jim said goodbye to his parents and set up to go to Jo'burg" (my transcript). Unlike Jimmy's, Zacharia's foray in Johannesburg is hardly a "voluntary" choice. Through an exposé of the real reasons behind black rural migration to the cities, *Come Back, Africa* turns the genre of films exemplified by *African Jim*—a genre crudely based on white expectations of "natives" in their "natural" environment—on its head.

11. Peter Abrahams's *Mine Boy* (1989 [1946]) offers an altogether different approach to the migrant worker theme. *Mine Boy* is perhaps the type of proletarian novel that more closely reflects the concerns Rogosin explores visually.

12. While the catalogue of apartheid laws (the Population Registration Act, the Group Areas Act, the Bantu Education Act, the Natives Resettlement Act, and so on) did not come into being until after 1948, segregationist policies were applied before that time. See Thompson 1990, chap. 5.

13. Millions of blacks were uprooted through forced removals from the mid-fifties onward. A notorious case in point is Sophiatown, the setting of much of the action in *Come Back, Africa*.

14. For a detailed account of how apartheid legislation sought to destroy family unity among Africans, see Elsa Joubert's *Poppie Nongena* (1980).

15. I am grateful to Lucky Makamba of the University of the Western Cape for his help in identifying these African languages.

16. On the development of the homeland system, see Thompson 1990, chap. 6.

17. It is important to keep in mind that many of the Sophiatown intellectuals received mission school education and developed their own versions of the urban-rural divide. Some had internalized a disdain for rural African forms. For them, urbanization was the way forward, as they viewed ethnic and tribal categories as impediments to African progress (see Nixon 1994, 11–41).

18. I am not suggesting Modisane's autobiography advocates specifically workers' rights to an urban identity, but rather that his defense of Sophiatown indirectly extends that right to all who lived there, most of whom were working class.

19. Both the underworld of township gangsterism and *Drum* magazine were almost exclusively male-dominated. The dearth of documentation on women's participation in these two spheres during the 1950s suggests an interesting area of research. See Dorothy Driver's "Urban/Rural Spaces: *Drum* Magazine (1951–59) and the Representation of the Female Body" (cited in Nixon 1994, 259).

20. Among *Drum* features one finds, for example, Henry Nxumalo, "The Birth of a Tsotsi"; Arthur Mogale [Maimane], "Crime for Sale"; James Matthews, "Dead End!" and Mokobo Manqupu, "Love Comes Deadly!" See Chapman 1994b.

21. In his autobiography, gang leader-turned-poet Don Mattera is quick to point out: "We were in the streets, and they [*Drum* journalists] were in the desks. We used to call such people 'situations.'" (cited in Nixon 1994). Paul Gready (1990, 143) brings up a most unexpected way in which the encounter took place: "Intellectuals were often asked or forced by *tsotsis* to recite a piece of prose; for example, Caiaphas Sodomo in Modisane's story 'The Situation' is forced by *tsotsis* to recite the funeral oration of Mark Anthony, and is amazed by their familiarity with the piece."

22. Far from attributing political militancy to Can Themba or, for that matter, to any of the *Drum* journalists, I am suggesting that *Come Back, Africa* marks a space where an incipient intellectual radicalization begins to be felt. The difficulty of incorporating a gang subculture into the mainstream of political activity and the partial fusion of these two historically divergent cultures has been studied elsewhere. See, for example, Beittel 1990, 1996; Glaser 1996.

23. Although Themba's prescription for dealing with apartheid may seem grossly naive today, it is worth remembering that *Come Back, Africa* was made a year before the Sharpeville Massacre irrevocably shifted the course of the political struggle. It should also be kept in mind that *Drum* journalists, rather than endorsing activism in organized politics, tended to advocate passive resistance and believed in the moral power of their argument to bring about change. Lewis Nkosi makes this point in an interview with Peter Davis. See part 1 of Daniel Riesenfeld and Peter Davis's documentary *In Darkest Hollywood* (1993).

24. For a detailed discussion of the emergence of the new African and antitribalism, see Masilela forthcoming b.

PART 3

Contemporary Debates

6

Framing South African National Cinema and Television

Jacqueline Maingard

There is no national cinema in South Africa, even though some cinema might seem—or seek—to represent or evoke a sense of "the national": recent examples are *Mandela* (1995), *Cry, the Beloved Country* (1995), and *Fools* (1997). In proposing this topic, therefore, the underlying question is: Why frame South African film and television as national? This question, the subtext to the chapter, in many ways remains unexposed and is not directly answered. The easy answer is that democracy is being made in South Africa and it is mediated through the images presented in film and on television. This leads to further questions about how South Africans, as participants in this national project of democracy, are being represented.

I make a number of assumptions about national cinema and television in South Africa. The first is that it encompasses both documentary and fiction film. In any case, the boundaries between the two are increasingly blurred, an argument that Bill Nichols elaborates in his book *Blurred Boundaries: Questions of Meaning in Contemporary Culture.* As he puts it, "documentary and fiction, social actor and social other, knowledge and doubt, concept and experience share boundaries that inescapably blur" (Nichols 1994, 1). My own research, and hence this chapter, focuses more strongly on documentary, though I recognize the need to embrace fiction as well.

The second assumption is that film and television are strongly linked. This is true universally, with films made as cinema being shown on television and films being made expressly for television, but in South Africa, the particular histories of film and television and the economic strictures that now face their production suggest that the link between them needs to be strengthened.

The third assumption is that there is no clear division between the apartheid era and postapartheid democracy. While there are moments and events that delineate points in history signifying change or the potential for change, there are ways beyond time in which, in the experience of life in South Africa, the syntagmas of history overlap: in the 1980s the term "postapartheid" spoke of the reach beyond apartheid and described the actions and movements toward it; in the early 1990s we spoke of the "transitional period," the historical "in-between" in the political processes initiated and developed toward the first democratic elections in 1994; now we talk of "democracy." But none of these are clearly demarcated, and lines of these pasts cross through and are entangled with the present.

The final assumption that I am making is perhaps more a position than an assumption: I am viewing national film and television in South Africa from within a contemporary perspective, rather than reaching back to cinemas of the past.

I begin with a focus on questions of representation that pertain to national identity in relation to specific productions. Two broad trends emerging in documentaries of the late 1980s and early 1990s are discussed with particular reference to the "voice" of the filmmaker—the authorial presence in the film's social statement—and to the notion of the "speaking subject"—how, to what extent, and to what effect the subject of the film is ascribed agency. This is tied up with a brief exposition on a theoretical perspective on questions of national identity.

While there is no sense of a national cinema and television in South Africa, as I have stated, it is possible to speak of its potential development through questions of representation. In doing so there are two structuring concerns that facilitate the investigation of representing national identities on our screens: the voice of the filmmaker and the notion of the speaking subject. The concept of voice in documentary film has been developed by Bill Nichols, a film theorist whose interests are rooted in the ideological constructs of documentary film in particular. He describes voice as "that which conveys to us a sense of the text's social point of view" (Nichols 1983). In other words, voice is how the filmmaker prescribes the film's social statement or, indeed, argument. This notion clearly relates to the ideological positioning that the filmmaker chooses, not only for the framing of the subjects in or subject matter of the film, but for the spectators. This takes the concept of voice into the realm of the ways in which the film works as a text: how it sutures or interpellates the spectator into its meanings through its inscribed rhetoric. This inscription occurs in the complex weaving of the text through what Nichols defines as three axes that structure the text itself—history, narrative, and myth.

In documentary, the historical axis binds the text to its referential reality, its historical context. The narrative axis frames and structures the film's exposition, its telling of that history. The axis of myth provides the spectacle from which the spectator gains pleasure. Seen in the light of these three axes, the voice of the filmmaker becomes "a level of authorial presence . . . that is felt and experienced by the viewer as different from the mere replication or reproduction of the world . . . [so that] what we experience is less the world reproduced than the world represented" (Nichols 1991, 128). The importance of this is precisely the fact that the authorial statement of the film is one that is "represented." Nichols implies that it is *consciously* "felt and experienced" by the viewer, but in effect it is the *unconscious* workings of the text to produce meanings for the spectator that is equally if not more significant. Questions, then, of how films render "the national" visible or meaningful for viewers through the inscription of ideology by the filmmaker become critical.

The notion of the speaking subject is more complex than that of voice, for it combines two concepts: speaking and subject. At the simplest level, it refers to the subject about whom the film is made, the person(s), the social actor(s) whose historical reality frames the subject matter of the film. The first point, then, is to identify who the subject is (and also who it is not, who is absent). Developing from this are questions as to how that subject is represented in the film. Put differently, with regard to the power and presence of the filmmaker in the text's social statement, the issue is the extent to which the filmmaker "allows" the voice of the subject to be represented. The notion of the speaking subject, then, refers not just to the ways in which the subject speaks, literally the words she or he utters, but to the extent to which all the workings of the text itself (through the axes of history, narrative, and myth) represent the subject.

This is further complicated when we add to this mix of representational issues and questions the ways in which the subject is ascribed agency within the text. This is related to the earlier point about the power the subject is accorded to determine the film's meanings. Theoretical perspectives on subjectivity in film point toward how classic narrative cinema represents the subject within the text. Specific codes and conventions conspire to maintain the sense that a seamless reality is being depicted. They also point toward ways in which the notion of "the subject" in film needs to be viewed from psychoanalytical perspectives, in which the subject is never a unified or unitary whole, but is always divided within her- or himself. Thus even where agency is ascribed to the subject, where the subject's "speaking" is primary in the meanings that the text evokes, the subject is still a site of "difference." This conceptualization of the "speaking subject" is significant for representations of "the national," for it relates to questions about who "speaks," who is given agency within the representational matrices of the film, for whom, and for what purpose (Hayward 1996, 82–87; Lapsley and Westlake 1988, 214–19).

There are two broad trends in representations of national identity to examine against this backdrop of the filmmaker's voice and the speaking subject, exemplified by the documentaries made by Video News Services (VNS, later called Afravision) and the *Ordinary People* series, made by Mail and Guardian Television. Comparing the two, it is clear that there are different strategies at work, resulting in different positionings of identity. I will note some of the general features of each category of documentary and illustrate these with examples from *Hlanganani: A Short History of COSATU,* made by VNS, and *The Peacemakers,* the first in the *Ordinary People* series. My overall focus is more strongly on the *Ordinary People* series since it is more complex on questions of identity and therefore more interesting for this discussion. It is also, in my view, a proposed or possible way forward for opening up the representation of national identity in South Africa, for it reflects multiplicities rather than fixed categories of identities and facilitates an engagement in the often extraordinary events of South African life with a subjective intimacy never before represented. It therefore warrants more detailed inspection.

Here it is valuable to note that there are some recent examples of fiction film that can also be seen as reflecting the filmmakers' interest in representing identities as less categorized or fixed and more porous. Both *Jump the Gun* (1996) and *Fools* (1997) (see chapters 8 and 9 in this volume) are compelling in laying bare particular South African realities and characters that have not been presented in cinemas before. And each film's stylistic and aesthetic features are innovative and inventive in ways that support these different perspectives on South African identities. While the present chapter cannot examine these and other fiction films in detail, the approach I have devised for examining documentary film can equally apply to fiction film, for how a fictional character is ascribed agency within a film is of crucial significance in representing identity and creating audience identification with that identity.

In the VNS documentaries, the filmmakers work on the basis of an ideologically derived political framework that proposes a symbiotic interconnection between the fight for the rights of workers—specifically the mostly black, urban, male workers affiliated with the Congress of South African Trade Unions (COSATU)—and the national campaign for political freedom and democracy in South Africa. The representational strategies that emerge based on this framework reveal a dominance of the voice of the filmmaker, because all the representational choices serve the political stance framing the film itself. It is a formulaic ideological prescription that acts as a structuring principle for the representational strategies selected. The documentaries are ideologically tight, even closed, promoting this specific ideological framework in relation to national identity. The subject is the urban, black, almost invariably male COSATU-affiliated worker, but he seldom speaks. When he does speak, however, uttering words about his own experience, his words are used in relation to other textual strategies to illustrate the broader ideological (pre)text on which the documentaries are based. Similarly, his textual representations as a subject who "speaks" are used illustratively rather than prescribing his agency within the text itself. His agency as subject is dominated by the ideological structuring principle that exists beyond the text, and it is in this ideological space that his agency exists, though it is unmatched within the textual framing of his subjectivity. This assigns to the spectator an observational position. The textual imaging on the screen is, for the viewer, two-dimensional. There is a solid dividing line between the viewer and the film's subjects. They speak *to* us and we watch and listen, without participation. The *Ordinary People* series, on the other hand, never allows the viewer to watch passively, for the camera is always moving with one subject or another, always allowing for shifting possibilities of identification and of identity.

The example of the documentary *Hlanganani: A Short History of COSATU* is especially significant, as it was "the first program made by the democratic movement to be shown by SABC TV."[1] Made for national television audiences in association with COSATU, it presents the history of COSATU in a linear chronology that begins with the 1973 strikes in Durban then moves to the formation of FOSATU (Federation of South African Trade Unions) and later of COSATU in 1985. It follows events in COSATU through each year after its launch, noting its successes and failures up to 1991 following the release of Nelson Mandela, the unbanning of political organizations, and the beginnings of negotiations about the first democratic election. All the way through the documentary, the point is made that civil liberties and the rights of workers are interlinked and that in the fight for democracy COSATU was a significant force.

The documentary interviews two workers, using them in strategic combination with other elements, including interviews with COSATU and union officials, illustrative imagery, a camera style that accords status to the workers and worker imagery in the frame, editing devices and the voice-over narration of a black female. This voice-over is not integrated with the subjectivities represented in the text itself; it appears to be tacked on after the making of the film rather than a fully integrated ideological positioning within the text and the meanings it seeks to produce. Every interviewee is male, and apart from the very rare representation of a woman within a crowd scene, women are entirely absent from this documentary as workers or union officials. Male subjectivities are therefore highlighted even more strongly by this apparently aberrant, and patronizing, choice of voice-over. Within the film's narrative and its ideological framework, women have no agency. In its historical context, the film demonstrates an enormous lacuna in this type of anti-apartheid documentary film: the representation of women, in this case women workers, in the fight for freedom in South Africa.

As a whole, within the limited and exclusive identities that the film proposes, the documentary is principally interactive (see Nichols 1991, 44–56), based on excerpts of interviews used in ways that clearly have been carefully prescribed, and not only in that they are all with men. They can be seen in three clusters: those with COSATU and union officials; those with commentators outside the union movement; and those with two workers, who represent the speaking subjects of the documentary. The speaking subject is, as I have already noted, not given any subjective agency within the text itself. Rather, the way the filmmakers link the words of the speaking subjects with those of the union officials ties their words about their specific experience into the documentary's argument—its ideologically based structuring principle that predetermines the strategies of representation and their relationship to each other in the framing and the making of the text.

An important feature of how the interviews are used in the documentary relates to the backdrop of each excerpt. The two workers are interviewed sitting on a chair in a factory with machinery in the background—a realistic worker setting. The exterior commentators are interviewed in realistic office settings, seated at desks. The COSATU representatives and union officials, however, are placed in front of graphic posters, depicting various worker-orientated slogans and images, that fill the background of the frame. This has the effect of harmonizing the words of the spokesperson with the words and images presented in the backdrop—a theatricalized context within which the interviewee speaks. In this way the particular or specific, represented in the words of the interviewee, is never disassociated from the general, represented in the background.

The selected ways in which each cluster of interviewees is represented strongly exemplify the concept of the voice of the filmmaker. For here, rather than follow convention and interview everyone in the same way, the filmmakers have constructed the "space" of each type of interview. This has the effect of highlighting the differences between them and enabling their selective and strategic incorporation into the film's voice in different ways. The primary interviewees are the COSATU and union officials. It is they who confirm the film's ideological framework, and the other interviews are used strategically to further that perception. Thus, although the speaking subjects are in relative terms a small feature of the documentary, their positioning, especially in terms of the documentary's voice, is crucial because their words verify and support the larger statements by the union officials. So the comments about the relationship between national liberation and workers' rights are represented not as mere political rhetoric on the part of the officials and leaders, but rather as primarily significant in the singular experience of individual workers. This is critical in relation to how the documentary sustains a link with its national audience, particularly attracting the identification of black (male) workers affiliated with COSATU.

The voice of this documentary hinges centrally, however, on the camera style used in the illustrative imagery. This chiefly involves the use of a low-angle camera that highlights the backdrops of all the scenes, especially crowd scenes and scenes at meetings. These backdrops are usually enormous banners, with graphics reflecting union names and logos. Each shot is carefully composed and framed to highlight the slogans and images on the posters as well as the militancy of the workers themselves. The aesthetic effects of these shots also relate to the colors in the images. The colors red, yellow, black, and white predominate, both in the posters and banners that make up the backgrounds and in the images of T-shirted workers in the foregrounds. For example, one of the shots of a worker congress depicts a crowd of workers in red T-shirts toyi-toying (the toyi-toyi is a dance performed during protest marches) in front of a large banner bearing the words "One Country One Federation" and "Unity is Strength" that fills the background of the frame. The low angle of the shot has the effect of framing the bodies of the workers at the waist and so highlighting their torsos, their masculinity, and the banner in the background. Another shot from a very low angle has a similar effect. The framing just below the shoulder level foregrounds the workers' shoulders and heads in red T-shirts with fists raised against the banner filling the background in red with part of the slogan "One Country One Federation" in yellow. The imagery on the banners and in the logos on T-shirts has its roots in Soviet revolutionary imagery of the 1920s, so the placement of the camera at a low angle, coupled with specific framing and composition, repeatedly highlights the revolutionary sentiments of the events depicted.

Intermittently, and sometimes linking sequences, the documentary uses a collage of images edited in strobe, which has the effect of breaking up the image and abstracting it from itself. Over these collages there is a reflective instrumental music in a township style. While these collages sometimes link sequences, they also momentarily remove the viewer from the mainstream narrative and allow reflection on the issues presented. In this way these collages act as an alienating strategy, a Brechtian device. They also, however, hold the viewer's attention within the framework of the broad political context within which COSATU was formed, especially when they represent images of crowds marching and demonstrating, and of police brutality. These sequences, then, serve primarily to entrench the broader political framework that exists beyond the specific environs of the workers' revolution, reminding the viewer of their interrelationship. This is reinforced with illustrative imagery that represents the events and historical moments during and following the formation of COSATU. This includes images of national meetings and congresses, police raids at COSATU House and union offices, and meetings between workers and "bosses." The union officials who speak as interviewees in the documentary are at times shown as part of these strategic meetings, confirming their credibility.

The narrational voice-over provides information, links sequences, and propels the narrative. At times it dominates the accompanying visual images, taking on the voice-of-God quality of didactic documentaries, described as the "expository documentary" (see Nichols 1991, 34–38). This didacticism is a strong feature of the film's closed ideological framework, for the spectator is led through the documentary with little if any opportunity to consider the subject matter for her- or himself. Rather, the preferred meanings of the filmmaker, the documentary's voice, are repeated, confirmed, and reinforced through each of the strategies selected and their combination.

In a general sense, the final message for the viewer is unquestionably that although political liberation is under way in 1991, there is a further struggle to be fought and won—the advancement of the rights of workers. Indeed, political liberation is not complete without workers being given the status of "the most important citizens of the country," as Cyril Ramaphosa puts it toward the end of the documentary. While this is in essence true, in terms of the subjectivities inscribed into—and absent from—the documentary, this primarily means male workers. The documentary's conscious rhetoric calls for action in the real world by creating a symbiosis between political freedom and workers' rights. It shows how these two features of South African life cannot be divorced from each other, and concludes by reinforcing its argument that the future of political freedom continues to rest centrally on the status of the worker in society. At the same time the representational strategies employed by the documentary, the limits of the subjectivities it represents, reduce the narrative framing of South African history to single, exclusive, categorized subjectivities—urban, black, male workers affiliated with COSATU.

I turn now to the *Ordinary People* series, which represents the second trend in representations of national identity. Like the VNS documentaries, the documentaries in this series are also based on what can be described as a formula. Here, however, the formula is not so much ideologically constructed as based on principles underpinning the selected representational strategies. In contrast to the VNS documentaries, the *Ordinary People* series allows for an ideologically open "swimming around" of possible positionings of identity, without ever being fixed in any one position. I will illustrate this with examples from the first documentary in the series, *The Peacemakers,* broadcast in 1993.

The *Ordinary People* series consciously engages with multiplicities of subjectivity in South Africa and represents a deliberate move to counter the singularity of the political documentaries made by VNS.[2] In 1993 the antiapartheid film and video unit Free Filmmakers and the *Weekly Mail* (now called *Mail and Guardian*), in a joint venture called Weekly Mail Television (now called Mail and Guardian Television), successfully negotiated the commissioning of the series with the South African Broadcasting Corporation (SABC). In that year seven parts to the series were produced and broadcast.[3] It was the first time that an independent production company had produced a current affairs program for the SABC. In 1994 and 1995 further parts were produced and broadcast on the SABC. One specific program, *A Day with the President,* was aired in a prime-time slot in May 1995, on the anniversary of Nelson Mandela's first year in office.

The *Ordinary People* series is a current affairs program presenting topical events and issues. While each part (approximately thirty minutes long, except *A Day with the President,* which is fifty-five minutes) stands alone as a documentary, it is significant that the series is driven by predetermined strategies that are repeated in each part. The series therefore has an overall coherence. Significantly for a current affairs program, the events represented in the *Ordinary People* series were not always widely reported in the media. The intent of much of the series was to inform viewers of events about which they knew little or nothing. Viewers were also taken to places and into situations where they had never before been. An example of this is the football match at the Lonehill prison between a prison team and the famous Soweto football team, the Orlando Pirates. Alternatively, very familiar events, situations, and places were presented differently from how they had been presented on television before—for example, the conflict between Inkatha and the African National Congress (ANC).

The key element of the *Ordinary People* series is that rather than individual perspectives representing the views of a mass organization or group, as in the VNS documentaries, the individuals presented stand primarily for themselves as "ordinary" people. This is so even when the individual presented is a leader or official. The way this is accomplished is explained by the four chief principles of this series.

The first of these principles is that each part is based on three or four key individuals who are connected to or who converge on a specific event or place. Each individual is followed and filmed by a cameraperson. In most cases the difference between the individuals is marked. For example, in *The Peacemakers* three peace monitors are followed through the day—one is from Inkatha, another from the ANC, and a third from the Peace Secretariat itself—as well as a member of the Internal Stability Unit; in *Tooth of the Times* the three individuals are a farmer, a farm laborer, and an auctioneer. The difference between the subjects varies from one part of the series to another. It may be based on gender, on race, on political allegiance, on occupation, and so on, or on a combination of differences.

The second of these principles is camera style. The camera is mostly handheld, an active participant in the proceedings, in the cinema verité style. This style is often used observationally in documentary, but in *Ordinary People* it is not an observing camera so much as a subjective camera, since the camera consciously seeks to represent the point of view of a particular subject. It does this by placing the camera alongside or behind the subject so that audiences view the world from her or his perspective.

There is an important distinction to be made here between the ways in which the VNS documentaries and the *Ordinary People* series represent a subjective point of view of the black working class. They achieve this, broadly speaking, by creating a sense of an ideological subjectivity, which also draws the spectator into identifying with it. There are times in the VNS documentaries when this is done by using point-of-view shots, similar to those in the *Ordinary People* series. One notable example is *Fruits of Defiance* (1990), where images of police brutality on the street are represented from the point of view of small children observing the action through the windows of their home. A domestic interiority is created that has powerful consequences for viewers' perceptions of that brutality. The subjectivity of the VNS documentaries emerges, however, from the *combination* of strategies rather than any single strategy on its own. In the *Ordinary People* series, on the other hand, the subjectivity is largely created by using the camera consistently as if it were the subject her- or himself.

The third principle on which the *Ordinary People* series is based is what I would term the personal-political line. Following the chapter "Many Politics" in *Dialogues* by Deleuze and Parnet (1977), I am invoking the concept of "lines" as a way of defining the line drawn by the creators of the *Ordinary People* series *through* each of its subjects as a personal-political line. The term "personal-political" might suggest a binarism, but the very use of Deleuze and Parnet's notion of "line" precludes such a connotation. Deleuze and Parnet (124) propose that "we are made up of lines and these lines are very varied in nature." The first of these lines is segmentary, clearly defined. A second type is more supple, allowing for thresholds to be crossed. A third kind is more complex, the line of gravity, the line of flight. But "the three lines are immanent, caught up in one another," and it is this entangled immanence, which Deleuze and Parnet (125) poetically describe, that I invoke here. In the series the representation of the subject as an ordinary person, no matter what his or her political position or status might be, is paramount. This occurs not as an obliteration of the political but as an interconnection between and around the many parts of a subject's life. Thus the notion of "lines" is an appropriate reference, for it allows for the sense of interconnection and relationship between these parts, rather than simply one position of a binary split between the personal and the political, with one being elevated above or away from the other. This idea has some relationship too to the concept of "hybridity," which I will return to later, for Deleuze and Parnet (131) write that "it is certainly no longer . . . a synthesis of 1 and 2, but of a third which always comes from elsewhere and disturbs the binarity of the two, not so much inserting itself in their opposition as in their complementarity."

The fourth principle is the conscious use of narrative[4] in the making of each part: "taking fictional principles and applying them to documentary film" (Gavshon 1997). Each "social actor," to use Nichols's term, is a "character" through whom the narrative cause-effect chain is motivated. Here there is a significant linking between the character in narrative time and space within a (fiction) film, and the "character" within historical time and space in a documentary film. Ultimately, this cause-effect chain leads to resolution and closure, at least in classic narrative structure. In documentary, however, while narrative may lead to closure of the filmic time and space, the historically real dimension of the film, the referential reality within which the film is located, remains open. This sets up a potential dilemma for the documentary filmmaker seeking to locate or position viewers/spectators in relation to the history that is in process beyond the frame of the text. Here, the fact that *Ordinary People* is a series facilitates the notion that there is no end to the ordinary people in South Africa. Even in the closing of each narrative, each part, there is the knowledge of another narrative/part to be opened up. Nevertheless, the challenge for the filmmaker is the positioning of the spectator in relation to the people and events of each part, with an incomplete sense of closure that might facilitate action on the part of the spectator in the real world.

The combined effect of these principles of the *Ordinary People* series is that three or four different points of view, usually on a single event, are subjectively represented within a filmic narrative structure. These three or four perspectives are represented by speaking subjects who both speak in personal narrational styles that explain and describe their lives, positions, and actions, and "speak" in the sense that their subjectivities are consciously and strategically represented in the film's textual framing.

This leads to a set of questions as to the voice or argument of each part of the series. Does this multiple subjectivity remove the filmmaker's voice? To what extent does the filmmaker defer his or her argument to the voices represented in the text? Or does this triple/quadruple subjectivity itself represent a clue to the ideological positioning of the filmmaker? It would seem that this is so, primarily because the text's social statement—its voice—in each case seems to be that these are "ordinary" people, no matter what their role in life or in society. The humanness of each individual, whatever his or her political orientation or social status, is primary. For South Africans in the early 1990s this was a powerful statement, given the polarized, brutalized state of the nation as a whole.

In a sense it might seem to be a liberal position that condones all and makes no judgment. Yet the nature of the series and its position in the early to mid-1990s, as well as its innovative form, seem to retract it from this potential. This is in many ways due to the fact that the images on television (and nontelevised documentaries such as those made by VNS) were largely based on categorizations of a polarized South African society. By contrast, *Ordinary People* was an intervention that opened up questions of identity. That it did so in humanist terms put it on a cutting edge that could have limited its success. On the other hand it is precisely because of this humanism that it was a successful and innovative intervention in the representation of South African identities to South Africans at that time. No longer were South Africans being identified on the basis of established categories, often in dichotomous opposition to each other—black/white, workers/bosses—but rather the human, shared ordinariness of all South Africans, across a diverse range of identities, was being exposed in a way that had never been attempted in televisual representation.

Furthermore, in presenting multiple subjectivities or identities in such a way that audiences are sutured (literally "stitched") into identifying with these subjectivities, "truth" is never fixed and is always open, allowing the viewer to derive her or his own meanings from the subjectivities represented. The viewer is not able to fix any "truth" onto *Ordinary People* because it represents three or four angles on any particular reality. In this sense, the "voice" of the documentary is quite simply that "truth" cannot be fixed onto South African realities. This has significant outcomes, for when truth is unfixed, it engages the viewer in having to produce meanings. In a Brechtian sense the viewer is therefore made to exercise her or his critical judgment. "Who is right?" seems to be the question that awaits an answer. And there is never just one answer, because the subjectivities represented are multiple and sufficiently diverse to make univocality highly unlikely.

There is no doubt that the primary strategy of this documentary series is the consistent focus on the representation of individual subjectivities. Unlike the VNS documentaries, which vary in the strategies used though they are all to the same ideological end, in *Ordinary People* the same formula is reproduced in each part of the series, and also to the same end. This primary strategy would not work as coherently if it were not for the fact that three additional strategies are tied to this one: the subjects are speaking subjects, the individual subjectivities are marked by significant difference one from the other, and the camera style enables these individual subjectivities to be represented so that audiences are sutured into positions of identification with each of them. And, at the time of their broadcast, the subjectivities represented took South African audiences into new experiences, or into familiar ones in new ways, through the eyes of subjects whose diversity meant that they would not all be subjects with whom any single viewer would usually identify. In effect, then, the *Ordinary People* series achieves a rejection of stereotypes. It personalizes categories of people that have been socially "fixed"—the farmer, the activist, the lesbian, the prison warder, the policeman, and so on. These categories most often also have a racial dimension; for example, the farmer is a white farmer, the activist is a black activist. Thus, rejecting these stereotypes is also an intervention in the racial attitudes that audiences might have. Furthermore, the identities of the subjects are not always encapsulated as whole or unfragmented: at times, individual subjects may reveal difference within themselves, and not only in relation to other subjects in the same part of the series. This adds to the complexity of questions of identity in the series.

The basic principles discussed above were visible in the series from the start, in the pilot program entitled *The Peacemakers*. Its narrative spans one day, Sharpeville Day, in 1993, when a potential clash between marchers of the Inkatha Freedom Party (IFP) and the ANC was averted by the presence of peace monitors. There are four subjects: Gertrude, an IFP monitor; Faith, an ANC monitor; David, a member of the Peace Secretariat; and Clive, a policeman in the Internal Stability Unit.

The choice of these subjects highlights the series' commitment to representing multiple subjectivities rather than singularized ones. There are two women, both black, representing opposite political stances. There are two men, both white, each representing a different "peacekeeping" function. The personal-political line is particularly strong in the representations of Gertrude and Faith, because of their particular political allegiances, and also because of the personalized subjective camera style. This style, which "marries" the camera to each individual subject, locates the viewer within the individual's subjective space, both physically and psychologically. For example, we follow Gertrude walking through the hostels in the area, greeting people as she passes them. Then later, after the events, in the closing of the narrative, the camera watches her, in her disappointment at the IFP's actions, sitting with a teacup hanging from her hand, her shoulders bent.

The personal-political line is also strong in Clive's character. This is primarily because the camera takes the viewer inside the armored troop-carrying vehicle from which he views the world. From this location he speaks of his fear of facing large angry crowds, as the camera reveals from within this space the shattered windows of the vehicle. From these individualized perspectives the narrative foregrounds the "ordinary" individual, and the polarities of the broader context become part of a personal-political line located in the individual's subjectivity and her or his "speaking" within and of that subjectivity. This is where the individual subjectivities play a crucial role in the film's voice. Precisely because the IFP monitor, Gertrude, has a position as speaking subject within the film, the aggression of the IFP supporters makes an even more powerful impression on the viewer. It is tied to the individual within it, in this case Gertrude, with whom the audience has been led to identify—the mass has been individualized—from the outset of the documentary. By contrast, in the VNS documentaries the focus is on the mass and the individuals are homogenized within it.

In the closing of the narrative—with regard to the text's ideological closure or openness and within that the holding open of the historical realm—while the event itself may be over, the conflicts that drive a wedge between groups and organizations and that can escalate into war are still there. We could ask, as the documentary closes: Violence has been averted but will it be averted next time? The narrative is complete, but historical reality is not. Furthermore, potential action on the part of the spectator within that history is exemplified by the actions of four individual subjects with whom we have been led to identify. History is not something that exists outside of individual, personal lives. Indeed, the speaking subject not only speaks about that history but has agency within it. This agency is tied not only to the subject's representativeness—of an organization, a political allegiance—but to the fact that he or she is an "ordinary" person like anyone else watching the program. Thus the subjects' ordinariness is the central feature that binds the viewer to the documentary's argument and to the possibility that action may follow. The documentary, then, is an intervention in historical reality, not only because of its strategies of representation but also because of its potential effects on viewers.

Let us now locate these two trends in representations of national identity in a theoretical framework that posits a perspective on questions of identity. In my view, perceptions of the multiplicities of identity in South Africa can be usefully developed within a theoretical framework incorporating theorists like Mouffe, Bhabha, Hall, and Trinh T. Minh-ha (see Maingard 1995; 1997). In an examination of the framing of national cinema and television in South Africa, Stuart Hall's paper "Cultural Identity and Cinematic Representation" has significant resonances. Hall (1989) asks questions about new forms of visual and cinematic representation, primarily in Caribbean cinema but also more generally in cinema of the diaspora. Invoking Fanon, he poses the question: Are these cinemas to be driven only by "unearthing that which the colonial experience buried and overlaid" or by the practice of "the production of identity" (69)? He describes this "*production* of identity" as "not . . . grounded in the archaeology, but in the *re-telling* of the past." In other words, identity is not only something that is there to be discovered and revealed. While it is specifically located, "positioned," it is also unstable, unfixed, constructed in "difference." Hall's conceptualization of identity, then, "lives with and through, not despite, difference; by hybridity" (80)—the "third" of which Deleuze and Parnet (1977) speak.

This concept of "hybridity" is one that Homi Bhabha (1989) has employed in his conceptualization of the Third Space—a space that is not positioned in one place or another, but that exists in between. As I have postulated elsewhere, this notion of the "in-between" is rooted in a Lacanian psychoanalytical conceptualization of the "I" of the conscious being divided from the "I" of the unconscious, so that the "I" of enunciation (the one speaking) is different from the "I" of that which is enounced (the one spoken of).[5] This conceptualization of identity is, I believe, still strongly bound within a binarist perspective, and I have proposed elsewhere that beyond this seemingly binary or dualist perspective, "we are always in multi-layered spaces of in-betweennesses" (Maingard 1997; also see Hayward 1996). Here, Trinh T. Minh-ha's perspective (Trinh T. 1996, 11) on difference as a "politics of articulation (or disarticulation)" is useful. In some senses she ties together the perspectives of both Hall and Bhabha that I have presented here by proposing that within this "politics of articulation" "we should continue to use words like 'in-betweenness' and 'hybridity' as tools of change, and we should keep on redefining them until their spaces become . . . saturated" (11).

In my view there is no fixed way forward, no fixed formula for framing national cinema and television in South Africa, nor for its making. Although there are some policies in place for the structural loosening up necessary to begin to make national cinema and television, the economic priorities of the nation are not going to allow for any significant funding of film and television at the level of the state. There will be some resources, however. Currently, a major resource is in those film and television education and training projects and programs already established and committed to developing some sense of national cinema and television.

I have sought here to propose that explorations of the multiplicities of subjectivities or identities in South Africa present a space within which representation in film and television can offer perspectives that *construct* identities that resonate within the realm of "the national," without delimiting "the local" or enforcing false continuities, in the very act of representation itself. In the past, in antiapartheid documentary films, representations of identity have followed two broad trends: first, an exclusive, categorized perspective on identity, which had a certain ideological necessity attached to it in that it played an arguably significant role in the broad counterhegemonic battle against apartheid; and second, a perspective on identity marked by the multiplicities of ordinary South African people. Through the analysis of additional individual fiction films and documentaries, perceptions of how identities are constructed in South African film and television will be further problematized. It is important to continue to locate the framing of these media in South Africa within questions of identity. The challenge lies in the making of a national cinema that accomplishes a complex interrelationship between refuting the singularized categorizations of identity enforced by apartheid, opening up multiplicities of identity from within the in-between blurred spaces that have not yet been explored, and recognizing and articulating difference.

Notes

1. This is the description on the video cover, which also notes that it was screened in July 1991, two days before COSATU's first national congress.

2. This is not to suggest that the makers of these different categories of documentaries worked against each other competitively. Indeed, they were all antiapartheid filmmakers and members of the Film and Allied Workers Organization; they collaborated as film activists in the late 1980s and worked on films together. For example, Brian Tilley of the VNS collective directed one part of the *Ordinary People* series.

3. My use of the term "series" refers to the corpus of *Ordinary People* documentaries from 1993 to 1995. The word "part" refers to an individual thirty-minute documentary from the series.

4. I am grateful to Harriet Gavshon (1997), producer of the *Ordinary People* series, for suggesting this as a fourth principle.

5. For a valuable treatment of enunciation and cinema, see Hayward 1996, 82–87.

7

The Race for Representation
New Viewsites for
Change in South African Cinema

Lucia Saks

Since the 1994 elections that swept the African National Congress into power with Nelson Mandela at its head, South Africa has been rethinking itself as a nation. This process has resulted in a complete restructuring of laws, institutions, economic regulations, and electoral and social policies, all with the aim of transforming South Africa into a progressive democracy and integrating the country back into the world economy from which it had been partially excluded. Such a profound transformation, however, cannot take place only at the institutional level. It requires an immense act of imagination to develop a further set of articulations that bind people together (often provisionally) and place them in a shared time and space, a national habitus. As a result, a new set of narratives requires construction, and a new set of terms for belonging compels representational form—hence the first part of this chapter's title, "The Race for Representation."

This chapter is an attempt to paint a picture of the changing role of South African cinema in that race for representation. In mapping those changes, I sketch out three areas—viewsites—from which to consider South Africa's cinematic desires, its attempt to produce a cinema under the sign of the nation. Given the problematic character of each national instantiation and the inner illusion, chaos, and systemic contradiction in each great social project of national reconstruction, there is a constant danger that the center will not hold; time is of the essence. Hence, the race for representation becomes a compulsion motivated by a deep and justifiable anxiety about instability, a way of regulating ambivalence through repetitive gestures and new inventions of gesture. As such, it is a race without a finish line, an infinite task, complete only at the moment of exhaustion, when all the runners give up or die—as happened in both segregation and apartheid, when the center could no longer hold. Fortunately, the postapartheid inauguration does not show any signs of exhaustion. But for now the race is to get started—and this is what betrays the peculiar anxieties and contradictions of the postapartheid moment.

The race for a national cinema is yet to begin. It remains at the furious level of state pronouncements, ideologies, policies, committees, research agendas, idealization, and utopianism. The role of cinema in South Africa is being debated within a context of global dependency and a general lack of institutional excellence, investment from abroad, media training, and audience (especially when it comes to an audience of color). What abounds is revolutionary proclamation, oversimplified ideology, governmental high-handedness, and—it must be emphasized—a genuine concern for the importance of media in the achievement of social justice and for the representation of diversity on the screen, and heartfelt debate about the autonomy of the cinema from the state.

Site 1: Putting Film on Paper

THE STATE STEPS IN

The first viewsite from which we may inspect the concept of national South African cinema relates to structure. Recommendations for the formation of a new statutory body were first made in the 1996 "White Paper on the Film Industry" issued by the Department of Arts, Culture, Science and Technology (DACST). This body, the National Film and Video Foundation (NFVF), would administer state aid for the funding of all aspects of film production, distribution, exhibition, training, archives, management, research and information, visual literacy programs, and the promotion of locally produced films and video both internally and abroad. Funding for the foundation would come from DACST and would be channeled to two funding initiatives: the Film and Video Initiative, to provide seed funding for film and video projects, and the Film Development Fund, which would operate as a training fund for students from, to use a current phrase, the historically disadvantaged communities. Its main object would be, according to the "White Paper" (DACST 1996, 13), "to effect redress across communities by providing funding for entry-level producers and first-time directors, bursaries for film study, and short, specialised film and video productions." Along the lines of the French Centre National de la

Cinématographie and its Africanized version in Burkina Faso, the foundation would also receive funds through a series of levies placed on nondomestic films shown in South Africa, video distribution, and television advertising for foreign films shown on public television in South Africa. In addition, local content quotas mandated by the Independent Broadcasting Authority (IBA) for both private broadcasters and the national one should give local film production a much needed injection of capital.[1]

Despite the passing of the National Film and Video Foundation Bill into law by the National Assembly at the end of 1997, the long-awaited foundation was inaugurated only in November 1999 at the Cape Town Sithengi Film and TV Market with the announcement of its fourteen board members and chairperson. Its predecessor, the Interim Film Fund (IFF), established in 1996 by the DACST as a temporary governmental source of production funding, met with criticism on issues of transparency and infrastructure. Much to the annoyance of local filmmakers, it lacked official application procedures and administrative principles. One just submitted a proposal, and then a committee comprising mostly industry players, leavened with a few academics, decided who would receive funding. Many first-time filmmakers felt the department should have been more open about its judging criteria, the logic behind success and failure, and the difference in the amounts awarded. Another sore point appears to have been the lack of a supportive infrastructure for nascent filmmakers once they had received the funds. New filmmakers lack the industry contacts and expertise needed to realize their projects; as a result, things can—and do—go horribly wrong. The situation is exacerbated by the lack of formal film training in the country and the idea pervading the industry that filmmakers are technicians, not artists or cultural critics. Although plans were included in the "White Paper" for setting up a national film and television school, nothing has yet materialized. The few training institutions that do exist offer a variety of courses at differing levels and tend to reinforce the technician approach to film by employing people from within the industry to "train" their students, thereby splitting theoretical and critical skills from technical ones.

A notable feature emerging from the desks of the state planners—notable in that it points to a general trend in future policy making—is the lack of regionalism. There have been some regional initiatives, with the setting up of film boards in the Western Cape and KwaZulu Natal, but the emphasis in state cultural planning is on centralization, which unfortunately conjures up echoes of the past, since centralization was the hallmark of apartheid's political economy of the media. DACST claims that its resources are too limited to develop more inclusive strategies that would support regional initiatives. Given the department's limited budget, this is probably true, but it is hardly an adequate explanation. A certain lack of inventiveness seems prevalent in South Africa's cultural funding policy: an inability to think laterally, as the economists love to put it, in ways that would generate new partnerships with local industry, with other government ministries and agencies, and with other countries. South African broadcasting policy, in particular, appears to be following what Richard Maxwell (1995, 33) calls, in his description of Spanish broadcasting policy in the 1970s, a "high policy" phase of democratization, or "democracy bestowed from above." We may look to Australia, the only Southern Hemisphere country that appears to have "got democracy culturally right," as a model for creative policy making in this area. The Australian film commission acts as a core funding body and facilitator, but it does not act alone. Its alliances with other government agencies, including those dealing with telecommunications and broadcasting, result in a strong, interlinked structural matrix at the federal level that works to support regional film initiatives.

LEGITIMIZING THE CINEMA

The need and desire for—indeed, the right to—a "cinema of one's own" have been legitimated in South Africa through the discourses of black empowerment, nation building, and the African Renaissance, President Thabo Mbeki's term for a continental African social and economic renewal. The concept of the African Renaissance in particular has captured the imagination of many since it offers a way of connecting the new modes of political assertion within the country to a larger discourse that involves the continent at large. Through it, the South African miracle can become the African miracle, reversing the pessimism that has settled in across the continent, fueled by thirty years of despotic military coups, internecine fighting, violent wars, genocide, and the ever increasing poverty faced by most Africans today. The idea of an African Renaissance draws on the heritage of *négritude* and Pan-Africanism—two powerful anticolonial discourses that emerged from the intellectual fervor of the 1960s, certainly a more optimistic era for the continent than the ensuing three decades—without inheriting all the Marxist baggage that went along with them. In short, it is a useful term, and it has found much use in industry and the politics of culture. It is a call to arms without arming anybody, a legitimizing ideology for cultural change, a poetic vision for the continent at large, and a self-help program for the individual. It is also a saleable slogan for attracting Western funding since it draws on the heritage of liberalism—a Western heritage—and evokes a historical period that arouses intense pride in the Western cultural imagination.[2] The term allays deep-seated Western fears by conveying the assurance that African nationalism is not an exclusive dogma based on the specter of reverse racism, but reaches out to all those who live on the continent and seek to participate in its development. We might at this point recall Frantz Fanon's distinction between nationalism and "national consciousness." In his celebrated dialectic of the deficits and benefits accompanying the idea of nationalism, Fanon preferred to speak rather of a national consciousness that formed the basis for an international one. This distinction is very much in place when President Mbeki states, "I am an African," for with that remark he claims to speak on behalf of all of Africa in the name of South Africa's Constitution, which does not define "Africanness" by race, color, gender, or historical origins.

The national aspirations embodied in cultural forms have been of pivotal importance for the theorists of the neo- and postcolonial, from Fanon's famous paper "On National Culture" to the work of Edward Said and his followers, to the point where such theory has run the risk of Hegelianizing the postcolonial field as a single, homogeneous shape defined in terms of these aspirations. Such theorizing has not been without reason, however, for the question of what kinds of nations would emerge out of the transitions from colonies to independent states has been a crucial one, and postcolonial thought has opened up creative ways of considering it. But it is also important to keep in mind that despite similarities with the decolonization of other African countries, South Africa's transition from authoritarian racist rule to majority rule cannot be considered coterminous with that process: it cannot be neatly incorporated into the postcolonial matrix. Mozambique, Zambia, Zimbabwe, and Tanzania, for example, have had fifteen and, in some cases, twenty years to shape their transitions from a postliberation era to a system of state governmentalism with internal structures and agencies, from which have arisen all number of social practices including different modes of identification and subjectivities. The length of time involved in each has allowed for what Ernesto Laclau (1990) calls "sedimentation" to take place, referring to the process by which laws and structures sediment themselves into the society through social practices that then, over time, become open to resedimentation and redefinition.

This process is beginning to happen in South Africa, but the original moment of change is still very present, and inevitably there are substantial continuities with the past in maintained social and political structures and policy orientations. The result has been, in the words of Patrick Bond (2000), "the constitution of new elites that largely recycle old ones." Few have gone so far as to accuse the African National Congress (ANC) of selling out, but there has been a strong call on the part of politicians and others attached to the ANC's leftist allies (the trade unions and the South African Communist Party) to abandon talk of a cultural renaissance and concentrate more on serving the material needs of the country. Only then can social policies begin to eradicate what Patrick Bond terms the persistent "uneven development" in the social and economic arenas marked by huge areas of local, social, gendered, and racial exclusion. Faced with the enormous social problems present in South Africa today, Bond's frustration at all this "cultural talk" is understandable and opens up a number of related questions: Are cultural renewal and its products really that essential right now to people who don't have bread, houses, jobs, or adequate health care? Is it not a luxury, a cover-up, or worse—a symptom of the government's despair at not being able to solve the country's real problems?

These questions are all part of the critical debate on the term "African Renaissance" among intellectuals and activists across the continent. The left wing accuses it of being obscurantist, since it "serves to obscure the class contradictions between [the] imperialist masters and the African masses who need a revolutionary renaissance, which seeks first and foremost to fundamentally change their terrible conditions by challenging the forces largely responsible for them: The World Bank, IMF and WTO" (Harvey 2000). Democratic analysts fear that if wrongly interpreted, the word "African" could be taken as meaning that only black people are entitled to be part of the renaissance, resulting in an intolerant future for the growth of a human rights culture in South Africa. Perhaps the most pessimistic, and certainly the most poignant, attack on the idea of an African Renaissance was made by the playwright and poet Wole Soyinka. Speaking at the University of Cape Town, Soyinka outlined the indiscriminate slaughter and systematic dehumanization that has become the norm in many parts of the continent, creating in Soyinka's phrase "a permanence of violence."[3] Elsewhere, he asked, "How does a sculptor begin to carve with only stumps for arms? How does a village *griot* ply his trade with only the root of a tongue still lodged at the gateway of memory? I do not hear in this travesty of the creative process, the annunciation of a renaissance, nor read the first flicker of its regenerating fires on our ever-receding horizons" (Soyinka 1999).

137

Does this pessimism apply to South Africa, where many see the move to democracy as the path to utopia, in much the same way as the newly independent African countries in the postwar period viewed socialism? There is no clear answer to be had, but there is an implicit warning sounded by the critics on the illusory nature of talking in terms of a pending renewal. As Soyinka (cited in Wilhelm 1999) notes, "I have always distrusted the horizon . . . especially its habit of constantly receding . . . receding steadily since that renaissance spirit of immediate post-independence." Warning words as powerful as these should leave one either silent or, at the very least, cautious of enunciating anything at all, let alone a renaissance. Yet people do continue to speak of it, not only as a potential on the horizon but as something that has already arrived, something in which one can participate, especially those involved in cinematic and media production. One of the best examples of this confidence is a new thirteen-part coproduction series of thirty-minute programs being made for television, radio, and the Internet under the title *The African Renaissance*. According to a press release of 17 March 2000, it is the "first Pan-African television and radio documentary series to capture the vision that lies behind the new wave of democratization in Africa."[4] This vision sounds very distant from the one Soyinka refers to when he speaks of a vast literature, not of renewal, but of conflict that has arisen in reaction to the continent's violence. It would appear that the very efficacy of the term lies less in its reality than in its ambiguity and mutability, which permit application and redefinition as circumstances require. In South Africa it continues to be used as an almost sacred benediction to conclude speeches (see Seepe 2000). It was in this role that it popped up at the inauguration of the NFVF, when the Arts, Culture, Science, and Technology minister stated that the continued enhancement of an African cinema aesthetic would "lend further credence to the renewal of the African continent, our African Renaissance." The newly appointed chairperson of the Film and Video Board, Shaun Moodley, also drove home the point by promising that the foundation would "embrace the challenge of the African Renaissance" in carrying out its work (quoted in "South Africa's Film and TV Foundation Launched," 3).

Getting into GEAR

Long before the appearance of "African Renaissance" as a term on the rhetorical landscape, South African state transformation was legitimated by the Reconstruction and Development Programme (RDP), a macroeconomic policy that became the ANC's 1994 election manifesto. Despite the ANC's history as a left-wing liberation movement, the RDP was no socialist tract. It was more of a "wish list" whose major tenets could be comfortably encompassed within the liberal Keynesian theory of state investment to stimulate growth. Patrick Bond (2000, 92) in fact describes it as follows: "There was no denying that the RDP document was influenced in part by right-wing ideas, such as maintaining excessively strict limits on state expenditure generally . . . , the promotion of international competitiveness and the endorsement of an independent Reserve Bank insulated from democratic policy inputs."

This view notwithstanding, the RDP was a people-driven document attempting to help those whose development had been deliberately hindered under the apartheid regime. While economic growth (defined as overall increase in output) was a basic goal, the document argued that it should not precede reconstruction and redistribution. Section 1.2.9 of the RDP specifically states that "attacking poverty and deprivation must therefore be the first priority of a democratic government." Its basic premise of growth through redistribution in order to achieve its aim—the transferring of economic, political, and cultural power from the previously empowered (the whites) to those who had been deliberately disempowered by the apartheid regime—made it acceptable to the left wing, who supported it as being capacious enough to encompass their socialist project. Leaders of the South African Communist Party (cited in Bond 2000, 93) argued that "by gradually infusing the RDP with socialist ideals and practices a socialist program for South Africa can be developed."

However, when the economic growth predicted by the state's economists failed to materialize and the rand took a dive on the financial exchange markets, a fiscal conservatism—or anxiety, perhaps—began to take hold. What emerged in 1996 was a new macroeconomic policy document, this time labeled Growth, Employment, and Redistribution—or GEAR. GEAR turned the redistribution and growth formula on its head by arguing that growth had to take place before any form of redistribution could occur. A cursory look at the document reveals the new policy to be a trade-off between two divergent and partially incompatible requirements: first, that of raising up a poor population through the redistribution of resources irrespective of economic growth, and second, the need to produce an economic climate that would attract international capital investment. What followed was what Patrick Bond (2000, 1) calls "official neoliberalism . . . adherence to free market economic principles, bolstered by the narrowest practical definition of democracy . . .

over an extremely short period of time." In real terms this meant cutting budget deficits and social expenditure, lowering taxes, relaxing exchange controls, and downsizing the public sector.

Against the barrage of criticism from those on the Left that the government had sacrificed the poor on the altar of neoliberal global capitalism, and amid applause from the Right that the government was finally beginning to make the appropriate moves in opening up the economy, the ANC denied that any fundamental differences existed between the two documents, a denial that has been challenged most forcibly by the Congress of South African Trade Unions (COSATU), which argues that its traditional constituency of unskilled black workers have emerged the losers. In May 2000, the confederation launched a national strike against job losses and other forms of industrial action. As COSATU recasts itself more as a labor movement than an arm of the ANC, industrial militancy as opposed to political diplomacy has become the order of the day, recalling its clarion call of the 1980s, "The struggle continues."

The most important point that emerges from the struggle to find a framework for South African globalization and regional integration is the obvious vulnerability of developing nations in the global arena. Certainly, economic policy deserves to be conducted in a more open fashion so that these debates can find greater public authorship (for an in-depth analysis of the reasons for the shift, see Bond 2000, 97–121). But no degree of transparency in debate can determine whether the multifarious economic processes that take place under the name of globalization will really deliver the goods: that is, help strengthen the local situation, attract financial investment from abroad, provide competitive wages for workers, reinvigorate state institutions, support regional initiatives, and so on. South Africa's economic policy will have to accommodate global market forces in a way that supports and strengthens national aspirations. It cannot just accept the typical global structural adjustment package forced on developing countries without searching for skillful interventions on behalf of its own citizens. To do so would be to run the risk of creating further internal economic and social disintegration.

SHAPING FILM POLICY

The background I have outlined had a strong influence on the shaping of the "White Paper on the Film Industry," which states its objectives as "meeting basic needs, job creation, developing human resources, improving the economy and democratising the state and society" (DACST

1996). What strikes one in the document, however, is the fluency with which it combines the fighting rhetoric one has come to associate with postcolonial academese with phrases that might be found in a reader on neoliberal economic policy. No distinction is made, for example, between the concept of a national cinema that "will enable South African audiences to see their own interpretations of their experience and stories reflected on local screens" and the creation of a film industry based "on a sound commercial footing in order to enable it to become internationally competitive." Chapter 2 opens with a sentence describing film as "an important dimension on the terrain of cultural expression and the exploration of social meanings." In the second sentence we read that film can "generate significant employment, income and investment opportunities" in the turbulent global media markets. In a later paragraph, the industry is credited with the potential to promote South Africa as a tourist attraction and a location for foreign film and advertising production due to the low costs of production in comparison with those of Western locations.

We may well ask what kind of a cinema is being envisaged in these phrases. Is it one that reflects the "petty bourgeois nationalism" that Frantz Fanon warned led to a "false decolonization," or is it a "combative" cinema (to use another expression from Fanon), a cinema that speaks to its own people in their own language irrespective of whether the outside world can understand it? While the words of the "White Paper" certainly do not reflect the statements of an oppositional decolonized subjectivity capable of giving shape to Fanon's ideas, they do reflect a way of solving what Elsaesser (1989, 3) has called, in his analysis of the beginnings of new German cinema in the 1970s, the "incompatible objectives of national cinema": economic viability on the one hand and cultural motivation on the other. The reconciliation of cultural and economic priorities in Germany's film subsidy bill of that period leaned heavily on a particularly German concept, something Kluge characterized as *Brauchbarkeit*. Roughly translated it means "usefulness"—that is, useful for the nation, for the industry, and hence for the general good. Similarly the "White Paper" tries for that same reconciliation by placing the institution of cinema within the broader South African framework of transformation, which, as I have described, negotiates a difficult path between the RDP and GEAR. Film policy rhetorically invokes both in its attempts to reconcile the cultural needs of the people and the marketplace, pragmatism and idealism, of which there can be no greater example than the utopian vision of a national cinema.[5]

THE FILMMAKER: CAUGHT BETWEEN SUBSIDY AND SELF

In view of these structural changes and imaginings, let us note very clearly that there must, in a national cinema, be an ongoing dialogue and surely a partial contradiction between the projection of state or industry planning and the subjectivity of the individual filmmaker. One of the difficulties of being progressive in a newly forming and progressive nation, especially one whose first president was Nelson Mandela and whose constitution is universally considered to be the model for democratic governance, is to remain autonomous from the dictates of social and cultural policy—or, in the case of industry initiatives, to avoid giving in to market dictates. Filmmakers may well agree with and benefit from the structures and ideologies put forward by the state or industry, but their autonomy will nevertheless consist in the way in which they resist subsumption by either. It is not easy to reconcile one of the major principles of cinema as an art—the right to self-expression and personal vision, the idea of art for art's sake, not for the nation—with the complexities of a state subsidy system conceived under the sign of cultural and economic renaissance, or with the demands of industry conceived under the sign of a free marketplace of goods. Elsaesser (1989, 44) notes these difficulties in the development of the new German cinema, which took the form of *Autorenkino,* or a cinema of authors. *Autorenkino* did not, he argues, eliminate the contradictions as much as disguise them. It determined the political and administrative machinery put in place to fund films practically and it furnished the criteria that validated filmmaking as an "art." Once institutionalized, the ideology of self-expression became a surrogate economic category that worked in two different ways. As an auteur, the filmmaker was able to access the subsidy system and exercise within it a certain amount of financial clout. At the same time, the system used the auteur as a commodity for marketing German cinema abroad.

Since the "new South African" cinema is still in embryo, we may look to the position faced by the universities in South Africa, particularly those that opposed apartheid and fought to operate outside of its laws, as an excellent example of this unstable position. Upon entering the main hall of the University of the Witwatersrand, one is confronted with a plaque declaring the university's autonomy from the dictates of the former regime. However, despite the introduction of a government that now shares the university's internal goals and mission, the issue of autonomy has not gone away. Indeed, it has resurfaced with enormous vigor and acrimony as South Africa struggles to come to terms with the deficiencies of the democratic process, a process that cannot please all of the people all of the time. As Peter Dirk Uys, South Africa's most pungent satirist, ironically puts it, "We fought for freedom, all we got was democracy." Such debates, however painful and disappointing to some, are of course a recipe for—and a sign of—a healthy public sphere. Therefore we may conclude that the first way in which South African filmmakers will remain progressive, innovative, and independent within institutional and market controls is to avoid giving in to either the dictates of a political correctness or the hegemony of the market.

PRIVATE LESSONS: THE INDUSTRY GETS ON BOARD

As an alternative to the run-of-the-mill training on offer, in 1998 the South African Screenwriters Association, with funds provided by African Media Entertainment (a large media consortium), Electronic Media Network Limited (M-Net) and the British Council, formed Scrawl, a writing laboratory. Inspired by the British Performing Arts Lab (PAL) and the Sundance Institute in the United States, the laboratory recruits aspirant screenwriters and brings them together with actors and directors, with the aim of producing ten full-length scripts a year. The emphasis for lab director Liza Key (cited in Haupt 1998) is on professionalism as opposed to what she calls the "missionary kind of funded courses" available in the townships in the 1980s. With good scripts in hand, it is hoped that the low investor confidence in South African film will be strengthened. So far, two such laboratories have been conducted, but no scripts have yet made it to the production phase.

In a more ambitious gesture, in 1993 M-Net, South Africa's first private subscription television service, began its New Directions initiative to help new filmmakers develop and produce their films.[6] Initially the project ran an annual competition for emerging directors and screenwriters from South Africa, selecting six proposals from the submissions, which where then produced and later screened on M-Net. Currently, in line with the idea that South Africa is now part of Africa in general and must participate in, and indeed provide the impetus for, an African "renaissance," the competition has gone continental to include scriptwriters, directors, and producers from six other African countries.[7] Since its launch, the initiative has produced twenty short films in South Africa, Kenya, and Nigeria and two full-length South African features, *Chicken Biznis: The Whole Story* (1998) and *The Sexy Girls* (1997).[8]

Also reflecting its commitment to the idea of an African Renaissance or as "South Africa's contribution to making itself aware of the

continent," was New Directions' choice of the Goreé Institute on Senegal's Goreé Island as the setting for a three-week training workshop
(Masemole-Jones 2000, 19). Twenty-one chosen participants from the
designated African countries traveled to the evocative setting—one of
the embarkation points for the American slave trade—to attend training sessions in acting, writing, producing, and directing led by Gaston Kaboré. The actors came from Senegal and spoke only Wolof and
French, while the filmmakers spoke only English and African languages
other than Wolof. Three films of the nine produced in Senegal were
selected for final production on 35 mm with a budget of R900,000
(U.S.$150,000). The date of release was October 2000, when they
were shown on M-Net to forty-four countries across Africa. Interestingly enough, there is to be no theatrical release for the films, since they
are not, according to New Directions, intended to make a box office
profit. It remains to be seen whether such altruistic interventions on
the part of industry can produce films that eventually might become
self-sustaining by meeting audience expectations.

FILM CULTURE: WINNING AUDIENCES

> Going to see South African cinema is at the moment a patriotic duty
> rather than what it should be—entertainment, fun, exciting.
>
> Bata Passchier, film teacher

One of the major problems facing the film industry in South Africa is
attracting local audiences. Is it that South Africans just don't go to local
films, having "grown up on American taste," as Anant Singh, South
Africa's only major international film producer, asserts,[9] or are the films
just not reaching the right audiences due to distribution and exhibition
constraints? There are many issues involved in trying to formulate an
adequate response to the public's rejection of local films. In the first
place, Singh is right in that South Africans have grown up on a diet
of American movies and imbibed along with that the idea that movies
are international commodities as opposed to national cultural products
like dance, theater, or even literature. Against this perception, the use
of patriotism or national feeling as a marketing strategy seems woefully
inadequate, especially in this post-struggle era, when going to a local
movie no longer means one is participating, however superficially, in
some antiapartheid act of aesthetic protest.

Interestingly enough, the perception of movies as global products
does not seem to hold when it comes to the medium of television, the
archsymbol of global acculturation. Very much in line with world trends

(Japan and Mexico are just two examples), television programming seems to have got the mix of local and global right. In what one might call "the soap wars" between local soaps and the established products imported from the United States, local soaps have proven popular, in some cases outperforming the imported ones in audience ratings. This represents a change from the early 1980s, when U.S. soaps broadcast on both the state-owned South African Broadcasting Corporation (SABC) and the private broadcaster, M-Net, cornered the South African market. But the changes in the 1990s challenged the commissioning editors to think local in their use of the genre, and the results have paid off. For example, in its six years on television, *Generations*, a soap opera set in an advertising agency and aimed specifically at the new and aspirant black middle class for whom interracial relationships have become the norm rather than the exception, has had audience ratings of 13.8 percent in comparison with America's *The Bold and the Beautiful*'s 12.8 percent.

While 80 percent of the audience for *Generations* is black, *Isidingo—The Need*, a local soap launched in 1999 dealing with the lives of characters living on Horizon Deep, a fictitious gold-mining community just south of Johannesburg, has managed to attract audiences across the color, gender, and age spectrum. Currently it has the largest audience share in its time slot, with ratings having increased from an initial 2.5 percent to 7.4 percent.[10] Very much in the gritty tradition of English soaps like *EastEnders* rather than the more glossy escapism of *Generations*, which models its aesthetics on *Dallas* and *The Bold and the Beautiful*, *Isidingo* is more issue-orientated, linking its story lines to the fluctuating fortunes of the South African economy, symbolized by the challenges facing the gold industry. And the market is far from saturated, according to the planners, who intend to launch five more local soaps targeted at specific audiences, such as Afrikaans and Nguni speakers.

Local soaps have succeeded not only on the home market but also internationally. *Generations* has been sold to Jamaica and there is interest in *Isidingo* from other countries in the Caribbean. *Egoli—Place of Gold*, the longest-running soap in South African history, is an M-Net product that has been firmly established across Africa since 1999, with the introduction of M-Net Open Time, a free unencoded one-hour prime-time window for nonsubscribers to the broadcaster's terrestrial operations in Ghana, Uganda, Kenya, Zambia, and Malawi.

While South African television programming seems to have found ways of satisfying its enormously diverse viewership both locally and across the continent, film production in the country is still struggling to find its place in the economics of culture as a viable commodity on the local circuit.

Regarding the distribution explanation, while it is true that many of the latest local films, such as *Kini and Adams* (1997), *Fools* (1997), and *The Sexy Girls* (1997), as well those in the planning stages,[11] use predominantly black casts, provide spectatorial identification through black role models, and tell stories that have historical and contemporary appeal to the black urban audience, yet they are still shown in predominantly "white" areas due to the lack of exhibition venues in the black townships, a spatial heritage of the apartheid past.[12] As a result, certain films simply do not reach the audiences for which they are intended and thus fail at the box office.

That is the argument put forward by Richard Green, the producer of *Chicken Biznis: The Whole Story* (1998), to explain the failure at the local box office of M-Net's second feature-length film made as part of its New Directions series. An extended version of the short comedy *Chicken Biznis,* which won a prize at the Festival Panafricain du Cinéma de Ouagadougou (FESPACO) in 1996, it follows the fortunes of Sipho, a small-time entrepreneur who has resigned his job as a messenger at the Johannesburg Stock Exchange to start a business selling chickens. With an all-black cast and using the liveliness of township slang and Sowetan street life, the film builds up its comedic depiction of this slick, small-time operator trying to make it "big" in the new South Africa, where the streets are lined not with gold but with foreigners and locals selling their wares as part of what in government-speak is called the "informal sector." The film eschews didacticism and polemics by refusing to treat South African life as a spectacular political event ("I hate this affirmative action bullshit," the director commented when questioned on his political position) and instead concentrates on the ordinary and the everyday. It speaks outside of apartheid or postapartheid modes of apprehension with sentiment and humor and a strong reliance on well-established generic conventions to present a humorous slice of township life. Yet despite all of this, and despite the reception of the film on the overseas markets (it won the best Anglophone film award at the 1998 M-Net All Africa Awards, the best first-time director award for Ntshaveni wa Luruli at the Milan Film Festival, and the Grand Prix at the Vue d'Afrique film festival in Montreal), the film was seen by only eight hundred people in South Africa.

Things are changing in terms of exhibition practices and distribution venues. The big South African distributors, United International Pictures, Nu-Metro, and Ster-Kinekor, have all expressed a willingness to distribute local films provided the producers agree to share some of the risk with them: as Jonathan Fox, the CEO of Ster-Kinekor, explained in a documentary called "The South African Film Industry" aired on SABC in 2000, "We are unwilling to commit financial suicide." According to the company's statistics, of all South African movies shown by Ster-Kinekor each year, only about 1 percent are financially viable. In addition, productions are expected to cover their own print costs of about R300,000 per print and come up with an advertising budget as well, a tall order for almost all local films. With shares of the profit going to the producer, the distributor, and the advertisers, a film must take four times its budget on the circuit before breaking even (Hooper-Box 1999). Therefore, although Ster-Century, the exhibition arm of Ster-Kinekor, announced its intention to open twelve new multiplexes in South Africa, some in black high-density areas such as Soweto, it is uncertain whether these will be used to exhibit the local product in any significant way.

This adherence to the bottom line by the distribution corporations has prompted calls for other approaches to solve the problem, such as Shaun Moodley's idea that the municipalities take control of certain cinemas and show local productions for a nominal entrance fee so that "anyone can walk in off the street and see a movie."[13] But will they do so? No matter how relevant the film's content, how diverse its form or appeal, or how it fulfills audiences' expectations through specific spectatorial positioning techniques, we cannot yet say, to use a popular South African phrase, that "local (cinema) is *lekker* (nice)." And it does not follow that increasing film production will necessarily alter local audiences' perceptions and expectations.

There is a further point to consider related to distribution, and since it is "abstract," neither a "factor" nor a "condition," it drops out of any analysis put forward by state and industry planners. Going to the cinema is not just a question of what's showing. It surely involves the much deeper question of subjectivity, of emergent forms of being, of the ways in which people see themselves participating in that ultimate enigma of modernity, the city, and city life. There is a vast literature linking the history of modernity to the history of the cinema. The cinema has been marked as a significant mode of modernity, the idea being that modernity was, in fact, cinematic even before the invention of the cinema, rendering cinema an effect of the times rather than an innovation. But, particularly in the case of South African cities, it is wrong to assume that everyone in the city has the chance to participate in modern modes of life. The conferral of citizenship on all South Africans does not translate into an urban enfranchisement, an ability to mingle and move, to engage in consumption and spectatorial experience, to try on new identities and new selves.

The gradual collapse of apartheid saw an immense urbanward shift, with profound consequences for the aspirations and abilities of residents to move into and around the city. Currently there exists a greater polarization between classes and colors among the residents of South African cities than could possibly be imagined in European and American cities, with people living in luxury urban enclaves surrounded by razor wire, abandoned factories, backyard shacks, and "single" family homes that now contain up to one hundred renters. What all this means is that merely occupying space in the city does not automatically give one a sense of place and community or set one on the road to greater cultural mobility. It can have the opposite effect, decreasing circulation and fixing people, especially the poor, the homeless, and the immigrant, into profound states of cultural immobility. The assumption, therefore, that brick-and-mortar plans for building cinemas in poorer areas or access to state funding subsidies to increase the number of local films on the circuit will remedy the problem and attract South Africans to the cinema results from a superficial analysis, not only of the role of cinema in creating new forms of identity but also of the spatial dimension of cinema: the fact that it not only shows the city on its screens but is implanted in the city itself as a spatial form, and cannot be separated out from broader patterns of urban circulation and development.

SOUTH AFRICA'S WINDOW ON AFRICA: FESTIVALS AND MARKETS

One way of breathing life into what is currently a fragmented and mostly profitless industry in search of both a cultural identity and a market niche is to look beyond local markets to regional and global ones. It is still the case, as it was in the time of the *De Voortrekkers* (1916), that local films cannot realize a profit at home and therefore must seek new sites for sales and marketing. The annual Sithengi market held in Cape Town has positioned itself as one of those sites, a new film trade route via the Cape. Begun in 1995 as a more regional initiative for Southern African film and television products, with considerable support from the government, the larger players in the film industry, and the Rockefeller Foundation, the market has developed into a successful trade fair cum film festival (with a touch of academic polemic on the side) for the continent, attracting not only African representation—

Ghana, Nigeria, and the Francophone contingent—but also delegates from France, Greece, Sweden, Italy, Britain, and the United States. The real significance of the market is that it represents important new nodes of redefinition for South African cinema.

First and foremost, it is an acknowledgment of South Africa's connection to the African continent in terms of shared histories of culture, struggle, expropriation, misrepresentation, and resurrection, the kind of connection proposed by the idea of the African Renaissance. It is a recognition that cinema in Africa and South Africa shares common challenges and problems—the cultural dominance of mainstream narrative codes, the lack of an audience, the mentality of the distributors resulting in the lack of exhibition venues, the lack of local funding and the concomitant reliance on foreign (Western) funding, a pervasive sense of cultural inferiority (especially in the arena of filmmaking), and a widely held concept of films as global commodities—and should seek common solutions, ones that do not always end up in trying to produce "Africa" on film solely as a saleable commodity to the West. In many cases, this desire to be successful in international markets is not just a matter of profits but a need driven by deeper perceptions of cultural and national identity and of belonging. As Marsha Kinder (1993, 6) argues in her work on Spanish cinema, "every national film movement seeks to win legitimation as the valid representative of its culture by striving for international recognition—the way revolutionary governments seek to be recognized by other nations." In its previous incarnation, official South Africa thought of itself as a Western outpost at the bottom of Africa, an accident of geography that should not be reflected in its cultural forms. It therefore sought validation from the countries that mattered, from the "world" that mattered—the Western world—with which it continued to maintain, despite economic sanctions and moral rejection, an imaginary bond.

Such misreadings, false perceptions, and inchoate displacements resist alteration, even when confronted with the material evidence of change, but change does come, especially when economics are involved. Thus the second recognition that has emerged, along with South African cinema's embrace of its African past, present, and future, is the industry's acknowledgment of an African media industrial market, an "African global," if you like, that operates not as an appendage to the "real" one in Los Angeles, New York, and London, not as equal to it, and certainly not in opposition to it, but as a viable commercial network of television and radio broadcasters, satellite broadcasters, video distributors, mobile video networks, and production houses, all of which can be used to produce, exhibit, and distribute films in partnership across Africa for both profit and prestige.

The marketing strategy for the *African Renaissance* series, which I have already mentioned, is an example of this new view of Africa as marketplace. Produced by a South African private production company, Ubuntu TV and Film Productions, in partnership with ICE Media, a Zimbabwe-based company specializing in the distribution of African audiovisual materials, and largely funded through donor aid, local corporate sponsorship, and coproduction financing from countries as diverse as Malawi, Algeria, Morocco, Angola, Namibia, and Cameroon, a pilot of the series was screened at the 2000 MIPTV Cannes festival. Significantly, the audience members, largely consisting of African television and radio broadcasters as well as noncommercial video distributors (nongovernmental organizations and video resource centers) were invited in order to secure their commitment to launch and promote the series. The Africa2Africa channel, one of the SABC's digital satellite channels, was also part of the proposed distribution network for screening the series, which would then reach an estimated one million digital satellite television subscribers across the continent.

From this situation emerges the third recognition, that South African cinema, or, to be more precise, the South African cinematic institution, is part of a larger media and entertainment industry, and cannot be bracketed off from those networks or seen as oppositional to them even if it claims to be national, alternative, diasporic, "Third Cinema," or, as Clyde Taylor (1985) puts it, "the last cinema." This recognition has been slow in coming to intellectuals, journalists, policymakers, and avant-gardists, especially those who have been involved in marginalized cinemas seeking to demarginalize themselves. Here the pervasive mentality has been one of casting cinema in national terms and contrasting it to television (the trope for all the other new media technologies), which is seen in the terms of the international, global information revolution (Rosen 1996).

Whereas this formulation has had a certain utility for scholarly discussions of identity and subjectivity, as well as for charting the specificities of the cinematic experience and legitimizing national cultural policy, it does not withstand careful scrutiny—not now and not in historical terms. As Philip Rosen (1996, 382) convincingly argues, the history of cinema has always been an international one in terms of distribution, finance, exhibition, and technology. Globalization can be seen as "simply another threshold in an internationalizing tendency present since the beginning of cinema." No radical rupture has occurred that would allow one to talk in terms of two opposing histories: the history of cinema and the history of the media. Instead, the history of cinema is part of media history, "just one historical stage," in Rosen's words, "in a world-wide proliferation of technological media."[14]

One can certainly understand the anxiety on the part of peripheral nations that accompanies this redefinition of cinema, for talk of globalization carries with it the specter of cultural imperialism, the domination of international capital through multimedia conglomerates, the decimation of a unique collective identity under the sign of the nation— in short, all the hallmarks of Western colonialism. But, as I have tried to show with the idea of an African global, the internationalizing character of cinema does not automatically spell the demise of local/national production. In fact, it can mean just the opposite. It all depends on how nations define themselves geopolitically, culturally, and economically, on how they define their markets and manipulate global technologies to reach them. At the Sithengi market, for example, the SABC concentrated its sales efforts on the Anglophone African market, according to *Africa Film and TV Magazine* (vol 24: 12), meeting with official and private broadcasters from those countries. The SABC reported sales of over 450 hours of programming in all genres, mainly sitcoms and soaps.

These facts of bookkeeping spell out in black and white the institutional convergences between cinema and media, convergences that point to a unity and not an opposition between the two. One can no longer talk of cinema versus television or national versus internationalization. This does not diminish the thorny issues surrounding the question of how cinematic institutions, particularly peripheral ones, can participate in global markets and still articulate national concerns. Nor does it resolve the shaky status of the nation as the synthetic framework for cultural unity (the focus of my second viewsite). But it does, as Rosen emphasizes, change the ground for future debates concerning the contemporary status of national cinemas.

Site 2: Putting South Africa on Film

How, then, shall we begin to talk about cinema in national terms—that is, the way in which the concept contains the potential for encapsulating or carrying the aspirations of the emerging nation? I can think of only two forms that have managed to date to incorporate diversity in a way that reflects a South African national consciousness. One is the foundational document of state and civil society, the Constitution of 1996. The other is the Truth and Reconciliation Commission, a body created to examine gross violations of human rights from 1960 to 1994. Both are about diversity. The Constitution gives recognition to a South Africanness based on diversity by proclaiming that education and other features of South African life must take place in the country's eleven official languages, and by acknowledging certain aspects of "traditional law" (such as polygyny), as long as they are not in conflict with constitutional law. The Truth Commission is about a diversity of victims and perpetrators whose testimonies cannot but force the construction of a new national history.[15] Both are foundational events for the nation. However, they are not cultural forms. Nor are they foundational texts, like the Bible, in terms of which a "people" may think of itself as a people.

Given cinema's lack of foundational status in the emergence of the nation, there is nothing whatever to assure that cinematic engagements with diversity can rise above the particular position they take and be of importance for "everybody" in the imagined community. To speak in the name of the nation is an act of hubris, a repression of difference, a violence to the diversity in whose name one speaks. Were there only one type of national film, its claim would be hugely undermined, given that its position would be particular and its audience limited. This is why an active, flourishing film industry is necessary, so that a number of different films, reaching differing groups, all in the name of nationalism, can emerge.

The question, then, of what it means to think of a cinema in the wake of the new emerging nation becomes one of the kinds of national aspirations that film is capable of representing—that is to say, the national character of such aspirations can only be evaluated in context. Since there is no such thing as a "national audience," particular kinds of films will (if they are lucky, considering the problems of attracting any audience at all) only reach particular groups, even if one resists retaining the racist stereotypes that decree that these groups remain divided into the old divisions of "colored," "white," and the like. Yet these facts do not diminish the crucial role of cinema in envisioning the new nation through a progressive/continuous state of vision and critique, even if the populations that constitute the great "rainbow" of the South African nation are so heterogeneous that the thought of cinema speaking "to and for the nation" is a modernist fantasy. As in the case of community media, different members of the nation may end up being "national" by imagining the shape of the nation in different ways. What is important to any notion of a national cinema is the retention and maintenance of these different imaginings. Whose imaginings have hegemony and whose are suppressed? And, granted that hegemony, what is the role of nationalism in dealing with all the other imaginings?[16]

These ideas are familiar from the work of Benedict Anderson, Partha Chatterjee, Homi Bhabha, and other social theorists on the character of what it is to imagine a nation and its structures. On the one hand, internal to the thought of national consciousness is the idea that one can produce unifying symbols. Yet, on the other hand, with the reconstitution of civil structures, respect for diversity in the texture of South African life makes such strivings problematic, reminiscent of the former regime whose policy the world deemed a "crime against humanity." The very circumstances of the times thus render the gesture of unification suspect, while at the same time making it of vital importance.

THE END OF COLLECTIVITY?

Do these tensions then ruin the possibilities for a collective identity to emerge from South African filmmakers in the future? In his discussion on new Caribbean cinema, Stuart Hall argues that divisions are, in fact, the material for constructing diasporic postcolonial identities. They underline not a shared history so much as one's relationship to a history. Using the idea of a diaspora, not in its usual sense of meaning peoples scattered from an original homeland but in the sense of a recognition of history, Hall (1994, 392–403) talks of an identity constructed through and within difference. To describe the play of difference within identity as a result of these factors, he draws on Derrida's wordplay between *difference* and *différance* (differ and defer). As a result of the one shading into the other, identity elicits new meanings while still maintaining the traces of its other ones. So instead of the two opposing grammars sketched by Bhaba in his double time of the nation, we are back at the idea of a dialectic of difference and similarity as opposed to an opposition out of which may (or may not) emerge a synthesis.

When read in this way, talk of hybridity and temporality (Bhaba's diachronic) does not spell the end of a collective consciousness but demonstrates how filmmakers at the margins could continue to negotiate a collective identity without imposition, repression, or appropriation. Collective identity can be staged in a way that openly acknowledges both the fault lines and the slippages implicit in the process, and the complete necessity of these characteristics as conditions of possibility. We are not talking here of truth or fiction, falsity or genuineness, but of an explicit process, a search (in the case of cinema) for a set of styles that can be put to use in imagining, but not obscuring, the nation. Hall (1994, 402) calls this search the "vocation of modern black cinemas."

Let us take the case of drawing and painting in South Africa as an illustrative model of what Hall is saying, since it has a much richer history than South African film. In the heady days of liberation immediately following the formal collapse of apartheid, the art world reflected a kind of utopian excitement. Inspired by vast quantities of liberated desire—the desire for a better society, for a new set of social relations, for fun and play, for experimentation, artists trained in quite different traditions and schools, and coming from the most diverse of social, economic, and racial groupings, began an intense exploration of the art of the "other." Finally the postmodern dreams of pluralist toleration and the panavailability of diverse cultural styles had become a possibility. African painters became fascinated with abstract expressionist painting while white abstract expressionists began to "Africanize" their works by injecting into them the rhythms and resonances of Venda woodcarving techniques, Ndebele beadwork patterns, and township "garbage" art. In this state of what could be called cross-pollination, it is not far-fetched to think that what was being expressed in these works were the utopian aspirations and dreams of a new nation in which the principle of diversity would be respected—celebrated, even. In this regard, visual art reflected the progressive imagination of a nation of difference, unified nonetheless through patterns of shared mutual interest and socioeconomic and political goals.

Site 3: African Cinema: From Didacticism to Pragmatism

> European critics label African cinema as if it was from one country. It's a continent of 54 countries with loads of different dialects. They'd never do the same thing in Europe. After all, Danish cinema has nothing to do with British cinema.
>
> Ramadan Suleman, South African film director

> As someone once said, responding to the fashionable idea of négritude, a tiger doesn't walk around thinking about its "tigritude." It's just a tiger.
>
> Gaston Kaboré

Since South Africa's acknowledgment of its connection to the rest of the continent has brought about significant changes in its film industry practices and view of cinema in general, I cannot end this chapter without a brief discussion of the changes that are taking place in African film production. The first wave of African cinema, which can be dated to the 1960s and 1970s, was first and foremost a political idea.[17] It emerged out of the early days of African independence as part and parcel of the thought that Africans could carve out for themselves not only independent states but also alternative spaces for making films outside of the Hollywood product. The reality they sought to depict was conceived not just in oppositional terms—that is, based on a desire to counter the stereotypical images of Africa and Africans found in mainstream cinema with more positive visions of African life in all its complexity—but as a way of realizing the national aspirations of the state (which was seen as the institutionalization of liberation) by showing the people the state of affairs: a social cinema, a cinema of liberation and purpose dedicated to educating, or rather reeducating, a new generation growing up in a new age. This definition of African cinema as an extension of the continent's independence and liberation from colonialism gave rise to a view of the filmmaker as teacher and revolutionary rolled into one and the film viewer as student, a position best summed up in Ousmane Sembène's famous description of African cinema as "night school."

But, as the quotations beginning this section illustrate, profound changes are taking place in the way filmmakers in Africa define themselves, their audiences, the films, and their position in a global entertainment industry. I use the term "filmmakers in Africa" rather than the more commonly accepted "African filmmakers" to signal this new attitude. Many of the leading filmmakers in Africa are rejecting the concept of an "African cinema" and concomitantly the label of "African film director." Even those who have made their name under that label argue that films made in Africa should not be placed in a box marked "African films" and separated from the rest of the world's films. To reject the label of "African filmmaker" is to reject being co-opted under the name of a state nationalism and being seen as important only in terms of one's contribution to the nation or the continent at large. As Gaston Kaboré (cited in Matshikiza 1999) sharply comments, "Just because you come from the African continent, why should you be expected to make films that represent the whole continent? Your film represents your own corner of life."

This does not mean that films made in Africa do not draw heavily on their African context or on a particular set of cultural modulations that inflect certain formal elements in the film—the sense of space and time, rhythm, language, and gesture. But these particulars, even if they are recognized as African, in the way that Japanese film is recognized as Japanese, should not be taken as representative of either a national or a continental consciousness. Africa, as Ramadan Suleman has caustically noted, is not one nation occupying a huge landmass, but an immense diversity of nations and cultures. To view Africa and Africans as a unity is a continuation of the colonial mindset. According to Kaboré, the fact that he makes films that mirror his African context does not make him an African filmmaker but reflects his own individuality and personal history. He calls African cinema an emotional rather than an ideological concept—emotional in the sense that it reflects, as do all art forms, the feelings of the filmmaker. Even Souleymane Cissé, who tends to be less resistant to the idea of an African cinema, talks of it as a pragmatic, by which he means a marketing position, a form of leverage that can be used to force the industry to show African films.

All of these "digressive trends," as Frank Ukadike (1994) glosses them, point to a redefinition of the film industry in Africa. The second wave of film directors in Africa are less concerned with the didactics and polemics surrounding filmmaking than with the practicalities of the industry and their own individual, as opposed to national, role in it (at FESPACO, students were rioting not about neocolonialism and cultural imperialism but about their grants). There is an emphasis on reaching a wider audience, both within the continent and abroad, and on finding solutions to the problems of distribution, inconsistent state funding, state censorship, and the fact that African cinema is an industry separated from its consumers. Contemporary directors want to reach a larger audience. If that means making films in English, appropriating the narrative codes of mainstream cinema (as Elsaesser 1989 notes, an audience-orientated film relies on mainstream genres and uses the same identification strategies as classical Hollywood cinema), or moving away from anticolonial movies to more layered and diverse subjects such as contemporary life in urban Africa (Idrissa Ouedraogo's *Kini and Adams* [1997]), women's inequality (Tsitsi Dangarembga's *Everyone's Child*), and the immigrant experience in Europe (Jean Marie Teno's *Clando* and Jean-Pierre Bokolo's *Aristotle's Plot*), then so be it.

Perceptions of the potential audience in Africa have also changed. They are no longer treated as potential revolutionaries who need to be educated and culturally transformed but rather as consumers, as participants in a worldwide entertainment and leisure industry. Ferid Boughedir notes that this businesslike attitude is more prevalent in Anglophone African countries than in the Francophone ones, for while French colonialism sought to legitimate its activities through cultural agencies and methods, the British approach was solely validated in economic terms, brute business being the order of the day. It seems that this is the dominant approach today. In terms of decolonization, the latter prevails since it translates more easily into commercialization than does the more didactic, culturally saturated former approach. It is not clear that Boughedir is right, although his point is an interesting one. At Fespaco, for example, Francophone filmmakers were talking of making films in English that they could then reroute through South Africa, the Hong Kong of Africa, so as to reach the larger global audience—a fact that tends to contradict his claim.

It would not be fair to end the chapter without acknowledging the continuing commitment of filmmakers in Africa to the continent. The move away from didacticism to entertainment should not be taken as an abandonment or a selling out to the West. Rather it should be seen as a way of broadening film production in Africa, a way of claiming for the filmmakers of Africa an autonomy outside of state regulations and structures and the hegemony of nationalism. By seeing themselves as part of world cinema as opposed to a world apart, filmmakers in Africa can forge their own affiliations with other progressive cinemas irrespective of geography or nation or race. As Kaboré (cited in Matshikiza, 1999) puts it, "The independent filmmakers of Britain are fighting like us to communicate how they see the world. We are happy if there is one guy named Ken Loach—his battle is the same as ours."

Notes

1. The IBA was created by the Independent Broadcasting Authority Act of 1993. The act enabled the IBA to take over those broadcasting tasks previously performed by the minister of home affairs and the postmaster general. It is a nonprofit organization funded by the government. Other funds come from various fees paid to the authority. All broadcasters, both private and national, are required to provide a full range of local television programming throughout the schedule and in prime time. Higher local-content quotas are required for the national broadcaster and community stations than for the private competitors. The national broadcaster had three years from the date of the regulation to achieve the following proportions of local material: drama—20 percent, current affairs—80 percent, documentary and informal knowledge—50 percent, educational—60 percent, and children's—50 percent. In total, 50 percent of the national broadcaster's programming must consist of local content. Compliance with local content quotas will be measured weekly. Private terrestrial free-to-air stations must achieve a local TV content quota of 30 percent. While no local content quotas are imposed on subscription broadcasters like M-Net, the act states that they are "expected to make a contribution to national development" (Independent Broadcasting Authority Act 1993, 16).

2. At the NFVF inauguration, the chairperson said he hoped the European Union would contribute R200 million, the equivalent of U.S.$33 million, to the new foundation in the form of coproduction financing.

3. Soyinka delivered these remarks in his 1999 lecture, "Arms and the Arts— A Continent's Unequal Dialogue." The lecture was part of the T. B. Davie Memorial Lecture series established in the late 1950s by University of Cape Town students and commemorates the former vice-chancellor's crusade for freedom of speech and human rights.

4. www.africafilmtv.com/renaissance/Press 9620Releases.htm.

5. The attempt to legislate a national cinema and film industry into being is not peculiar to South Africa—it has a long history in postcolonial African states. Manthia Diawara's survey (1992, chap. 4) of the labyrinthine history of the Federation Panafricaine des Cinéastes (FEPACI) clearly shows it is easier to put film on paper than to put products on the screens in front of audiences.

6. M-Net was launched in 1986. It is Africa's premier pay-TV service with almost 1.2 million subscribers in thirty-seven countries across the continent. In South Africa it operates a daily two-hour open window from 5:00–7:00 P.M. for unencoded programs, such as the country's longest-running local soap opera, *Egoli—Place of Gold*. New Directions is managed by Letebele Masemole-Jones and produced by Richard Green.

7. These are Nigeria, Kenya, Ghana, Ethiopia, Tanzania, and Zimbabwe.

8. *The Sexy Girls* was released in South Africa by Ster-Kinekor and grossed U.S.$17,507. I could not obtain box office figures for *Chicken Biznis*.

9. Anant Singh, quoted in "The South African Film Industry," a documentary broadcast on the SABC2 television channel on 15 June 2000.

10. SABC audience ratings, www.isidingo.co.za.

11. Examples here would be Ramadan Suleman's project *Zulu Love Letter*, which explores the rift between a mother and her daughter through the language of Zulu beadwork, Teddy Mattera's *Max in the Crying Business*, a contemporary satire about a professional mourner, and Khubu Meth's project entitled *What's Going On?*—a complicated thriller about a young black journalist's discovery that her husband, a prominent antiapartheid activist and double agent, is the murderer of her former lover.

12. "The South African Film Industry."

13. Ibid.

14. Rosen (1996) offers an insightful and brilliant discussion of the viability and utility of the trope cinema versus television and the kind of schema that it generates in terms of identities, the subject, culture, and the audience. Rosen argues that these oppositions, though widespread among film scholars and cultural theorists, do not hold. The concept itself has utility in film history as a way of stimulating and organizing research and pointing to the possibility of using cinema as a sphere of resistance to certain global practices.

15. Victims of apartheid and of antiapartheid cadres were given a hearing at

the Truth and Reconciliation Commission, revealing an extraordinarily complex picture of the ways, means, and extent of violence under the apartheid regime.

16. For example, Partha Chatterjee's research (1993) shows that the diaries of Bengali women in the 1890s reveal quite different imaginings of the nation from the ones that have taken root.

17. This brief sketch can hardly do justice to the subject. I have included it as a background to the current situation, a situation in which South Africa is, for the first time, taking part. Anyone seeking a deep and full analysis and overview of the last thirty years of African cinema should consult Ukadike 1994; Diawara 1992; and Martin 1995.

PART 4

Into the
New South Africa

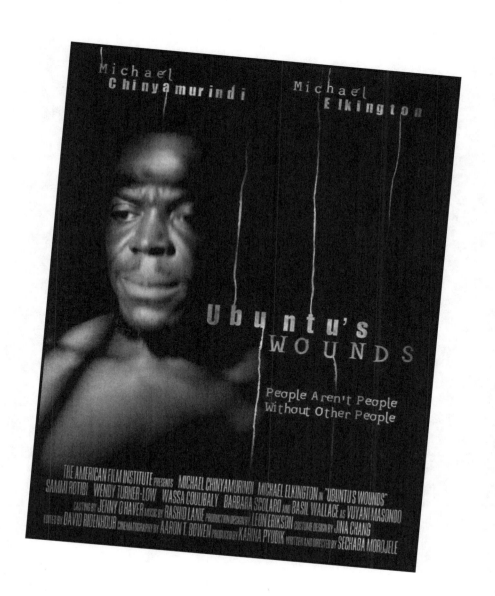

On the preceding page:
"UBUNTU'S WOUNDS." Sechaba Morojele's award-winning Short thesis film from the American Film Institute. Title designed by Suppasak Viboonlarp.

8

Jump the Gun
Departing from a Racist/Feminist Nexus in Postapartheid Cinema

Laura Twiggs

There has been little academic writing on Les Blair's *Jump the Gun* (1996), and that is a shame. It is a shame because the film radically departs from old models of representation, particularly with regard to gender, and has the potential to enliven theoretical debates and further understanding not only of gender representation but of representation per se. In the very core and fabric of this film lurks a model that could be revolutionary for the cinematic representation of women and for understanding the nexus between the way that women are represented by men and how they choose to represent each other and themselves. It also could point the way toward a criticism that incorporates differences of class and race at the same time as gender.

This chapter examines pivotal scenes from *Jump the Gun* in the context of feminist psychoanalytic film criticism. The assumption of viewing relationships between "spectator" and "text" centered on the "male gaze" has been a cornerstone of feminist psychoanalytic criticism since the work of Laura Mulvey (1990). That film was constructed to answer the male pleasure-seeking impulse has always informed film theory. I propose that an analysis of *Jump the Gun* disturbs this assumption and suggests a way forward for filmmakers and theorists.

Jump the Gun was made in 1996. Set in Johannesburg after the 1994 elections, the film exhibits a contextual awareness far more progressive than that of any South African predecessors that have treated relationships between black and white characters. Up until that time, only films that dealt with black people in isolation could claim to have any genuine contextual awareness, but these were largely unconcerned with the dynamics of gender representation or with the forging of real bonds between black and white. What, or who, the reader/viewer is that is produced by the meanings liberated through the relationship between the viewer and *Jump the Gun* is an important consideration, located (though not exclusively) around the central female characters of Gugu and Mini, who are thus the focus of this chapter.

Jump the Gun exhibits a self-awareness of its Third World context and demonstrates a comparative perspective that will drive it toward its revolutionary conclusion. From the title sequence at the beginning to the last scene of the film, the cinematic emphasis on transport figures as a trope of the Third World. An analysis of the opening sequence demonstrates how *Jump the Gun* can be said to be progressive in a thorough and ongoing sense, particularly in the ways in which the characters of Clint and Gugu are first given contrasting representation, which has far-reaching implications for the rest of the film.

The film opens on the drilling gear at the top of a mineshaft, shortly followed by a train moving across the screen. Then we see a white man, Clint, asleep in a first-class train compartment. He wakes, confused and disoriented, and attempts to gather his bearings. We now see inner Johannesburg through the train's window. A few frames later we see two black women in a crowded, communal third-class compartment of the same train as they prepare to disembark, the younger one, Gugu, "our heroine," in profile. Gugu is distinguished by her comparatively modern clothing: she wears an orange miniskirt and a brightly patterned, skintight bodysuit. We see her disembarking alone, her only luggage a large plastic hawker's bag. She walks almost directly toward the camera before we are returned to a now wide-awake Clint, who has left the train and is walking in the same direction. Gugu climbs a flight of stairs and is assimilated into a crowd of departing passengers, still recognizable by her distinctive dress. She walks toward sunlight, and Clint walks across the station plaza with a sports bag in each hand, surveying his surroundings before looking upward. We see what he's looking at: the bright sun is reflected, creating a blind spot and an image that resembles a chart demonstrating retinitis pigmentosa, portending blindness. We then see him in the back of a taxi, being driven through the streets of Johannesburg. He looks out of the window, turns to the driver, and says: "South Africa's getting quite African lately, hey?" Black people stand on the pavement, seen through the rear window of the taxi.

We next see a crowded minibus taxi rank in a black township, with litter piled in the streets. Gugu crosses the road and holds up her hand to stop a taxi from running her down. She crosses another road and is seen next to a black street fruit vendor. There are throngs of black faces in this sequence and an absence of white ones. The piece of paper in her hand shows she is following directions and is actually not as much at home as she may seem. Next, we see Clint's yellow taxi stop outside a building where the words "Ladies' Bar" are prominently displayed.[1] Clint gets out of the taxi and enters the Troyeville Hotel. After this short sequence, the camera cuts again to Gugu, walking across another busy township road and up a driveway to Sis Buleng's Place, a shebeen.

Why this point-by-point retelling of the opening scenes? Indeed, why such detailed opening scenes at all? The existences played out comparatively in the opening sequence deliberately speak of difference on several scores. First and foremost, Clint and Gugu inhabit very different spaces, worlds that, in the apartheid era, were destined never to coincide. The physical spaces they occupy simultaneously (the train, the station) house both "worlds" together, but the worlds in *Jump the Gun* are spatiomental, not merely geographical locations. Clint, as a white male, effectively is the representative of the pinnacle of racial patriarchy as epitomized by apartheid, while Gugu, as a black woman, is the representative of the lowest rung of that now defunct system. No particular difference is specifically highlighted: gender, race, and economic class all figure concurrently. The comparison is produced by the intercutting between the two worlds and is especially evident in the frame: both the white male and the black female occupy the same structural positions in relation to their contexts and in relation to the viewer. As composites or amalgams of the furthest points of these simultaneous differences, Gugu and Clint are cinematically forced into a relationship of equality in terms of their relative power in two independent strata. Neither Clint nor Gugu acts as a prioritized reference point, and neither conveys a feeling of being at home or entirely comfortable in their environments. The piece of paper Gugu consults signifies her status as a stranger, and Clint's continual surveying of his surroundings and his words "South Africa's getting quite African lately" indicate the foreignness he experiences; even though he certainly was in Johannesburg before the dismantling of apartheid, he finds it an entirely different place now.

This fact in tandem with the "blind spot" represented in the glare on the windows serves as a powerful indicator of the film's shift from the sort of assumption upheld in earlier South African cinema. Monolithic notions of patriarchy are disassembled in the film's construction and in South Africa's social fabric. *Jump the Gun* treats Clint's flawed mode of seeing as a character trait that undermines the perpetuation of hegemonic traits. Likewise, the film destabilizes potential assumptions held by the audience and disallows a mode of reading or decoding the representations within the text in terms of a Western monolithic notion of patriarchal power relations. The fact of the changed South African context resists such an extrapolation: it is not white men who are in political power but black men and women. In the face of this given, the entire "patriarchy" monolith needs to be reformulated, with dire consequences for old models of representation.

Other factors compound the subversion of the dominant trends of cinematic representation. The first face seen is that of the white male asleep—not only do his closed eyes indicate that he does not control the phallic gaze, but his sleeping image evokes vulnerability. Added to this, his visible psychic disturbance at not knowing where he is when woken by the conductor and his less than heroic appearance, bordering on the comic, render him a site of identification fraught with problems for the white male spectator anticipating pleasure (and, by inference in the pyramid of power relations, for the white female spectator as well). As he steps out of the taxi under the sign "Ladies' Bar," his emasculation in the opening is complete, for not only has he exhibited a lack of the controlling power of the gaze in sleep and a lack of a complete perception in his view of the glare reflecting off the window, his image is now associated with the "lack" represented by the female in the script under which he is represented.

Within the comparison set up between two newcomers to Johannesburg, Gugu is far less out of place than Clint. Gugu exhibits greater agency than he does, as she is seen negotiating her way between the taxis and even making them stop as she crosses the road, thus orienting herself, whereas Clint is driven and then delivered right up to the door of the hotel. While symptomatic of Clint's position of financial privilege, this privilege is not ultimately represented as empowering, as the "Ladies' Bar" sign attests. In spite of the Third World signifiers of the minibus taxi rank, the third-class crowded compartment, the litter in the township streets, and the African street vendor, Gugu resists representation as "Third World Woman" with incumbent connotations, explained thus by Chandra Mohanty (1988, 65):

> [The "average Third-World woman"] leads an essentially truncated life based on her feminine gender (read: sexually constrained) and being "third world" (read: ignorant, poor, uneducated, tradition-bound, religious, domesticated, family-oriented, victimized, etc.). This, I suggest, is in contrast to the (implicit) self-representation of Western women as educated, modern, as having control over their own bodies and sexualities, and the "freedom" to make their own decisions. . . . These distinctions

are made on the basis of the privileging of a particular group as the norm or referent.

Although thus far in the film there is not enough evidence to refute each one of these negative connotations, the overall impression made by Gugu even before she has opened her mouth is that this description is inappropriate, largely because the first term (sexually constrained) is inapplicable to a woman exuding the sexuality that Gugu does. Gugu's style of dress and confidence speak of an independence and savvy distinctly at odds with the notion of "Third World Woman" detailed above. And yet, the film suggests her "Africanness" rather than "Westernness" in the juxtaposition of Gugu and Clint—"Africanness" in the sense meant by Clint when he remarks, "South Africa's getting quite African lately."

In the remainder of the film, Gugu's resistance to stereotypical representation becomes an almost point-by-point rejection, or subversion, of the "Third World Woman" assumption. However, this is not to say that women are in any way idolized or sanitized in the film or that there is necessarily anything lofty about "Africanness." Few if any of the characters are to be trusted at face value. Both Gugu and Mini—the white prostitute with whom Clint falls in love and through whose friendship with Gugu the parallel worlds of black and white are brought together—seem not entirely above reproach in their own self-representations. However, there are differences in the ways in which the representations of male and female characters are seen to be signifiers of "untrustworthiness," and the importance here of the female relation to what Mary Ann Doane (1990) has called "masquerade" will be essential to this discussion.

The scene in which Clint meets and falls in love with Mini provides a nexus of the two concerns of spectacle and masquerade.

[Mini, the white prostitute, has a drink in her hand.]

Mini: I must thank you from the bottom of my heart for being such a nice person, Clinton.

Clint: Can I offer you a cigarette, Gloria?

Mini: Yes, please. [She leans forward and takes one. He is about to light his first when he sees hers extended. He lights her cigarette, snaps the lighter closed.]

Clint: I prefer "Can Harm Your Baby."

Mini: [softly]: I beg your pardon? [He indicates the packet of cigarettes on the table.]

Clint: This one says, "Smoking Causes Cancer." I prefer "Can Harm Your Baby."

Mini: You say something like that, and I thought you were a nice person. I am a good mother. [He looks confused.]

Clint: Are you all right?

Mini: I thought everything was supposed to change. I thought I was going to get my baby back. [He is bewildered.] But they won't give me my baby. You know that not all Afrikaners are bad people, and when I talk about Afrikaners, I'm not talking about Terre'Blanche who gives us a bad name. It's not a thing people understand.

Clint: Some people can ride horses and others can't.[2] [Mini starts to unbutton her shirt, almost in tears.] Are you . . . are you hot?

Mini: [semidressed, her bra showing.] I'm not suitably dressed. [Male and female patrons stare at her. One woman in the bar audience turns away, then looks back again. A black male spectator in the background looks at her, and another male in the foreground turns to stare as well. Clint is caught between the stares.] I'm going into mourning for my lost child. [The proprietor, J. J., walks toward Mini.] I'll just have to wear this.

J. J.: Christ, Mini, I've told you before . . . if you wanna change, do it in the toilet.

Clint: I thought your name was Gloria. [Mini is drunkenly trying to put on a white shirt.]

J. J.: Do you want me to call a taxi? [Face offscreen.]

Mini: I don't want to go anywhere. [J. J. bends down, holds her arm tightly, and looks her in the eye.]

J. J.: Just—and I'm going to say this very quietly, okay?—take your things, and FUCK OFF! [Loudly.] My customers have got better things to look at than your tits!

Mini: Oh, go suck your mother's balls!

J. J.: That's it! You're out of here! [Cut to Clint, watching as J. J., offscreen, pulls her to her feet and manhandles her through the people in the bar, her bag in his hand. Clint turns to look as they exit the frame behind him.]

The comic drunken posing that sets the scene is prefigured by what has been established about the character of Clint; Mini is as yet an unknown entity. Clint's self-conscious gentlemanliness, his bumbling display of manners and etiquette (lighting the cigarette, his formal posture and tone, and his desperate and flawed attempts at clever repartee—"Some people can ride horses and others can't") are all an assumed mask of "breeding" or class, which he evidently feels he lacks. In assuming the signifiers of "the upper classes," Clint attempts to add to this meeting a dignity he does not have, which exaggerates his comic function. This is not to say that his function is that of the "clown," a stereotype demanding a specific response from the viewer. As the catalyst for viewer response, Clint is more complex than that, being at the same time a part of the spectacle provided by Mini when she strips off her shirt, the onlooker to the spectacle that is Mini in her seminakedness, and the unwitting instigator of her spectacular actions.

The characters of Mini and Clint here provide the bar audience with a pair of spectacles through which to view a complex dynamic of the same forces at work in cinematic identification/objectification. The spectator is encouraged into a series of responses predicated on this mirrorlike structure between the bar audience and itself as part of an intricate viewing dialectic of desire. Because Mini strips of her own volition and for her own inexplicable reasons, the notion of the female as spectacle cannot here be viewed as the simple one of a vehicle for male pleasure, for her own desires are an integral part of her actions. It has been argued that

> the split between spectacle and narrative supports the man's role as the active one of forwarding the story, making things happen. The man controls the film fantasy and also emerges as the representative of power in a further sense: as the bearer of the look of the spectator, transferring it behind the screen to neutralise the extra-diegetic tendencies represented by woman as spectacle. . . . As the spectator identifies with the main male protagonist, he projects his look onto that of his like, his screen surrogate, so that the power of the male protagonist as he controls events coincides with the active power of the erotic look, both giving a satisfying sense of omnipotence.
>
> (JOHNSTON 1972, 34)

However, in this instance it is the spectacle provided by the woman that moves the narrative forward. Furthermore, the point of the greatest distance, the most "removed" and voyeuristic gaze of the onlookers, that

169

of the "ultimate" voyeur, is seen to belong to the female in the bar audience, made most explicit in the shot that foregrounds the male patron staring at Mini from the female bar-audience member's perspective. The configuration of "looks" represented on the screen is complicated by the presence of the black male onlooker in the background, who structurally engages in a more direct relationship with the cinema audience through being situated directly opposite their line of vision. In the hierarchy of looking relations, therefore, the white male patron and the black male patron compete for control over the image offered by Mini as spectacle directly at the middle point between them. Most importantly, both of their looks are mediated by a female onlooker (explicitly at the point mentioned above, to which attention is drawn in the film by the fact that she looks away and then back again, which highlights the fact of her looking).

If J. J., the proprietor, who intervenes and removes the threatening presence of the female as spectacle, is seen as the vehicle of the controlling male gaze through which the "sense of omnipotence" is created in the viewer, this is not unproblematic either, in relation to the role of the female figure.

> [I]n psychoanalytic terms, the female figure poses a deeper problem. She also connotes something that the look continually circles around but disavows: her lack of a penis, implying a threat of castration and hence displeasure. Ultimately, the meaning of woman is sexual difference, the absence of the penis as visually ascertainable, the material evidence on which is based the castration complex essential for the organization of entrance to the symbolic order and the law of the father.
>
> (JOHNSTON 1972, 35)

If this is true, then what is most visible here as a sign of sexual difference is not lack but presence: the presence of Mini's breasts. The evocation of the masculinized, sexualized, and incestuous woman in Mini's words, "Oh, go suck your mother's balls!" adds something deeper than the castration threat mentioned above. This evocation further disrupts any placation of the "neurotic needs of the male ego" (Johnston 1972, 39), assumed as a given to any theory of cinematic identification, in its appropriation of the phallus by the female, who simultaneously bears the mark of sexual difference in the presence of her breasts. This is compounded by the fact that it is "for [her] lost child" that Mini becomes a spectacle in the first place, wanting to encode on her body a sign of mourning for loss of a different nature: that of her child. If the child is seen as a fetishized phallus, as Freud suggested, then this loss of her child must provoke a different response to Mini's "lack" as a woman, "lack" being predicated on original absence and "loss" being predicated on original presence.

The association between the female and the phallus gains deeper significance throughout the rest of the screen action, leading to the destabilization of the phallic signifiers in the film and posing additional problems in terms of the radicalization of the phallic gaze.[3] The importance of the black male as the active phallic signifier is further established in relation to the sexualities of Gugu and Mini. Again, a comparison is set up between the worlds of Gugu and Clint in the construction of markedly similar scenarios involving each of them, in this instance extending to a comparison between Clint and Zoo (the wheelchair-bound gangster with whom Gugu has a strategically motivated affair) and between Gugu and Mini.

The first scene I wish to analyze in this light opens with Gugu and Zoo in bed. In the foreground is a night table on which a bedside lamp is burning. Gugu is on top of Zoo, her arms flexed on either side of his head. Her face is mainly obscured by Zoo's, and he is seen sucking her lips like a baby, even continuing to suck the air in this way when she moves her face away. The shot focuses on his pleasure and the glow on his face afterward when Gugu rolls off him and lies behind him, propping herself up on one elbow. He is in the light cast by the lamp, she in comparative darkness. She smiles, looking at him.

Zoo: Was it good?

Gugu: I didn't know you would be able to do it. [She strokes his face with her forefinger.]

Zoo: Now you know. My feet can't do it, but the boy is still sharp! [Zoo makes a fist for emphasis.]

That black sexuality, a subject characterized by a "great silence" (Gaines 1990, 209), receives cinematic representation at all is a marked departure from previous South African films and the body of Western film as well. The fact that this scene is one of several in *Jump the Gun* that represent black sexuality and that the common denominator to every such scene is Gugu, the black woman, is indicative of the progressive cinematic modus operandi at work in *Jump the Gun*: the black woman is represented as a fully constituted subject, with both the sexual and racial terms of her identity exerting equal pressure on the narrative. Indeed, it may be said that it is Gugu's sexuality and her blackness that provide the impetus for the largest proportion of narrative development in the film, as it is through her agency, through what are shown as conscious decisions on her part, that the scenes depicting black sexuality come into being. This constitutes a radical revision of the terms on which "the unfathomability" of black women's sexuality is based. According to Hortense Spillers, this "unfathomability" arises "because the opportunity to codify one's sexuality belongs only to those in power; even as feminists have theorized women's sexuality, they have universalized from the particular experience of white women, thus effecting a 'deadly metonymy' " (cited in Gaines 1990, 209).

The dialogue following the sex act between Gugu and Zoo is mainly in Zulu, although the black characters in the film generally converse in a mixture of English and Zulu, which indicates the willingness of the film to engage with black sexuality on its own terms, thus breaking the "deadly metonymy" to which Spillers refers. It can therefore be posited that the film acknowledges and embraces the fact of black power, as black characters have the opportunity to codify their own sexuality. Because Gugu is the common denominator in the scenes featuring black sexuality, it follows that the greatest opportunities to codify black sexuality in the film are given to the black woman. On this score, then, *Jump the Gun* is several steps ahead of other films, like Elaine Proctor's *Friends* (1994), in which the black woman's sexuality does not merit even the "universalization" argued by Spillers, but receives literal textual "silence."

Again, then, the accepted terms of hierarchical racial patriarchy are challenged by representation within *Jump the Gun* and provoke the question, Who is in power? the answer to which runs counter to cinematic theories of filmic pleasure. Furthermore, Gugu's and Mini's sexual roles offer an inversion of the racial stereotypes of female sexuality (Gugu becomes a "kept woman," albeit temporarily, and has no children, which indicates her control over her reproductive capacity, while Mini is the prostitute as well as the "dysfunctional" single mother who has had her child removed by welfare). Neither Gugu nor Mini approaches "pure" or sexually "innocent" representation, the implication for the viewer being that both inversions are fraught as sites for objectification and for identification as they go against the grain of culturally dominant assumptions of the "relativity" between black and white female sexuality (black women being relatively "loose" and white women relatively "pure").

When Gugu and Zoo are seen in bed after their second act of lovemaking, they occupy the same positions, Gugu again further removed from the forefront of the screen, her face similarly obscured by darkness and by her hair and Zoo's face again bathed in the light of sexual after-glow illuminated by the bedside lamp. Again the figure of the mother intrudes into the image, but in this case she appears in Gugu's speech as a carefully constructed ploy through which to gain money from Zoo. Gugu says, "I have something I want to ask you, but I'm frightened it's too soon." She then asks for money, "one grand," which she explains is for her mother, to whom she has not yet been able to send money. Questioned, Gugu elaborates that the money will be used for electricity, water, and food. Zoo responds by saying that the money will be the first installment of a dowry (meaning that he is to marry Gugu), after asking her: "Do you love me, or do you just want to fuck me for my money?" and telling her that if the latter is the case, he will kill her.

Gugu responds at the end of the scene by looking up at Zoo and saying coyly, "You wouldn't shoot a woman." It is here that Gugu's ulterior motives in her sexual relationships are made most explicit. This duplicity must be seen as an instance of what Joan Riviere and Mary Ann Doane have called "masquerade": "Womanliness . . . could be assumed and worn as a mask, both to hide the possession of masculinity and to avert the reprisals expected if she was found to possess it. . . . The masquerade, in flaunting femininity, holds it at a distance" (quoted in Doane 1990, 49). Gugu's "flaunting femininity" has already been intimated in the appearance of her dress when first seen by the audience, a reason for her representation breaking the "Third World Woman" stereotype as explicated by Mohanty. That mode of dress is not limited purely to her first impression, however; consistently throughout the film Gugu is seen to take enormous care with her appearance. In the second bedroom scene, Gugu directs her request for money as much through her coyly downcast eyes as through her alluring sexual body (she fondles Zoo's nipples throughout). The moment at which Gugu says, "You wouldn't shoot a woman," her body language is particularly that of the female seductress: she is languid, her head is cocked slightly to one side, and she looks up at Zoo through her long eyelashes. The result is that, as she speaks these words, the image she presents to Zoo is pure "womanness," or, to borrow Laura Mulvey's term, "to-be-looked-at-ness" (Mulvey 1990, 33).

However, the scenario presented to the spectator is not as simple. What is highlighted in the way Gugu is shot by the camera is her adoption of this female masquerade as much as her foregrounding of the masquerade itself. According to Doane, the foregrounding of masquerade poses problems of comprehension for the spectator: "The idea seems to be this: it is understandable that women would want to be men, for everyone wants to be elsewhere than in the feminine position. What is not understandable within the given terms is why a woman might flaunt her femininity, produce herself as an excess of femininity, in other words, foreground the masquerade" (Doane 1990, 48). The incomprehensibility of her masquerade and the doom-laden quality behind Gugu's confident utterance are enhanced because, as she speaks, she is being shot by the camera, and her manipulation of "to-be-looked-at-ness" is seen not only as being inviting to the male gaze, but as actively soliciting that gaze. Her invoking the female body in this way in her speech by drawing attention to her sexual difference ("a woman"), while at the same time acting it out, means that, while in the field of looks played out on the screen she is seen to disguise herself in a suit of impregnable armor (by removing "herself" from the scene and having this surrogate "woman" stand in for her); to the audience she is seen as setting herself up as a target with her sexual difference as the bull's-eye for the phallus/gun/gaze. This is a result of the consciousness with which Gugu adopts the masquerade as a manipulatory device through which to increase her own power (as an independent woman) and to fulfill her own desires.[4]

The levels of distance and closeness at work in this scene,[5] therefore, complicate the spectator's relationship to both of the characters and hinder actual spectator identification with the look (of Zoo? of Gugu? of the "shooting" camera?) or actual spectator objectification of the image (the masquerade? the discernible entity behind or assuming the masquerade? the composite image of Gugu manipulating Zoo? Zoo himself?). The subversiveness of Gugu's masquerade thus leads to the subversion of film theory based on the omnipotence of the masculine gaze in that it leaves available to the spectator none of the theorized possible positions in relation to the image.

> The masquerade's resistance to patriarchal conditioning would therefore lie in its denial of the production of femininity as closeness, as presence-to-itself, as, precisely, imagistic. . . . Masquerade . . . involves a realignment of femininity, the recovery, or more accurately, simulation, of the missing gap or distance. To masquerade is to manufacture a lack in the form of a certain distance between oneself and one's image. . . . [Masquerade] works to effect a separation between the cause of desire and oneself. In Montrelay's words, "the woman uses her own body as a disguise."
>
> (DOANE 1990, 49)

The "patriarchal conditioning" mentioned here by Doane applies equally to theories that posit the omnipotence of the male gaze and are themselves patriarchally conditioned. In the scene, the masquerade not only "work[s]" to effect a separation between the cause of desire and oneself," but is also based on an original objectification of the subject to whom the cause of desire is presented. Thus a confusion between the identity of the object and that of the subject leads to a similar confusion on the part of the spectator, uncertain of which look to identify with. The spectator is encouraged into a masquerade of his or her own, based on the female model and inevitably leading to the spectator using his or her own bodily image as a disguise, enabled by the split that occurs in this process to entertain more than one position at a time in relation to the image. This is because the spectator's essentially voyeuristic nature is foregrounded to himself or herself. By this I mean that the spectator is made acutely aware of the fact that he or she is in possession of the reference points that Zoo lacks. This leads to the uncomfortable apprehension by the spectator of privy knowledge, gleaned through the act of voyeurism with its "peeping Tom" and "unwholesome" connotations. The "masquerade" entered into by the spectators is thus an attempt to distance themselves from the illicit nature of their own essential voyeurism, or "looking-at-ness," while maintaining the position of "innocent" onlookers. For a moment, then, spectatorship is constructed as a mask, but rather than being a "decorative layer" it becomes an "invisibilising layer" that conceals not "identity" in the sense that Doane or Riviere intended, but the specific identity of "invisible-ness" as a cover for voyeurism.[6]

Finally, the issue of the racial hierarchy of the gaze and that of the ultimate "overthrow" of dominant-looking relations as power play comes into effect in two later scenes. In the first of these, Gugu auditions for a place in a band and liberates her voice. Gugu and Thabo (a band manager) approach a run-down brick building, a township recording studio and practice room, where they are greeted by a young black woman who all but sneers at Gugu and fawns over Thabo. Thabo explains to two other black men that he has brought Gugu for an audition. They are skeptical, accusing him of using the band to bed women, but Thabo persuades them that Gugu could be brilliant. She overhears what he is saying and projects all the sexual magnetism she can toward the other two men as she waits nervously for their verdict. Finally, she is handed the microphone. A musician starts to play and asks her to sing along. Nothing happens; she cannot make a sound. This goes on and on unbearably until the unwelcoming woman from the scene's beginning giggles to herself at Gugu's ineptitude. Thabo is beside himself with nerves and impending embarrassment; the musicians are bemused and on the point of irritation. It is an excruciating screen moment. Then Gugu starts to sing, softly, her eyes cast down timidly. Soon the sounds become richer and stronger. The men all smile at her as her voice lifts in a spine-tingling crescendo of nonverbal noises. Thabo blinks with relief and disbelief as Gugu now forms words from the long chains of sounds. She sings, "Baby, baby" several times and her voice grows deeper and fuller by the second. The unwelcoming young woman casts an anxious, lingering sidelong glance at Thabo, then looks at Gugu, her smiles and giggles gone. Gugu's voice comes easily and naturally. The scene ends as she softly sings the words, "Baby, baby," before lapsing into a series of quiet, melodic, rhythmical nonverbal sounds, her now wide-open eyes on Henry (one of the musicians), Thabo, and the woman, her mouth wide open as she sings.

A key position here is held by Thabo, whose situation is analogous to that of the male spectator in the problematic instance of Clint's objectification. The woman's position in relation to the female image is similarly analogous to that of the viewer when confronting the duality of the masquerading Mini, or "Gloria." If Thabo and the second black woman are seen as Gugu's audience, it is the case here that the literal silence that the woman Gugu represents, the actual "gap" or "lack" in the discourse, which she initially does not fill, causes enormous psychological distress to Thabo, but not to the black woman spectator, for whom the silence is relief and the sounds the distress.

Furthermore, the sounds or "babble" that Gugu produces, the fact that the only discernible word is "baby," and the echolalic sounds of Gugu's name beg to be related to what Julia Kristeva has said characterizes the Lacanian Imaginary, or the "Maternal Realm." The Maternal Realm is that which the subject inhabits prior to his or her movement toward the Symbolic in which, through the acquisition of language, he or she may constitute the self as a separate entity and articulate the self-affirming "I am." All three of these features relating to Gugu can be aligned to Kristeva's notion of the "semiotic disposition," a practice of communication without signification particular to this Imaginary/Maternal Realm, important here because they rest on heterogeneity, or to use Kristeva's term, "heterogeneousness":

> One should begin by positing that there is within . . . language . . . *a heterogeneousness* to meaning and signification. This *heterogeneousness,* detected genetically in the first echolalias of infants as rhythms and intonations anterior to the first phonemes, morphemes, lexemes and sentences; this heterogenousness, which is later reactivated as rhythms, intonations, glossalalias in psychotic discourse, serving as ultimate support of

the speaking subject threatened by the collapse of the signifying function; this heterogenousness to signification operates through, despite, and in excess of it, and produces in poetic language "musical" but also non-sense effects that destroy . . . accepted beliefs and significations. . . . The notion of *heterogeneity* is indispensable, for though articulate, precise, organised, and complying with constraints and rules . . . this signifying disposition is not that of meaning or signification: no sign, no predication, no signified object and therefore no operating consciousness of a transcendental ego.

(Kristeva 1980, 133)

Gugu, with her name and her affinity to the "semiotic disposition," becomes synonymous with heterogeneousness, aided to a large extent by the masquerade, which has been seen to create a split, a multiplicity of heterogeneous "selves," within the female subject. In this way, one of the most radical shifts away from a problematic system of representation that homogenizes the black woman into a universal signifier "Woman" occurs, not only subverting but inverting that homogenizing system. The result is that the black woman, Gugu, is the agent through which the represented audience of Thabo and the second woman (and the spectator in the cinema auditorium) experience their exposure to, and are drawn into, the space created by the semiotic disposition.

The fact that Gugu manifests this signifying disposition by directing the one sign, the one predication, the one signified object of the word "baby," both at the mixed-gender audience of Thabo and the second woman in the studio and at the spectators seated in the cinema auditorium, where the only sounds available to both sets of recipients create the synchronic effects of drives and pulsations and the diachronic effects of contact with the archaic mother, indicates that at this filmic moment both cinematic representations and spectators inhabit the same space created via the semiotic disposition. This is characterized by rhythms, pressures, gurgles, and babble—an organic musicality: "the *chora*, receptacle, unnamable, improbable, hybrid, anterior to naming, to the One, to the father, and consequently, maternally connoted to the extent that it merits 'not even the rank of a syllable' " (Kristeva 1980, 133). That Gugu is thus aligned to the Maternal and Imaginary, through whom both onlooking characters and auditorium spectators are drawn into this state anterior to the father, anterior to the law, and anterior to language, means that in these moments the binary oppositions created by language (such as man/woman, black/white) cease to be valued, operative terms. The tones and cadences in Gugu's voice create an "amniotic fluid" that envelops and incorporates all spectators, exaggerating the "womb" metaphor that may be applied to the auditorium.

However, this is complicated by the cinema auditorium offering fantasy as a "real" experience at the level of auditory and visual perceptions (Cowie 1990, 165). The images projected onto the cinematic screen encourage the spectator into a process of identification (Mulvey 1990; Metz 1982), evoking an analogy between the film screen and the mirror of Lacan's "Mirror Phase"—the point of departure from the Maternal or Imaginary phase, and the point at which the Symbolic realm of the phallus, of law, of the father, and of language is entered into by the now-constituted subject. Yet this is precisely what the scene challenges, amounting to a challenge against the entire basis of psychoanalytic theories of the gaze that depend on the a priori privileging of the male. Part of this challenge is its demand that the figure of the black woman be taken into serious account as a (potential) catalyst for the dissolution of the conventional structures that regulate viewing power relations. Moreover, if the cinematic experience reactivates the Imaginary, encouraging a "regression to an infantile state" (Mayne 1990, 37) during which the spectator/child within the darkened "womb-like" auditorium seeks a reflected image of itself through the gaze of the (m)other (the camera of the filmmaker, the actual eyes of the characters) and through the mirrorlike surface of the screen, then the figure of Gugu here is responsible for the double evocation of the Maternal.

This double evocation is compounded by the fact that the maternal state/motherhood has been described as "the black continent" in relation to the extent of it that is unknown and unexplored (Groen 1993, 97–105). This exists in an obvious parallel to Africa, the archetypal "black continent" and the origin of the motherhood metaphor. Thus, Gugu's being a black African woman not only in a maternal role, but in the role of the entire Maternal Realm, results in her emergence as the archaic, primordial mother, the mother of all mothers, and yet a mother who does not rely on difference from men, or difference from fathers, or on biological function for her status (Gugu has no children).

Perhaps in this can be discerned a metaphorical reason for the tremendous threat experienced by white feminists in relation to the voices of black women, as seen in the earlier film *Friends* (1994). These voices house the potential for radically reordering the signifying system, being the most "outer," the most "other" and anterior voices to the dominant male order. This means that the black woman's voice may be far more effective as a means of provoking radical change, mistakenly interpreted as a loss of power for white women, a loss of control over signifying practice as it has been inherited from the patriarchal order for white middle-class women.

However, *Jump the Gun* exposes the unwarranted paranoia behind such fears of white women. It does so, in the first instance, by depicting Zoo's (unsuccessful) attempt to oppress Gugu, who has been collapsed into a mother of all while still maintaining her own racial specificity. Here, through her black female body, Gugu further signifies in a manner aligned to a world removed from the Symbolic when she cries and when these tears are foregrounded on the screen, encouraging empathy.

Of chief importance in the crying scene is neither the ethical issue behind Gugu's actions nor the accuracy or inaccuracy of Zoo's accusations. What is important is the signifying function of the tears within the discourse of cinematic representation. The presence of the tears becomes even more effective as a signifying practice that resists that of the Symbolic (thus being the visual equivalent of Kristeva's "semiotic disposition") because it exists outside not only one (verbal) language, but two (when taking into account the subtitles). It is thus a counter to both Western, white, male signification (the English component) and African, black, male signification simultaneously, and does not replicate the homogenizing impulse of the phallocentric order found in much Western feminist discourse. The value of the tears is that they mark the limit of the ability of both racial phallocentric language and "phallogocularcentrism" (Jay 1993, 493–542) to signify, and as such point toward a positive development of the feminism latent in *Jump the Gun*.

The scene can be viewed as a virtual answer to the challenge put to feminism by Derrida as summarized by Martin Jay. Only a feminism that knows the value of the veil of tears, "that tears are the essence of the eye—and not sight," can preserve the insights provided by "revelatory . . . [and] apocalyptic blindness, which reveals the very truth of the eyes." Only women who resist mimicking the dominant male scopic regime can avoid merely inverting the hierarchy that it supports (Jay 1993, 523). Furthermore, Gugu's tears are aligned with the Kristevan notion of the abject, a notion that film critics, particularly of the horror film genre, have found to be fertile. Through the application of this notion here, it becomes possible to posit the effect of the tears on the spectator.

> Images of blood, vomit, pus, shit, etc., are central to our culturally/
> socially constructed notions of the horrific. They signify a split between
> the two orders: the maternal authority and the law of the father. On
> the one hand, these images of bodily wastes threaten a subject that is
> already constituted, in relation to the symbolic, as "whole and proper."

> Consequently, they fill the subject—both the protagonist in the text and the spectator in the cinema—with disgust and loathing.
>
> (KRISTEVA, CITED IN CREED 1989, 70)

Yet these feelings of abjection, of "disgust and loathing," are not ends in themselves:

> they also point back to a time when a "fusion between mother and nature" existed; when bodily wastes, while set apart from the body, were not seen as objects of embarrassment and shame. Their presence in the . . . film may invoke a response of disgust from the audience situated as it is within the symbolic but at a more archaic level the representation of bodily wastes may invoke pleasure in breaking the taboo on filth—sometimes described as a pleasure in perversity—and a pleasure in returning to that time when the mother-child relationship was marked by an untrammeled pleasure in "playing" with the body and its wastes.
>
> (KRISTEVA, CITED IN CREED 1989, 70)

Although equally a bodily waste product, however, tears cannot be seen as directly and unproblematically interchangeable with blood, urine, or excrement and do not provoke the same audience response of "disgust and loathing." The bodily release of tears is less straightforward than the expulsion of by-products from necessary metabolic processes, being seen as the cornerstone of the human ability to move beyond seeing and knowing (Derrida, cited in Jay 1993, 523). The veil of tears thus provokes the recognition of the initial separation from the amniotic fluid of the mother's womb and a recognition of feelings of sadness and loss resulting from the split with the archaic mother, as well as the loss of the maternal as the sole originary tactile vehicle for all human sense experience. Tears conjure up a melancholic nostalgia for—and the resurfacing of acutely painful repressed memories of—original tactile experience and thus inarticulable "closeness" unmediated by the Symbolic realm of language. The figure of Gugu (with "her waters breaking") is thus a signifier for the Maternal Realm, and furthermore the power relations of the male scopic regime are subverted because it is she who is seen to exhibit the greatest degree of human specificity in relation to animale rationale (Derrida, cited in Jay 1993, 523), as it is she who manifests the sign of human (r)evolution.

Mini, as the white woman, receives a different signifying capacity and is not as depleted as Clint in terms of her signifying potency. Whereas Clint leaves Johannesburg, the final scene of the film shows

Mini and Gugu together, with Mini having greater access to plurality than Clint by virtue of her gender.

> [Mini and Gugu are seen from a distance in profile, Mini sitting in front of Gugu, who braids Mini's hair. There is a stratum of rock with grass growing over it on which they sit.]
>
> *Mini*: What's a prostitute? [Cut to a close-up shot of both of them from the front. Mini is sipping wine from a glass. Gugu giggles.]
>
> *Gugu*: "Makhoshe," or "skabberish."
>
> *Mini*: [pulling a face] Skabberish! Sies! [An expression of disgust; Mini turns her head to look at Gugu.] And what's a star?
>
> *Gugu*: A star?
>
> *Mini*: Yeah, like you . . . [She looks off left.]
>
> *Gugu*: [shakes her head] There isn't a word for it. I'd say, "ntzo-duma." What are you going to be?
>
> *Mini*: My future's been; I haven't got a future. [She looks down and sips from her glass.]
>
> *Gugu*: [putting her arms around Mini and patting her] It's okay, babes. You come stay with me; I'll take care of you. [Gugu rocks Mini in her arms and begins to sing in Zulu. They smile together. Cut to a distanced shot, with Johannesburg seen in the background and them on an outlying green field. As Gugu sings the camera retreats.] Come on, join in: "You can come and stay with me, baby, come with me, baby. . . ."
>
> [This fades into the soundtrack. Cut to the trains, one arriving in Johannesburg and one leaving (bearing Clint away). The camera pans, then circles. The soundtrack develops into the song Gugu sang in her moment of triumph with the band at J. J's: "A Better Place to Live." Fade to black. Credits.]

Again, Gugu falls outside the Symbolic system of language, there being no word that can adequately convey what Gugu "is," what is her essence. She cannot be held and defined by masculine discursive practice, existing before and beyond it in the same way as the Imaginary exists before and beyond the Symbolic, while at the same time exerting a power over it as it is she who here provides the meanings for the words in question. The importance of this becomes clear with the consideration of the following words by Trinh T. Minh-ha (1989, 48): "[N]aming, like a cast of the die, is just one step towards unnaming, a tool to render visible what he has carefully kept invisible in his manipulative blindness."

The potential site of power provided by the nonthreatened exchange between the black and the white woman, particularly in learning the names given by each to themselves and to things of personal and specific relevance, is the note on which the film ends, and is the same site as the nexus between theory and discursive practice. It is crucial that in this represented discourse, difference is not suppressed and that the "tool of survival" (read: theory) is here shown as being actively "rethought in relation to gender" in the practice of this theoretical discourse, with the focus on the meanings of words such as "prostitute" as an identifying signifier of one woman and "star" applying directly to the other. This bears an uncanny relation to the directive given by Trinh that "theory as a tool of survival needs to be rethought in relation to gender in discursive practice." It is even more uncanny that this final, important scene revolves around an interracial female couple not only teaching and learning words and their meanings, but deciding on their meanings and creating new ones on the outskirts of dominant discourse (literally represented by their removal from the city with its phallic skyscrapers). Why this may be termed "uncanny" will become clear if the following theoretical extract is taken into account:

> Mastery ensures the transmission of knowledge; the dominant discourse for transmitting is one "that annihilates sexual difference—where there is no question of it." . . . [W]omen "are constantly moving, they recount, among other things, the metamorphosis of words from one place to another. *They* themselves *change* versions of these metamorphoses, *not in order to further confuse the matter but because they record the changes*. The result of these changes is an avoidance of fixed meanings. . . . They agree upon the words that they do not want to forgo. Then they decide, according to their groups, communities, islands, continents, on the possible tribute to be paid for the words. When that is decided, they pay for it (or they do not pay for it). . . . Those who do so call this pleasantly 'to write one's life with one's blood,' this, they say, is the least they can do." . . . It is a way of making theory in gender, of making of theory a politics of everyday life, thereby re-writing the ethnic female subject as a site of differences.
>
> (Trinh T. 1989, 43–44)

The roles and actions of Mini and Gugu at the end of the film can be related directly to the practice of "[writing] one's life with one's blood" and to accepting and embracing differences. The implications of this, and the implications of *Jump the Gun*'s representational strategies up to and including this moment, have potentially far-reaching effects for progressive film theory and for feminist criticism in general. The closing image of Mini and Gugu and the parallel that can be drawn between their interaction in this sequence and "[writing] one's life with one's blood" exhibits a (r)evolutionary tendency—a direct result of the film's attention to teetering (especially white) patriarchal power played out through the representation of the phallus/gun/look signifier and its limitations and impotence in relation to the central black female character, Gugu.

In addition, an overt inversion occurs in relation to notions of the "future" and to whom the future belongs (or to whom ascendancy belongs in terms of justified social, economic, and political power). Whereas certain predecessor films, like *Friends* (1994), suggest that white South African women have an essential and necessary role to play in the future of black South Africans and intimate that without the help of white women a future for blacks is untenable (thus supporting a patronizing colonial mentality), the opposite is the case in *Jump the Gun*. At the end of *Jump the Gun* Mini recognizes, accepts, and verbally acknowledges the expendability of the white woman in the scheme of further development when she says, "My future's been; I haven't got a future." It is the thought of this potentiality that may be said to characterize white women's fears of their black counterparts, fears to which films like *Friends* pandered. Nowhere in *Jump the Gun* is there a suggestion that it is directed at a white-only audience, nor does it in any way support the idea of a threat posed to white women by black women's ascendancy. This threat is an illusion, unsubstantiated by any cinematic or external reality, and Gugu is seen in *Jump the Gun*'s end scene to be maternal and nurturing to Mini, comforting her and negotiating a way for the feasibility of their joint survival ("You come stay with me; I'll take care of you.").

The homoerotic charge that permeates the closing of *Jump of the Gun* applies to the interracial pairing of Mini and Gugu. It is emphasized when Gugu repeats the phrase, "You come stay with me," associated with heterosexuality and originally spoken by Zoo in the tears scene—there an indication of his intention to "own" her. However, Gugu's using these words of Zoo's does not indicate her adoption or replication of the male role, position, or discourse, or any related wish to "own" Mini. The important difference between Zoo's and Gugu's use of these words is that Gugu incorporates them into gentle, rhythmical song, that she sings them to Mini much as a lullaby that bears the mark of the "semiotic disposition" in its nonverbal element (as discussed in relation to the audition scene). More than drawing Mini into the Maternal/Imaginary that is evoked by the semiotic disposition, Gugu encourages Mini to "join in" that signifying practice. Yet this is not to suggest the collapse of differences between Mini and Gugu into one homogenized signifier of the "Maternal" or of "Woman." The closing image of Mini and Gugu corresponds to "*affidamento*," an Italian term explained by Luce Irigaray (1994, 193–94) as "a bond between one woman and the other based upon a recognition of the qualities which distinguish one woman from the other."

This *affidamento* is seen in the way that Gugu and Mini do not attempt to find a word that can describe both of them together; in other words, they do not seek a common signifier. The words for which Mini asks translation apply either to Gugu or to herself, and yet Gugu and Mini are seen to share a common future—in the sense that they will be together, rather than that their individual futures will comprise the same events or the same experiences. It is with this sense that the cinema spectator is left at the end of *Jump the Gun,* a sense that is concretized by the song to which the film's end credits play out: "A Better Place to Live." The future is actively evoked by the final song's words, "a better place for all." *Jump the Gun* is thus proposing a forward movement, a progression that is applicable not only to the South Africa represented in the text but to, and in, the text itself.

Jump the Gun's representational inclusion of the black male gaze, its representations of black (and specifically black women's) sexuality, its encouraging of the spectator to assume a mask of "invisibility" along the lines of the female "masquerade," and its representations of interracial hetero- and homosexuality (the first being a threesome sequence not discussed here and the second being the "charge" between Mini and Gugu in their last scene) distinguish it from previous films in terms of the spectator-text relationship. These features separate it too from any parallels between representations of black women in itself and the homogenizing "blind spots" in Western feminist discourse that lead to the suppression of black women's voices. The final scene between Gugu and Mini may provide a lesson for white middle-class feminists who maintain their hegemony because of "determined" ignorance, or due to fears of being dominated by black women if they lose "control" of "the right of admission" into their discourse. For, according to Irigaray (1994, 194), *affidamento* (such as that between Gugu and Mini witnessed at the end of the film) "can act as a guarantee of freedom for women who are afraid of being dominated or obliterated by other women."

In an analysis of *Jump the Gun,* the definite progression under way in South African film becomes palpable. The particular context that informs cultural production in South Africa is conducive to the continuance of a radical and (r)evolutionary development in cinematic representations of racial difference, the most important for feminism being those among women. It becomes possible to predict an outcropping of South African films that will afford feminist film critics opportunities to consider the implications of looking and racial taboos, such as looking at white female characters through the gaze of black male characters (already discernible—but as yet undeveloped—in *Jump the Gun* in the scene in which the black male bar patron looks at Mini as she strips off her shirt).[7] Areas such as this must be addressed by feminist film critics and South African filmmakers if their theories are to be defendable against accusations of elitism, which their bias toward privileging the (white) spectator, male or female, have justifiably provoked in marginalized black women on the periphery of their discourse. South African films of the near future will very probably provide subjects for analysis that will lead directly to this necessary reworking of theory, already under way in *Jump the Gun.*

Returning to the specificity of South Africa's sociohistorical context, the stress on actual and spatiomental spaces defined by race and class are of particular importance given apartheid history, South Africa's own time and place/space particulars, and the way that these inform and frame cultural artifacts such as films. The rigid control of space during the apartheid era as a separating mechanism between race groups has led to a heightened sensitivity toward such issues and to the inherent politics of cinematic representation so pertinent to current feminist film theory. The progression under way in South African society is reflected in the shift in representational strategies from *Friends* to *Jump the Gun,* and the emphasis in this chapter on race and class as these intersect with gender enables the engagement with current feminist debate from a climate in which (un)ethical spatial constructions have been glaringly obvious at all levels of social practice. As cultural artifacts, postapartheid South African films may serve as new models through which to reconceptualize film theory that has arisen from contexts in which specificity has not been as dominant a political issue as in South Africa. When it is borne in mind that the shift between representational strategies in *Friends* and *Jump the Gun* occurred during what in future may be seen more accurately as a transitional period rather than "postapartheid," the realization of a vast potential for yet more radical representational strategies at the intersection of race, class, and gender becomes inevitable.

185

Notes

1. In South Africa, a "Ladies' Bar," historically, is a restaurant or lounge where the sale of liquor to women is permitted.

2. Clint is here referring to a story reported in the press about Eugene Terre'Blanche, whom Mini mentioned as "giving Afrikaners a bad name." Terre'Blanche, the head of the white right-wing extremist group the Afrikaner Resistance Movement (AWB), allegedly arrived drunk at a rally and fell off his horse, to the amusement of the press and news crews documenting the event.

3. Unfortunately, space constraints prevent an analysis of the gun shop sequence. I am referring here to the inclusion in this scene of a young black male's mastery over a firearm and of his ability to aim the weapon. In this sequence there are several shot-reverse-shots that lead to the intermingling of white and black male "gazes."

4. The film suggests that Gugu does not seek power over men to have access to their money, she wants a career in the music band and financial independence.

5. I am indebted to Doane's work on "proximity and distance" (see Doane 1990, esp. 44–46).

6. "[F]emininity itself is constructed as a mask—as the decorative layer which conceals identity. For Joan Riviere, the first to theorize the concept, the masquerade of femininity is a kind of reaction-formation against the woman's sex identification, her transvestism" (Doane 1990, 48).

7. This optimism is based on the notion that *Jump the Gun* is symptomatic of changes that are observable and rapidly accelerating in the social sphere. In addition, the popularity of the film has been amply demonstrated at the box office, which implies a certain political effectivity as well.

9

Sexuality, Power, and the Black Body in *Mapantsula* and *Fools*

Kgafela oa Magogodi

Scholarship on South African cinema has been overwhelmingly preoccupied with racial politics, with little consideration given to the politics
of sexuality. The focus of this chapter is on the gendered body in the
context of racial politics and power in apartheid South Africa as depicted
in Oliver Schmitz's *Mapantsula* (1988) and Ramadan Suleman's *Fools*
(1997). The centrality of the gendered body in *Mapantsula* was largely
ignored until Jacqueline Maingard's (1994) intervention, in which she
problematized the film's male point of view, which, according to her,
underplayed women's struggle. Conversely, the thematic foregrounding
of rape in *Fools* inevitably invites a discussion of the politics of sexuality
and sexism. *Mapantsula* was created during the heat of political upheavals and racial tensions in the late 1980s; *Fools,* as a film produced in
the "postapartheid" dispensation, raises questions of gender in the context of more recent political preoccupations. It appears that Suleman's
concern is anchored in the relationship between racism and sexism in
processes of domination. This chapter explores the gendered body by
drawing on assumptions about masculinity and femininity as apparent
in the sociopolitical and historical contexts that are presented in *Mapantsula* and *Fools.*

Rethinking Black Sexuality

Mapantsula reflects on the political upheavals and apartheid repression
of the late 1980s. It is the story of a township gangster, Panic, who is
imprisoned because he is mistaken for a political activist. Panic reflects
on his life before his incarceration, his flashbacks of memory unfurling
his gangster life in Soweto and the inner city of Johannesburg. Blending
with these flashbacks is the narrative of Panic the prisoner, subjected to

continual police interrogation and torture. Shown within the film's dual narrative structure, Panic's experiences encompass family life, romance, and petty crime as well as his imprisonment and developing political consciousness.

In *Mapantsula,* Schmitz presents a Manichean split between a white and a black visual world. There is almost a sense of a geography of whiteness, characterized by opulence, mansions, and beautiful gardens, juxtaposed with a geography of blackness, whose poverty is marked by filth and overpopulation. Blacks are not allowed into the white world unless they are servants like Pat, Panic's girlfriend, whom Panic is not even allowed to visit.

In *Fools,* the bulk of the action takes place in a black township where the only whites to enter are authority figures—men—such as the school inspector and the police. In fact, white women do not exist on Suleman's screen. By implication, white womanhood, as apartheid custodians would have it, must not be tainted by any contact with the black world, specifically contact of a sexual nature.

Fools is the story of a teacher, Zamani, who rapes and impregnates one of his pupils, Mimi. Mimi's misfortune occurs on the day she visits Zamani's home to present him with a gift, a live chicken, from her mother, who wishes to thank the teacher because her daughter has passed the dreaded matric examinations given in the final year of secondary school. Zamani's crime implicates him in a series of tensions with various members of the Chaterston community, including his wife, Nosipho.

Although the film is set in 1989, against the background of police suppression of political activities in the township, Zamani's rape does not have political motives; the rape in *Fools* is political only insofar as it shows the consequences of oppression on the powerless Zamani, who can victimize only those weaker than himself.

When Zamani first appears on the screen in *Fools,* he is portrayed as an emasculated figure. Zani, a young activist, verbally abuses him, from which we learn that Zamani's sharpness as a young man has been blunted. Zani calls the likes of Zamani "masters of avoidance" who have abandoned the struggle against apartheid for drink.

Zamani is not revealed to have any craving for "white flesh." Rather, his aggression gestures inward, into the black township community. Yet Zamani's criminality is not a matter for police investigation and incarceration. Zamani's castigation and isolation from the community lead him to introspection and consequent rehabilitation. Suleman's strategy seems to be two-pronged. First, the rehabilitation of Zamani is indicative of the community's sense of justice, which is not premised on violence. Indeed, this peaceful justice is evident in the protection that MaButhelezi, Mimi's mother, offers Zamani against the wrath and hatred of Busi, Mimi's sister, and the very fact of her offering the teacher some home-brewed beer in a mug that belonged to her late husband. Second, the community's sense of sexual morality is implied in the initial act of suspending Zamani from his duties as a schoolteacher. In essence, Suleman, through the community's condemnation, seeks to challenge assumptions about the rampant and wild sexuality of black people.

Despite the rape, Zamani's lack of virility debunks myths about the insatiable lust of "natives." This is revealed in a scene in which he is unable to ejaculate; the prostitute with whom he is engaged tells him, "Let's blame it on the weather," and insists on payment for her time. Similarly, in *Mapantsula*, Panic does not exemplify a "native" with a "perpetual erection." The morning scene in Panic's room shows Pat refusing his request for lovemaking. Panic, though he accepts grudgingly, does not display Zamani's sexual decadence or the urge to rape. None of the characters in *Mapantsula* or *Fools* conform to the stereotype of black people with untamable libidinal instincts. Instead, the directors present scenes of believable human sexual exchanges.

The Gendered Nature of Power and Black Masculinity

The following statement in Désiré Ecaré's film *Visages de femmes* (1985) provides a springboard for this discussion: "Our bank is our thighs, our breasts and our ass; with these we have got all the power; with my backside, mother, I can get the government toppled tomorrow if I want. I can get a new Ambassador appointed to Paris, to Peking and even to the Vatican. The Pope won't twig, God and women always see eye to eye" (cited in Ukadike 1996, 199). According to Nwachukwu Ukadike, T' Cheley's "acerbic proclamation" in Ecaré's film is in dialogue with "female sexual power," which "cannot be dismissed as a stereotypical image of African woman." As Ukadike (1996, 199) suggests, the narrative points to "the potential of a future sociocultural revolution and challenges the viewer to reflect upon black sexuality."

Similarly, in Henri Duparc's *Rue Princesse* (1993), the female protagonist, Josie, tells her boyfriend, Jean, that when she became orphaned at a young age, her uncle took her to a brothel, but she later became the "manager" of her own body when she operated independently as a prostitute. Underlining the economics of her project, Josie calls her room a plant where, presumably, sex is manufactured at a cost.

Through Josie, Duparc reflects on the need to free the female body from patriarchal control, and yet the voyeuristic gaze of the camera on her body seems to locate her only within the biological realm, as one who is absorbing her world more sexually than intellectually.

The notion of "bottom power" is foregrounded in both Ecaré's *Visages de femmes* and Duparc's *Rue Princesse*. In Duparc's film, for instance, prostitutes climb the social and economic ladder by selling their bodies as delicacies to members of the ruling elite—the mayor, the police commissioner, the bank manager. Simultaneously, Duparc is able to deconstruct power by exposing the illicit sexual conduct of men in authority positions who publicly condemn prostitution but covertly purchase sex. Yet the ambiguities of this power can be noted when one considers that the elite is still being "serviced."

Like Duparc, Ousmane Sembène in *Xala* (1974) shows men in positions of power as suffering from impotence and picking up sexual diseases like everyone else. The sexual impotence of the main character in *Xala*, El Hadji, is symbolic of a sterile postcolonial social order, which is a responsibility of the new ruling elite after political independence in Senegal and, by extension, throughout Africa.

The gendered metaphors that flow from these observations allow for novel reflections on *Fools* and *Mapantsula* beyond a tired celebration of the fact that these movies contain stories about black people. For instance, Zamani's sexual impotence in *Fools* can, like El Hadji's sterility, be figured in political terms. Pat's entrapment in a love triangle in *Mapantsula* invites a comparison with depictions of women in *Rue Princesse* and *Xala* whose movements are within the biological realm as sexual partners, not partners in the shaping of the destiny of "the nation." As such, it seems that women are credited with nothing beyond their sexual power(lessness) or partnership in an African nationalism that is defined in masculine terms. Essentially, these constructions and deconstructions of power, race, and nationalism, as brokered on the gendered body, inform and are informed by history.

In *The History of Sexuality,* Foucault (1976, 38) discusses the manner in which sex is "put into discourse." He proceeds from the assumption that human sexual behavior is riddled with the issue of power, which "penetrates and controls everyday pleasure." For Foucault, the centrality or privileging of conjugal sexuality engendered "the appearance of peripheral sexualities" like sodomy, adultery, incest, the sexuality of children, and prostitution. These peripheral sexualities came under the category of the illicit. In effect, there were laws that sought to police sexual behavior so that sex within marriage was the norm and any other forms of sexuality not only became "a moral infraction" but also, in the case of certain acts like sodomy and prostitution, were legally punishable. Foucault (1976, 39) states that the "agencies of control" or "mechanisms of surveillance" saw a shift, with the industrial development of society "since the nineteenth century," from religious to medical control of the sexual body. While religious control puts emphasis on morality, the "medicalisation of sexuality" also brings to bear certain types of power "on the body and on sex" through labeling as mental pathology "unorthodox sexualities" such as "the sexuality between doctor and patient, teacher and student, psychiatrist and mental patient" (Foucault 1976, 38, 39).

Foucault's model, based on his study of the history of sexuality in Western society, is also applicable within the African context, though there are variances. Conceptions of black or African sexuality constructed in the West, with underpinnings of racial stereotypes, existed in a separate category within the Western imaginary. Nonetheless, there is a sense in which Foucault's assumptions are transferable to African societies that came into contact with Christian morality via colonization as well as through the discourse of Western medicine on the sexual body. For instance, central to the thematic concerns of *Fools* is the prohibition of sex between a teacher (Zamani) and a student (Mimi). Crossing that barrier brings about the expulsion of the teacher, who is also judged guilty of raping his pupil. This thematic concern, one may argue, is inspired by the social referent in South Africa's black townships. In the eponymous short story by Njabulo Ndebele that inspired the screenplay of the movie *Fools,* the writer bemoans what was apparently then an epidemic in township schools. In the short story, Zani addresses Zamani about the moral bankruptcy of teachers: "Some of them, like you, are paid to be killers of dreams, putting out the fire of youth, and to be expert at deflowering young girls sent to school by their hopeful parents" (Ndebele 1983: 164). Ndebele links sexual intercourse between teachers and students with the decadence of apartheid education, implying that the apartheid state sponsors the degenerate sexual activities of the teachers.

Zamani, as a married man, is also guilty of adultery, for which he incurs the wrath of his wife, Nosipho, who refuses any further sexual contact with him. Nosipho's rejection leads Zamani to purchase sexual favors from prostitutes. During one such incident, he has to flee from the police, who, as custodians of the moral law, are in charge of arresting prostitutes and their clients. Through this series of illicit sexual activities Zamani is implicated in all sorts of peripheral sexualities, which are brought to bear on his body, as indicated in his eventual loss of sexual virility. This point comes across in Ndebele's story (Ndebele 1983, 200–1) when the reader enters Zamani's stream of consciousness:

> After reading a book on civilisations, I put out the paraffin lamp next to me, and rose to go and sleep. After undressing I sat naked at the edge of my bed and looked at Nosipho breathing regularly in her sleep. And I felt how worn out my body was. So unfit. Too unfit for any hard task. The sagging breasts with wrinkles going across; useless strands of hair around the nipples; a navel closed shut by flabs of stomach; and from the depths of where a sagging stomach met with tired thighs, peeped the point of a circumcised penis, too tired now to be a release for passion. Had it been consumed by the fire of its own corruption?

Zamani's sexual impotence, it can be suggested, is a consequence of his profanity. The authorial voice of the text suggests that Zamani's moral and political baseness is to be punished with senility.

Similarly, in Suleman's interpretation of Ndebele's moral impulse in *Fools*, Zamani's body is made to suffer from sterility. To underscore the moral and political sterility of teachers during the struggle against apartheid, Suleman uses a similar strategy to that of Sembène in *Xala*, where El Hadji's sexual impotence is symbolic of the failure of the new ruling elite to overhaul the oppressive and exploitative social conditions. Zamani's political sterility in *Fools* is exposed by the young activist Zani, who interrupts Zamani's class to teach a history lesson based on the struggle against apartheid. Effectively, Zani challenges the idea of pupils having to commemorate Dingaan's Day, a celebration institutionalized by the apartheid government of the "victory" by the Dutch settlers over Zulu warriors in 1838 at the Battle of Blood River. Zani's lesson to the pupils not to celebrate their own defeat is rudely terminated by the school's headmaster, Meneer ("Sir" in Afrikaans), the apartheid agent in the story, who comes storming into the classroom threatening both Zani and Zamani with violence. It is only Zani who is able to stand firm against the headmaster's abuse, and he even asks Meneer why he speaks rudely to his teacher before the pupils.

As Zamani's political sterility is underlined in this sequence, it is compared with Zani's youthful virility, which is figured in both sexual and political terms. Zamani's friends warn him about the comrades, who will "ask you to march, . . . and behind your back they declare independence with your wife." But Zani's friendship with Zamani's wife proves to be no more than fraternal. Zani is therefore, unlike Zamani, morally and politically redeemed because of his faithful commitment to both his girlfriend, Ntozakhe, and the struggle against apartheid. Notably, Zamani, in a state of drunkenness, threatens to beat up Zani, whom he suspects of bedding his wife. He swings a fist at Zani and misses, falls flat on his stomach, and blacks out on the floor. When Nosipho walks over Zamani's unconscious body, she metaphorically tramples on his failing manhood. Yet Zamani insists on his status as the patriarchal figurehead of the family. Significantly, Suleman's juxtaposition of Zamani's aging body and Zani's youthful physicality dramatizes the idea that the sexual body is a text for sociohistorical processes.

The similarity of Suleman's strategy in *Fools* to that of Sembène in *Xala* is visible in their attempts to explore the gendered body. Zamani's sexual decadence is highlighted during a gathering with friends who compare pictures of their young girlfriends despite their age and the fact that they are married men. One of Zamani's friends says to his colleagues, "Look at my latest sugar baby!" The other friend retorts enthusiastically, in township slang, "Die ding [the thing] is strictly fresh, no preservatives." Women, to Zamani and company, are seen as edible, their bodies as food. In township slang, men would boast about "go ja bana [eating the babies]" after acts of copulation, thus expressing the desire to consume a woman's flesh via the act of sexual intercourse.

Significantly, Mimi brought a live chicken as a gift from her mother to her teacher, Zamani, after she had passed matric. Perhaps Mimi's misfortune can be explained in township lingo, which describes statutory rape as "chicken murder," for, in the aftermath of the rape, Zamani literally kills the chicken by breaking its neck. With the chicken's blood splashing all over his face, Zamani says, "I am a respectable man." Does the spilling of blood beget his manhood? The image is reminiscent of the ritualistic shedding of the blood of a live chicken on a marriage bed as a sign of broken virginity in *Xala*. The notion of a chicken as a gift or sacrifice also relates to the body of a woman as an offering on the altar of phallocentric manhood.

In *Fools*, acts of copulation are for men attempts to contest colonial masculinity, while in *Xala* men copulate to celebrate the fruits of independence. Women's bodies are seen by the likes of El Hadji as "fruits of uhuru" (the results of independence), while the likes of Zamani invade women's bodies as terrains for the reconstruction of their emasculated virility.

In *Fools*, Zamani's expulsion from school is lifted by the community elders, all male, because, as they claim, the community needs teachers. Zamani's violent act of rape is pardoned because, as one of the elders puts it, they want to see a shovel in his hands soon. Nosipho, on observing the easy manner in which Zamani is let off the hook, says to her husband, "You men have no shame." Through Nosipho's mumbling, Suleman reviews the system of patriarchy within black townships where women's voices were muffled and their bodies violated.

On another level, Suleman portrays the emasculation of the black man as implied in the activities of Zamani, who is submissive to white authority at the school where he teaches but insists on his manhood at home. When Zamani warns his wife not to behave like "those women who wear pants in stockvels [stock fairs]," he is really addressing Nosipho's potential invasion of his masculinity. Like Chinua Achebe's character Okonkwo in *Things Fall Apart* (1988), who is emasculated by colonial invasion, Zamani and his circle of friends draw their masculinity from deflowering young girls, and yet their bodies are cowed under the yoke of apartheid oppression. On hearing about the arrest of Zani, one of Zamani's friends expresses his fear of the wrath of the apartheid police when he says that "heroes die young." All Zamani and his friends can do is to philosophize in a rather sterile manner about revolutionary icons like Nkrumah and Lenin. Their sense of purpose proceeds mainly from lording over women's bodies.

Someone once said that woman's place during the struggle against apartheid was lying on her back under a man. This is reminiscent of how, during the 1980s, the period in which Suleman's movie is set, young women were raped under the pretext that it was part of the struggle to produce soldiers for the revolution. By implication, Suleman raises the gendered metaphors that were born out of black nationalist discourse. He problematizes the idea that African nationalism was constructed around masculinity, that the success or failure of a nation depended on its abundance or lack of virility. In nationalist literatures Africa is also referred to as "Mother Africa" and colonialism understood as the political rape of the continent. The idea of the female body as victim is made apparent in this eroticized construction of history. When people like Jomo Kenyatta in the story "Gentlemen of the Jungle" write about "colonial penetration," sexual symbolism is used to define the colonial encounter. African nationalist rhetoric usually equates the lack of freedom with femininity. Theorists have written extensively about how the political conquest of the African man by the European man is often marked by sexual violence committed over the bodies of the conquered.

The gendered metaphors of the struggle are critiqued by Suleman when, ultimately, the pregnancy resulting from the rape is terminated. But it is not clear whether Mimi aborts the fetus or has a miscarriage.

She is bleeding in an outside toilet when her sister, Busi, cries for help from Nosipho, who works as a nurse at a local hospital. A few moments later Mimi comes out with a blanket around her waist, without a baby in her arms, supported by Nosipho. The importance of the scene is its suggestion of collectivity among women (which is initially threatened by Zamani's act) and the peripheral location of men (such as Zani, crying on the margin). In the symbolism of abortion or miscarriage, Suleman may be tacitly suggesting that so long as patriarchy reigns supreme and justifies violence against women, there will be no forces of renewal in this society.

Perhaps Suleman makes a similar point to that of Sembène in *Xala*, where part of the failure of El Hadji and his colleagues in the chamber of commerce is that they exclude women from participating. Far from being equal partners in shaping the destiny of the nation, women are seen as mere sexual partners in Sembène's Senegal. Suleman's black South African township in *Fools* also shows the exclusion of women from important community matters, such as the decision about Zamani's future as a teacher.

Even Ntozakhe, Zani's girlfriend, with whom he studied in Swaziland, exists on the fringes of both the struggle and Suleman's film frame, despite the fact that, like Zani, she "might have read many books." Zani, on the other hand, is introduced to Zamani's students as having leadership qualities and "possessing the truth of light" because of the many books that he has read. Why Ntozakhe is not credited with leadership qualities becomes a problematic issue, although it is possible to suggest that Suleman's depiction is perhaps very close to Ndebele's in the short story (male complicity?). But we see that Zani's books do not simply confer leadership, seeing that he remains marginal in the township because of his intellectual snobbery. Zani's encounter with Mazambane (a cameo character in the film who drives around in a flashy BMW terrorizing the community with his violent tendencies but also sometimes ferries the young comrades to their political meetings) illustrates this point. The school pupils are attracted to Mazambane's brand of "comrade *tsotsi*" (a cross between political activist and common thug) leadership in spite of Zani's derogatory assessment of Mozambane as a "chicken brain."

While the notion of masculine leadership is treated with ambivalence, it could be said that Suleman's portrayal of Ntozakhe as a mere girlfriend derives from the social referent he is attempting to represent. Alternatively, Suleman can be faulted for not inserting a female character at the center of his narrative. Rather, women in the movie are credited with a fragile form of sisterhood, as they are seen bickering among themselves during the preparation for a wedding celebration. Busi provokes Nosipho into a fight and directs obscenities at her when the latter walks away. The only time women are seen working together is when Mimi is bleeding in the toilet scene, where we see MaButhelezi, Mimi's mother, passing a bucket to Nosipho. But these women operate silently in this sequence. Are the women mere bodies without voices?

Such is the case with Ntozakhe's body, erotically revealed in the opening sequence of the movie. Zani and Ntozakhe are seen naked, kissing and embracing, inside a moving train. Instead of showing the apparently impending sexual act, the camera cuts to the outside, showing the train releasing steam as if to suggest the desire between Zani and Ntozakhe. Soon the camera cuts back to the two characters looking contented. The editing logic suggests sexual intercourse. In the story that follows, however, it is only Zani's character that is developed, while Ntozakhe, whose breasts fill the film frame in the lovemaking sequence, exists merely as his girlfriend. While Suleman deconstructs the myth of masculine adventure and phallic potency, it remains rather unfortunate that Ntozakhe's agency, which is paralleled to that of the prostitute, is confined to love and its making.

Jacqueline Maingard (1994) speaks about the inability of Schmitz in *Mapantsula* to give voice to women's struggles. While she acknowledges some effort to depict Pat's exploitation by both her boyfriend, Panic, and her employer, Mrs. Bentley, Maingard regrets the fact that Pat's libertarian impulse is spurred on by another man, Duma, the trade union leader and political activist in the story. For Maingard (1994, 238), the film is dominated by a male viewpoint:

> While the film's text is representing a black view, it is also a male view and the perspectives of black females are marginalised. In a scene that evokes the despair of domestic workers this is underlined. Panic waits for Pat in her room at the "Madam's" house. She comes in and collapses exhausted into bed. As they converse about her request for more pay, in an over-the-shoulder shot from Panic's point of view, we look through the window at the silhouette of Pat's employers chatting and drinking from mugs. The shot makes manifest the alienation experienced by domestic workers, but although this is Pat's experience, textually, it is Panic's point of view that is confirmed. It is his anger that is expressed and furthermore his frustration that is vented at Pat abusively: "Hayi fuck you, Pat! You must wake up, man!"

Where Pat's viewpoint is allowed "a brief space in the film's center," Maingard further argues, it is only to serve the already established "black perspective," which is "primary." Maingard (1994, 239) offers an example of Pat's view of her Madam when it is just the two of them in Mrs. Bentley's house, which is "stereotyping her as a white 'Madam'" while "the film maintains its black perspective."

Panic's story is influenced by his romantic affair with Pat. It is revealed that the two are sexually involved when they both wake up in the morning after a night of boozing and dancing in a nightclub. The following conversation, in Panic's room, as written in the published screenplay of *Mapantsula,* draws attention to their sexuality:

[Panic closes the door and jumps back to bed, moving closer to Pat]

Panic: Sithandwa vuka tu! (Sweetheart, wake up please)

Pat: Hayi, awungiyeke. (Leave me alone)

Panic: Ngiphe kayi-one tu. (Give it to me once, please)

Pat: He-e! Hayi bo! Kufanele ngiye emsebezini, manje kukhona uthi ngikuphe! (Hm! No, no. I must go to work, you are asking me to give it to you now!)

Panic: Ungabi impossible man. (Don't be impossible man)

Pat: Impossible! Ebusuku ubudakiwe la, ungayifuni kukhona uyifuna manje! (Impossible! At night you were drunk and you didn't want it, now you want it!) [She wriggles loose and looks at the alarm clock]. Hawu, Thixo! awubheke isikhathi! (Oh, God, look at the time!) [She frees herself] He Panic, asikwazi ukuba wolova sonke. (Hey, Panic, we can't all be loafers.)

[She gets out of bed and starts dressing. He lies back, disgruntled].
(MOGOTLANE AND SCHMITZ 1991, 69)

Schmitz, while highlighting the sexuality of the body, allows for a reading by which Pat upsets the patriarchal imaginary supposing a woman to be readily available for the pleasure of a man.

However, the control that Pat appears to have over her body is short-lived—she seems to jump out of Panic's bed only to land in Duma's. Could Pat not have joined the South African Domestic Workers Union (SADWU) without being romantically involved with Duma? Pat appears to move into spaces where she is physically exploited. While the Madam is only interested in the labor of her hands, Panic exploits the labor of Pat's entire body in his persistent demands for money and sex. Duma, who is supposed to help her rid herself of exploitation by both the Madam and Panic, appears to take advantage of Pat by offering his political consciousness in exchange for her love. More injuriously, given the historical reality that domestic workers in South Africa are generally women, Schmitz commits the error of giving the SADWU leadership to a man. Clearly, then, Pat's movement, despite her potential for growth politically, is limited to a love triangle that serves to build the characters of male heroes in the story, a typically Hollywood formula.

Are we therefore to conclude that female subjectivity in films directed by men is open to mistreatment? According to Ukadike (1996, 194): "Female subjectivity in Africa, as elsewhere, has often been defined by men rather than by women. Black women have fallen victim to a tendency to 'de- womanise Black womanhood'—to paraphrase the Nigerian playwright Zulu Sofola. Consequently, films made by African women and men are attempting to re-humanise portrayals of women and to reassert their identities." While Ukadike (195) acknowledges the need to give black women "access to the medium of film" so that by "taking more control of the camera and the cinematic apparatus" they can attempt to portray womanhood in a positive light, he argues that a number of black male filmmakers have also contributed to the challenge of "re-imaging" African womanhood. Ukadike recalls Sembène as among the men who have attempted to portray women positively. For instance, in *Xala* Sembène can be said to explode the myth of masculine power both in sexual terms and in relation to African nationalism. We have noted how African nationalism has been constructed around masculinity. El Hadji's lack of virility is used in the film to figure the failure of a nation led by a corrupt and decadent elitist breed. But while El Hadji's body is figured as a political spectacle, the body of Ngoni (El Hadji's third wife) is essentialized as an erotic spectacle.

Clearly, whatever potential the filmmaker shows in reviewing traditional gender relations is limited by his failure to transcend the patriarchal trap in which women are placed in sexual roles as opposed to engaging in politics. In *Xala,* politics is the province of male characters. Laura Mulvey (1990) comments on how women, portrayed as spectacles of erotic pleasure, are rendered powerless in male-directed films, which assume the power to inscribe sexual appeal on their bodies or emphasize their libidinal values while underplaying other aspects of womanhood. The camera's gaze over bodies of women becomes politically suspect. This is apparent when Ngoni is stripped naked and her buttocks fill up the movie screen in the same manner as Ntozakhe's breasts in *Fools*. After El Hadji's failure to deflower Ngoni, one of his in-laws is heard complaining, "A girl like that could arouse a dead man."

Significantly, she draws the viewer's attention to Ngoni's sexuality as opposed to other qualities she may posses as a woman or marriage partner.

Mapantsula offers a series of relationships that exist outside matrimony. The relationship between Panic and his girlfriend, Pat, is not blessed by the church or sanctioned by law through the institution of marriage. Even when Duma takes over from Panic as Pat's boyfriend, there is no potential for wedding bells ringing. The idea of a woman as wife seems to be absent here. Schmitz also depicts female-headed families like those of Ma Modise and Pat's aunt, where there is no sign of a husband. MaButhelezi's household in *Fools* provides another example of matrifocality; as a widow, she is in charge of the family. These are independent women who are portrayed as self-sufficient, but their roles are marginal compared to those of the males in the stories. Ma Modise can also be said to fit the stereotype of a woman as mother. Reference to women's bodies as vessels for childbearing or tools for procreation cannot be overemphasized. Ma Modise is the opposite of Nosipho in *Fools*, whom Zamani refers to as "bloody barren toad"—in line with the patriarchal imaginary, within which a woman is castigated for not bearing children for her husband. In *Mapantsula*, however, Ma Modise has children, but they are not for her husband. Can a deduction therefore be made that by providing a female-headed household, Schmitz is operating by a different imaginary, one beyond patriarchal impediments?

In relation to black masculinity, both in *Fools* and *Mapantsula*, women's bodies are treated with ambiguity. Both Suleman and Schmitz display pointers toward refiguring the woman's body by problematizing the gendered nature of power in black townships as both internally derived from traditional ideas about sexuality and externally occasioned by apartheid masculinity. While there are limitations in the strategies used by Suleman and Schmitz, it would be unfortunate to conclude that male-directed films are inherently disabled with regard to reviewing, progressively, the gendered body. Perhaps Schmitz's fault lies in displaying only a passing acquaintance with the gendered body while he emphasizes the black perspective in line with the contemporaneous political events he represents. The director of *Fools* narrativizes the gendered body by politicizing the rape of Mimi, and therefore summons thoughts on questions of sexuality.

The discussion of the body in *Fools* and *Mapantsula* marks a shift from the emphasis on racial politics in South African film scholarship. This, of course, not to suggest that racial politics have become insignificant. Indeed, racial politics remain the subtext here, given the consequences of the racial past. But questions of sexuality are important political questions that can no longer be trivialized. For instance, the new dispensation in South Africa, by institutionalizing women's rights in the Constitution, politicizes gender. The Constitution further recognizes that women in South Africa were previously treated differentially and therefore black women were worst hit by apartheid policies and laws. From *Fools* and *Mapantsula* we can note that the filmmakers take the initiative of demonstrating that black women are marginalized by and suffer under both white rule and the callous treatment meted out by black men themselves. If African filmmakers and scholars do indeed have a radical agenda, questions of sexuality and gender need to be addressed. The need to release black sexuality and gender portrayals from colonial, apartheid, and patriarchal imaginaries must be stressed, particularly in terms of what that means for women.

Afterword
Future Directions of South African Cinema

Haile Gerima

Zimbabwe, Round One: The Southern African Film Festival (1984)

I am in a Zimbabwean aircraft bound for Harare. Coincidentally, President Banana and his official entourage are also on the plane, occupying parts of the first- and second-class cabins. White former Rhodesians are also scattered about. One of them, a gentleman (to the extent I can identify and classify white Rhodesians), is right next to me. We are still at London's Gatwick; looking out the window, I see bags and bags of luggage being loaded on the plane under the pretext of "diplomatic pouch." Afraid of flying and of heights, I can't imagine how the plane will be able to take off with all that luggage along with all these people.

Though President Banana was subdued and dignified on the flight, lacking the usual manufactured aura of African leaders, his entourage, some in civilian clothes and others in military uniform, drank themselves to oblivion. I sat there vicariously aching for the stewardesses, who stayed on their feet all night serving all types of liquor and food and also being groped and fondled by this rowdy bunch. The returning whites simply smiled, and the one in my row talked to me all the way about his return from self-exile. He kept saying that initially he had thought blacks, as he put it, were going to massacre the whites, but as this had not happened, he wanted to return, wanted to reorganize his life and bring back his family, temporarily staying in Europe. He kept bringing up the idea that blacks could not manage the country without white people. And he was very adamant about that.

201

We finally approached the international airport in Harare. The pilot headed for landing but was suddenly made to circle the airport for a long time. Later we were told it was because the troops preparing to welcome the president were not in position. To feel the plane fly in circles at a very low altitude made my heart jump into my throat. I was relieved when we were finally allowed to land. It was early in the morning when I made it through immigration, customs, and all of the other bureaucratic stops at the airport. Two Europeans, a Frenchman and an Englishman, met me, and I remember being puzzled when they took me to the private residence of the French cultural attaché.

While I quietly waited to be taken to my hotel, I was obliged to overhear a discussion of the first motion picture that would be made in Zimbabwe about the history of the liberation struggle. The gentleman from England and my French host gave me the impression that the project was threatened by a disastrous conflict between competing forces. The disputing factions were referred to as "incompetent Zimbabweans" said to be utterly corrupt and inept. The discussion took place around me without my participation in it until they finally asked me whether I would make such a project into a film. I told the two gentlemen that I did not do films that came at me in the manner this one had been deployed. I told them that I also had my own project entitled *In the Eye of the Storm,* which I hoped to shoot in and around Mozambique and Zimbabwe. I advised them that it would be quite an error to make a film on such a vast theme and that it would be wiser to break the project down into smaller, personal film projects, the way the early Russian filmmakers (Eisenstein, Pudovkin, Dziga-Vertov, Kuleshov, and others) had addressed their social upheaval from the perspective of diverse individual filmmakers. I suggested that they look into some of the concrete examples from the Cuban film industry (Tomás Gutiérrez Alea, Julio García Espinosa, Sara Gómez, Sergio Giral, and others). I went on to relate the tragedy of Algerian cinema and its experience of failure after the making of a major big-budget film entitled *The Chronicle of the Ambers,* with the economic bankruptcy it brought about for the whole of Algerian national cinema. In no uncertain terms, I let them know that most of all I was not interested in this kind of cultural manifestation that comes about by political assignment.

After that, I was taken to my hotel where I met most of my friends, including Pedro Pimenta, who had come all the way from Mozambique to participate in a discussion on Zimbabwean cinema. Djibril Diop Mambety, from Senegal, was also present.

Two important and typically African problems arose in the midst of preparing the logistics of this conference. One was triggered by conflict between two ministries, a battle of "turfs" between the Ministry of Information and the Ministry of Culture. There was a dispute as to which one had jurisdiction over motion pictures. (I was relieved that the Ministry of Sports had not entered the fray.) In fact, because this workshop was organized by one of the ministries—the Ministry of Information, I think—the other instructed its employees not to attend. The second problem was the unresolved issue of race—namely, the privilege of whiteness, the legacy white supremacist governments in Southern Africa had left, and the divisive racial contradictions inherited by the newly formed African governments.

Besides local Zimbabwean filmmakers, there were filmmakers from the Southern African region attending the conference. Some of them were Zambians and Namibians, and there were three groups of South African filmmakers representing the Pan Africanist Congress (PAC), the African National Congress (ANC), and white independent directors who did not belong to either organization. Others were representatives from the South West Africa People's Organization (SWAPO) and the Committee for African Cineasts (CAC).

One of the contradictions that continued to manifest itself was the issue of white South African filmmakers who had been privileged enough by apartheid and white supremacy to have made most of the films screened at the workshop. None of the black South Africans had any film projects to present; their not having the economic and technical means to express their own story was the underlying cause of the conflict. Most of the films by the white South Africans were about black people. Hiding behind class-based ideological protocol, the ANC representatives were constrained not to address the issue of white privilege publicly, but members of PAC made sure this contradiction surfaced during discussion, even as they knew that this would not result in any lasting solution. I remember a South African woman painfully articulating the lack of everything, including the political freedom, to make a film about her own story. Years later, in the "new" South Africa, I was to encounter some of the individuals who had attended this conference, but I will come back to their reality later.

The Harare conference ended with a resolution to work toward strengthening all filmmakers in the Southern African region and to create the necessary communication avenues with other African filmmakers, including participation in the Festival Panafricain du Cinéma de Ouagadougou (FESPACO).

Britain, Zabalaza: The London Film Festival (1990)

In the early 1990s, just after the release of Mandela, I was invited to attend a cultural extravaganza in London that included a program on cinema entitled "The Future of South African Cinema." I was asked to address the topic. In an auditorium full of Africans, I found myself with a group of panelists who, I think, were all South Africans. Three of the four were white and the other was Lionel Ngakane—one of the oldest African filmmakers, whom I had known for quite some time; I had often seen him at FESPACO and other international film festivals profiling African cinema.

A most interesting concept thrown carelessly around at this panel discussion was so-called "nonracial cinema." When it was my turn to speak, I organized my thoughts on the future of South Africa in the following manner. First, I stated that there was no such thing as non-racial cinema, especially not in South Africa, a country founded on the notion of white supremacy. With independence, cinema would have to celebrate all races and specifically African people, whose image and story had been so brutally suppressed. I felt that in the new South Africa, film would have to dramatically dynamize culture. In fact, I went on to suggest, in order to correct the past abuse of color privilege, most of the white filmmakers would need to refrain from future film projects and take responsibility for producing and financing the filmmaking of Africans in South Africa. The whole auditorium exploded. Most of the whites lost their center of intellectual gravity. However, I went on to suggest that by virtue of their credentials and professional experience, which they had attained in the old South Africa, white South African filmmakers would continue to be in prominent positions and still be able to make films about other South Africans strictly because of their very privileged historical background.

Ngakane, who was more sobered by age and experience than I was, could express himself only according to the official ANC line, which prioritized class over racial politics. I have a personal experience to relate, one that made me realize his complexity and the implications of his years of exile in England. I do not know when exactly it was that I was fortunate enough to come to his home as a guest, along with Med Hondo, Gaston Kaboré, and Ngangura Mweze. There I witnessed the most unforgettable symbolic representation of what it means to be truly exiled. While surveying Lionel Ngakane's residence, my eye caught a very strangely shaped bottle sitting on what looked like a shelf or a mantelpiece. When I asked him what this bottle was and what it contained, he said, in a matter-of-fact way, that it was his father. His meaning did not register right away because I thought that he might be referring to a photo, but there was no photo near the bottle. When I asked him what he meant, he informed us that the bottle contained his father's ashes because he had not been allowed to return to South Africa to attend his father's funeral during the apartheid era. I think that his family had shipped this bottle containing his father's remains to console him. I do not know for sure, but I was struck and remained frozen for quite some time.

While all of them, including Ngakane, were booing and cheering the World Cup soccer match between England and Cameroon, I sat there transfixed, starring at the bottle containing the remains of his father. I shifted through a number of emotions. This story was full of the conundrums of African history. The bottle and Lionel Ngakane could be subjects for cinema. A documentary might be suitable because the bottle symbolically represented a society that had tragically inherited a divisive time—a time for a rite of passage. If I could follow Ngakane on camera on his return with the remains to a free South Africa, it would be a film of healing for those capable of transcending false and shortsighted political coexistence. A film idea crossed my mind, but I was automatically discouraged by the reality of the absence of resources. Like so many other stories about our ancestors and us, this one would also be lost—never to be shared with future generations.

To go back to the London conference, there was a special group of young South African aspiring filmmakers who had been brought to England for a brief orientation. I joined them in several workshops and befriended most of them—to name a few: Morbane Modise, Masepeke Sekhukhuni, Mickey Madoda Dube, Seipati Bulame-Hopa, and Bridget Thompson. I earned their friendship through candid discussion of cultural politics. Most of them, irrespective of race, belonged to different ideological camps. They were all genuinely full of passion about the future of South Africa.

Zimbabwe, Round Two: The Harare Film Festival (1987)

I had to return to Zimbabwe for another round on the issue of cinema and Africa. I had met a white filmmaker on my first trip to Zimbabwe who had modestly told me that he was not a filmmaker, he had just done some video work for the Ministry of Agriculture. What I remember most about this gentleman is the fact that he was very humble, all the way to his physical demeanor. When I returned years later, he had positioned himself as the kingmaker of Zimbabwean cinema. At one point in the conference, he headed a panel and challenged all of the African filmmakers present on the parameters of African cinema. Sitting in the audience were Med Hondo, Gaston Kaboré, and Souleymane Cissé. To this day, this gentleman continues to harass most Zimbabwean filmmakers. They fear him because his privileged status grants him the power to offer filming and financing opportunities to those with an affinity to whiteness.

Indirectly, this case has implications for South African filmmakers. Many of the young aspiring South African filmmakers who came to Harare were divided into political factions. When I was in discussion with one of the groups, the other three or four groups would not come near us. A few days into the film festival, I got tired of all these political divisions and invited all of them for a private discussion in which I would mediate among them. I brought Gaston Kaboré with me. Thanks to the respectful relationship I had been able to develop with each group, most were able to attend the session. I was nervous, as there was high tension between the different groups, to such a point that they did not even look one another in the eye.

My talk to them went along these lines. First I underlined, in no uncertain terms, the freedom of individuals to associate and be part of any political organization. I further emphasized that to be politically aware and active and to be abreast of all kinds of politics was critical for all filmmakers. I also mentioned that the most positive aspect of young groups of filmmakers coming out of South Africa was not the politics they adhered to but their contribution to the rhetoric of cinema and culture. They were the necessary dynamo to energize the future of the dwindling intercontinental African cinema. As far as filmmaking was concerned, I informed them, they all belonged to one group or entity. By virtue of their common interest in cinema, they could and should struggle together, bonded by a common destiny: On the crucial issue of resources—be it funding or the very technology of camera and lights—they were one and the same. I told them they had to harness their collective energy in order to forge a new system of production: that is what they needed to show us, the rest of the African filmmakers.

I told them of my way of thinking, a thinking that comes out of my student days at UCLA. I too was ravaged by the political division of my generation, which often diverted me toward a temporary political agenda. Politics is often a short-term objective, but culture, on the other hand, has a wider umbrella. If we put our cinema at the service of culture, where each one of us empowers our stories, then, however insignificant they may appear to be, in the vast field of culture they will matter. "You have the common benefit of all the individual stories that each one of you tells," I explained. "I am not giving you a prescription," I said, "but for me, politics is, after all, too narrow to contain the imagination of the film artist." Our cinema should transcend politics. The story of our grandmothers and our grandfathers demystifies false politics; politics must be subjected to the microscopic judgment of culture. We cannot make politically tribalized films to serve the objectives of political parties. They do not need films. Politicians can use leaflets, banners, and billboards. Cinema is too expensive. It should encode the wrinkles of our grandmothers and grandfathers, the memories of our childhood, the millions of untold stories that are the root cause of our destabilized existence.

I talked for hours along these lines, at times repeating myself, drowning in the widening gap of their division. I told them that I had brought Gaston Kaboré, the general secretary of the African Filmmakers Federation, because I wanted them to be connected to a larger entity of impoverished filmmakers—for they needed a perspective on the experience of African filmmakers who had been active for the past thirty years. Kaboré, once more, reinforced the importance of unity among filmmakers. With positions still hardened, our meeting ended.

Zimbabwe, Round Three: The Southern African Film Festival (1998)

On my third visit to Zimbabwe, Zimbabwean cinema was still under siege by unspoken racial conflict. Except for some individual independent filmmakers, most of them acted like bodyguards or Man Fridays for the very few white filmmakers who made films about everything but their own personal stories. The first film dealing thematically with the liberation struggle of Zimbabweans was, in neocolonial fashion, made by a white filmmaker. The film project I mentioned earlier, which had been conceived by the newly independent intelligentsia of Zimbabwe, was all but forgotten. In fact, Zimbabwean filmmakers had failed to bring about a clearly coherent national policy on cinema. I did not even know to which ministry cinema belonged or was attached. Any Zimbabwean feature, even if the director wanted to make a film about his or her mother or father or grandfather, had to include in its script a theme relating to development, ecology, or environmental concerns. The young filmmakers I had met in the early 1980s were no longer wide-eyed excited young artists. They all walked around diplomatic film-functions, hustling more as politicians than as filmmakers. Their gossip about each other was unbearable and counterproductive and created a deadly environment for cinema. Most of the white filmmakers were well connected with development agencies and European funding and institutions. In fact, often they were a necessary point of reference to vouch for the credibility of the black filmmakers. The humble position whites had projected immediately after independence was no longer there. Not only were whites content with their privileged position, they accused the black intelligentsia of reverse racism.

During this visit, the festival was marred by a divisive climate. In fact, under the leadership of some of the white film aficionados of Zimbabwe, an international festival had been organized to undermine the Southern African Film Festival, which had been struggling to survive for quite some time. In this climate of political intrigue, the most constructive aspect of the festival for me was to come across my young aspiring filmmaker friends from the Newtown Film and Television School. I spent my time with them for many different reasons. At that stage, they had already become embroiled in the divisive nature of Southern African cinema. In my trips to South Africa, I have spent many hours with these young people in their film school. The survival of this school, constantly faced with hostility and debasement, continues to inch along under the leadership of Masepeke Sekhukhuni—a very determined sister who has decided to devote her time, so far, to the school. The students hail from many African countries. I will return to them after a detour to narrate my experiences in South Africa and my Rashomon impressions of the contradictions inherent to what is to be the new South African cinema.

South Africa, Round One: The Weekly Mail Film Festival (1993)

During apartheid, I had consistently refused to participate in the many film festivals organized in South Africa. In the early days of the new, "free" South Africa I quickly accepted an invitation to attend the Weekly Mail Film Festival in Johannesburg. This was an important occasion for me, if only to demystify my overall fixation with the new South Africa. At the festival I was slated to premier *Sankofa*. Without going into detail about my impressions of the country, I quickly surmised there were some unresolved contradictions—a fact common to newly independent African countries. Some of the events that struck me as significant follow.

Predominantly, the attendees of the Weekly Mail Film Festival were white and very mobile. Talking to them, I realized many could have caught my film at the London Film Festival or, for that matter, in Paris or Berlin. To fulfill an arrangement I had made with the festival organizers at the University of Cape Town, I flew to the "Mother City." Throughout my brief stay there, I was totally alienated by a crowd of pretentious intellectuals who came to the verge of intellectual paroxysm as they shuttled and surfaced on the ocean of "world film awareness." I was more interested in being in the midst of the so-called "nonracial South Africa," a South Africa that would bring together all of the different nationalities and, most specifically, Africans with whom I had an important, direct common cultural interest. The initial dinner in some nice white person's home in my honor was not attended by a single nonwhite person. Whether individuals were good or bad, genuine or not, no attempt to engage me by way of benign chats could make it easier for me to survive the occasion. Once being there became an overbearing reality, I quickly resorted to the classic African American technique of the double personality. That enabled me to cope with a state of contradiction.

The evening *Sankofa* was projected, the theater was full of—again—white people, except for one person who to me was black, but who might have preferred to be called colored. The black Africans who were supposed to be imported from some reservation did not show up. I do not understand what happened. During the question-and-answer session following an almost private showing to psychologically besieged white South Africans, someone who was either the belligerent Boer type or keenly aware of the contradiction asked me in a challenging tone what I had felt showing *Sankofa* to an all-white audience. I told him to ask the organizers or himself. That night I reflected once more about the privilege and continued power of white people who literally had brought me to South Africa to test African film expression. I asked myself whether these ideologically sound white individuals did not have a black African friend, an East Indian African friend, a colored African friend or, for that matter, a neighbor that could have come along to share my offerings, which they turned into their own offerings.

The next day, I was at the University of Cape Town participating in a panel discussion on African cinema. Again, the majority of the participants representing nonracial South Africa and multiculturalism belonged to the white race. I concluded that for this group, African cinema was a form of exotic intellectual entertainment. There was something disingenuous in how they talked about African cinema. Most of them sounded like explorers and discoverers, photographers, anthropologists, and missionaries. They were totally unaware of the inherent political and activist nature of African cinema, an African cinema that wants to express itself through the stories of censored ancestors. And in order to do that, the aesthetics of African cinema and the required linguistic visual grammar have to emerge out of the transaction of traditional and repressed stories.

When I finally returned to Johannesburg, Teddy Mattera, a very disillusioned aspiring black filmmaker whom I was introduced to by my white sponsors, took me to a radio interview. On our way to the interview his car radio was on, and I heard the radio host making a very distressed appeal: "We have to stop the killing. I want to hear from white callers! Please, you white people out there, call us and be part of the discussion! We black people are killing each other! You can help us stop the killings!" A white woman called in to answer his plea; in an Afrikaner accent, she said, "We white people have been trying to tell you that you are going to take South Africa down, like the rest of those African countries! You black people are not fit to rule! You will not stop with killing each other only; you are going to destroy this country! We tried to tell you and tell you, you black people cannot make South Africa a better country!" I looked at Teddy in total shock, expecting some kind of explanation. Instead, he told me that this was the station where I was going be interviewed.

After entering what looked like a fortress, I was led into the studio, where the African host I had heard on the car radio was sitting. As soon as I sat down next to the microphone, his first concern was to address the idea of forgiveness. I knew all along that I had come to speak about *Sankofa* and African cinema in general. For a second I thought he had mistaken me for a clergyman. So I quickly said to him that I was the filmmaker, to which he hastily responded, "I know that you are the filmmaker, and we will get to filmmaking and your own work. However, in the new South Africa we have a good opportunity to forgive and forget for the well-being of our country. And our people need to hear your views, especially about forgiving." At this point I was totally derailed, and I did not know how to recover. While I understood the political implications of his question from a cultural point of view, I found it fraudulent. To go on and extrapolate my idea would have confused and not helped matters. I staggered my way through the issue of forgiveness because I could not imagine anyone incapable of forgiving. If I recollect correctly, I spoke of the importance of history, and of letting go of the past, and of always upholding the humane way in resolving contradictions. I do not know if he ever got back to asking me about filmmaking before the interview ended.

The radio interview reminded me that the majority of the powerful institutions of mass media rest in the hands of the white race, which implicitly demonstrates who still controls the economic power structure of South Africa. If anyone is intimidated, it is the nonwhite intelligentsia. The power structure, in terms of economics as well as the ownership of information, remains in the control of white people—and their riches stretch from Europe to America to Australia. Every incident that takes place in South Africa is processed and midwifed by the white intelligentsia. It is to them that the greater metropolitan centers call for the clarification of the political reality of South Africa.

Hand in hand with the film festival a book fair was taking place. Pedro Pimenta, a friend from Mozambique who happened to be in Cape Town, invited me to one of the bars near the fair. There was a young white man, Jeremy, who was introduced to me as one of the South African filmmakers. At one point in the evening a black South African I knew from the United States approached and welcomed me to his country. I soon noticed that he was very uncomfortable. When I asked him whether he was all right, I realized that such a question was all he needed for the floodgate of rage at the new South Africa to break open. He told me: "Even the first documentary film, on the ANC, was commissioned to a very young white kid at a budget of half a million rands." As he vented his frustration, I tried to comfort him by reminding him about the good work in mass media he had done while he was in the United States, telling him that it was something to be proud of and that he should not let the new conditions destroy him. Later that night I discovered that the young white man named Jeremy was the target of my friend's hostility.

One of the most positive experiences I had in South Africa was spending time at the Newtown Film and Television School, where a group of black and white people were running a very serious film school geared at underprivileged South Africans and students from the Southern African region. My encounter with the school and the discussions I had with the students were profoundly enriching.

South Africa, Round Two: The SABC and the Newtown Film and Television School (1996)

When I returned to South Africa it was for a fund-raising workshop organized by the South African Broadcasting Company (SABC) and

211

the Newtown Film and Television School. After a screening of *Sankofa,* the funds would be directed to the Newtown School to help generate income for future training projects sponsored by the SABC. The workshop at the Newtown Film and Television School, an extended one, dealt primarily with the state of African cinema, and I felt my contribution there was satisfactory. The workshop at the SABC was about the nuts and bolts of film directing. Limited to just one day, it should actually have been allocated at least two weeks; a lot of information had to be compressed. Nevertheless, I tried to establish a fruitful relationship with the attendees.

South Africa has a very rich tradition of stage techniques for acting and directing. The transition from this to film is going to be a challenge for any serious filmmaker; those who want to make the transition will need to recognize the points of mutation. In other words, theater acting and directing constitute a primordial trust fund for any South African who wants to leap toward the cinematic medium. But at a certain point in the transition, all those techniques will need to be converted into a new state of existence; filmmakers will have to subjugate those theatrical skills to the cinematic medium. While television, by nature, can accommodate this rich drama tradition by simply recording it, cinema requires the breakdown of a given narrative, moment by moment, by implementing parts that make it a narrative whole when the master concepts of a visual entity are clearly constructed. To unleash this process is in itself a protracted engagement. I think most filmmakers continue to struggle to master film narrative.

A few of my South African filmmaker friends took me out for tea one afternoon. One of them, Mandla Langa, I had met as far back as at the first Southern African gathering in Harare in 1984. He was one of the ANC representatives at that meeting. Now he is one of the most widely published poets in the country. Present were also some of the young filmmakers, theoreticians, and historians who adhered to the principles of the Newtown Film and Television School: Masepeke Sekhukhuni, Morbane Modise and Mickey Madoda Dube. All of them had attended film schools in the United Kingdom and the United States and were full of dreams, and like many other filmmakers, myself included, they fantasized that some day their version of the story would appear on the motion picture screen. Outside of our fantasy there was nothing tangible except that we all had plans for an experience that would transcend the devastating realities of our countries. The day we met for tea South Africa was being represented at the Cannes Film Festival. We learned from the CNN news that, ironically, a majority of those at Cannes, if not all, were white South Africans. There they were, benefiting from a nonracial South Africa. For me, the news confirmed what I had witnessed in Zimbabwe years earlier.

South Africa, Round Three: Robben Island and the South African Film Market (1997)

I returned to South Africa for a third time. Caroline Carwe Maseko, a white South African I had first met at the Newtown Film and Television School and later saw again at the workshop I gave on film at the SABC, had extended an invitation to me to attend a workshop on Robben Island. She was a radical individual who deep down recognized the explosive nature of race in the new South Africa. She had heard me talk mercilessly, straight up, on the issue of white supremacy, on the subliminal power of the culture of whiteness, which was the most unpopular topic of discussion not only in South Africa but also in Europe and, most importantly, in the United States. Unfortunately, it seemed that in South Africa they had chosen to deal with the issue of race in the superficial manner of the United States, Europe, and Australia—that is, a tradition in accordance with the white settler psyche. After hearing my views, my access to people was curtailed. Some even went so far as to block from me meaningful endowment that would help my work. But Caroline Maseko—out of what I call an honest relationship—wanted my views presented at the workshop she had organized for the SABC at Robben Island. The idea of a film workshop on Robben Island blew my mind and I accepted immediately. I cancelled everything, even lucrative honoraria in the United States. Mickey Madoda Dube, an independent filmmaker who had graduated from the University of Southern California, was also going to be present.

After a night in Cape Town, I boarded the boat to Robben Island. Sailing toward Robben Island, I was suddenly stricken by a deeply embattled sense of terror. For me, as for many others the world over, this island represented, literally, the brutalization and confinement of all our sentiments of freedom. From the time we first heard the names of Winnie and Nelson Mandela, the island hovered on the outskirts of our consciousness. I mention Winnie Mandela because it was she who first showed me the island where the father of her children had been confined. It seemed that the idea of peaceful resolution was held hostage on the infamous Robben Island.

We stayed there for two weeks. We were dispersed around the island, sleeping and living in and around the ghosts of the place. You

213

cannot avoid the stench of history there. Once you are on the island, away from your physical everyday reality, the place makes you dream an already conjured image of untold historical drama. Morning and evening, like everyone else, I walked around. The island's spiritual custodians, whose stories have never been told, would constantly whisper those stories, especially when they found you alone. Even the animals—the deer, the penguins, and the pigeons—seemed endowed with the individual striking personalities of a human spirit. One minute you would see them and the next moment they would disappear, so elusive were they. And they all told stories. Every squeak of a rusted door is almost a human call there. The wind was impermanent, but when it wanted to make its presence felt, its sound waves could be decoded into a narrative of waiting souls exiled to the island, uttering the mourning of many nationalities. Every turn, every corner there, is a place waiting for a camera angle to take in any story ripe enough to be visually translated.

In the workshop made up of ten aspiring individuals, eight, on the basis of my own consciousness, I will call black. Without wanting to deal with the daily exchange rate of the constructs of race, two participants were white and, to be politically correct, one was of English and the other of Dutch ancestry. They all came to the island with assets and deficits. And there, suddenly, the history of South Africa was sitting in front of me, magnified in the faces of those ten people.

Eighty percent of the workshop members were undereducated, if we are to judge by the script they wrote in English. Our main goal was to cultivate storytellers, and so the first step was to demystify writing one's story in English. I went on to address the issue of caution when one translates local stories that are born in our minds into a language that does not have corresponding expressions to accommodate particular metaphors and symbolisms. Such translation, I stressed, would lead them to inflect their story with the judgment of conventional standards, which were basically Eurocentric. So a great deal of time was used to tell the story without validating the standards that came with packaged formulas. In this process we isolated individuals on the merit of their particular stories, after hearing their well-written scripts—"well-written" not in terms of the screenplay per se, but because the imperfect English sounded empowered, and that encouraged those class members who did not have a full command of the language. That is why it was important to concentrate on these people and on the narrative of their history, to accentuate the aesthetics of these nuances. In fact, more and more, we found that the ones who had complete command of the language were already intoxicated with the formulas of Hollywood cinema. Their stories, without their knowing, had fallen into the experience of narrative rape. They too needed a different process of narrative development from the formula.

Once we succeeded in redirecting them from the formalities of the standard, they became challenged. When the standard was reigning over the workshop it arrested the participants' development, so concepts to counter it were thrown around. Only then could they see how one becomes incarcerated by the formula in standardized political commitments in storytelling. Political commitments, when superimposed at the expense of the story, become equally disfigured. Some individuals at the workshop needed to be dislodged from these superficial, wrongly placed political situations. I lectured on the importance of a world outlook as a governing umbrella, daily evolving in and around our consciousness. In the creative process, we should keep this world outlook in its geographical location with the confidence that when we tell our story in an effective way, we can tell a nondidactic story capable of transcending our so-called political position.

The story has to be trusted and left to wander in our consciousness until it acquires a ritual dimension. I went on to elucidate that through the screenplay writing process a given storyteller may, by the time he or she finishes the script, no longer believe in the political position held in the first draft. My initial work was to first empower the storytellers and then have them write their story. Once they had tested the pleasure of that experience, I would, in fact, no longer be needed. I have always hoped to teach students so that in the process I become obsolete. Once the storyteller is empowered, there is no need for teachers. After empowering their story, we then went into the physical aspect of the creative process of directing. All I know now is that within ten to fifteen days we were able to see the unique accent or voice of the different storytellers. They imperfectly succeeded in telling their story through their own aesthetics.

One aspect of the workshop involved professionals coming from the mainland as supporting teachers. This approach worked effectively and I give credit to Caroline Maseko for it. When the workshop was over, each participant in his or her own individual way, empowered and trusting, looked as if he or she mattered, as if each story mattered. If South Africa is going to be healed, it is the right of all to tell their stories. When storytellers are terrorized and not allowed to tell their stories, what remains in their mind is a wish for social and political calamity. When storytellers are free and audacious, noncompromising, they have the ability to heal their communities and societies. It is at this early stage of introduction to the art of filmmaking that we need to be very cautious not to preempt the filmmakers' ability as storytellers in their own cultural context.

In conjunction with my obligation on Robben Island, I was to appear at the South African Film Market that took place at the end of the workshop. I could not say until the last minute how I was to participate, though I knew that as part of the market component there would be an organized funding possibility for independent filmmakers, so before reaching Robben Island I had sent proposals to seek funding for future projects. Most of the people at the Robben Island workshop also attended the Film Market. The day I arrived I was treated at one of the best restaurants in Cape Town. Food in the Cape always reminds me of what a good life the whites have created for themselves. Then I was taken to the main office of the Film Market, which was staffed by whites—with a few token blacks. I say "token" because in a liberal postcolonial arrangement one will seldom see individuals who represent the historical experience of otherwise excluded people.

The visual logo of the South African Film Market merits some comment. The first year the Film Market took place, the image the organizers came up with as the new nonracial South African cinematic logo were the faces of Greta Garbo and Marlene Dietrich. This logo was protested and they have finally come up with the image of an African woman—perhaps an improvement, but hardly a challenge to the established aesthetics. As I walked through the corridors of the Film Market heading toward the office that was going to deploy me, I saw one filmmaker's interpretation of nonracial South Africa imprinted on a film poster. On the advertisement, there was a large picture of a white man in bed with a black woman on his left and a white woman on his right. Holding these two Barbie dolls, his chest bulging, the man triumphantly shows us his ultimate trophy.

When I finally got to the office, a woman asked me to be a panelist, so I automatically assumed I would be involved in a film discussion and asked her what the topic would be. She said that she wanted me to sit in a room where South African filmmakers would be coming to pitch their stories to me. I informed her that I was looking forward to pitching my story as well. Then I asked her what I, a struggling filmmaker myself, could give these filmmakers. "You can comment on their pitching ability and suggest how to improve it." I knew something was wrong—and I am good at detecting that. So I declined the invitation. I told her I would prefer her to give this responsibility to real producers. That night the Film Market's opening took place in an auditorium that belonged to some unseen capitalists. I cannot even begin to describe the banquet; all I can say is that the cost of the food alone could have produced seven African films. Speeches were made and James Dean reigned all over the TV monitors.

By day two of the Film Market, the students from Newtown Film and Television School had arrived. When I looked at them their eyes disarmed my warrior mentality and made me finally relax. Otherwise, I perceived the whole environment of the market as hostile and racist. Every symbol, every corridor, every poster attacked the integrity of being an African. Images of old capitalists insisting on culture remaining the way it was still abounded. Africa's presence was literally nonexistent. So the Newtown Film students, in a makeshift restaurant hallway, would surround me for hours talking about the politics of African cinema, the aesthetics of African cinema, from film language to the struggle of expedition. I felt totally useful only then, despite the conscious or unconscious attacks the film culture around us represented.

One of the added features of the Film Market was a series of authoritarian lectures delivered by a group of British filmmakers, sponsored by the British Film Institute (BFI), an institute that has already closed down its London African section. The auditorium was full of white people except for maybe seven blacks, two of them from Zimbabwe. Though personally I did not know who these British filmmakers were, having had experience of the British and American film markets over the last twenty years, I was interested in hearing what they had to say. I asked myself, "Why have they been allowed here? Isn't British cinema dead? Do a few grunts here and there, if you will, testify to a culture that Hollywood has destroyed?" With an air of arrogance, the British offered fabricated, unrealistic, untested film formulas. Was this the new "nonracial South African cinema" reaching out to the mother country, England? In fact, I heard they had already had a session on white Australian settler cinema. "Something funny going on here," I thought to myself. Isn't South Africa in Africa? Aren't they supposed to make reference to and know the struggle of South African cinema for the last thirty years? Although I knew that it would not amount to anything substantial, a film market in an African country with the filmmakers of old mother colonialism, what were we to surmise from this challenging contradiction?

I finally couldn't take it any more, especially the arrogance of a British facilitator and their mystification of the status of "British Cinema." White British filmmakers at present, by and large, make films that I classify as application forms—unabashedly directed toward catching

217

the attention of Hollywood recruiting agents for possible integration into that film industry's monopoly. In the hallway a few people stopped and asked me what I thought of the panel. I only told them what James Baldwin once said on television to a very arrogant Anglo-Saxon woman: "My dear lady, it used to be said that the sun never set on the British Empire! And, my dear lady, now the sun couldn't even find the British Empire."

As each day went by, black South African filmmakers were getting more enraged. For therapy, we would sit around the coffee shop to discuss what was taking place. Some of them were very insulted, especially those filmmakers who had believed in the Film Market and submitted their developing projects to these staged, brutal pitching sessions, to people who were impersonating European producers. Later we heard that these producers were vacationing. After all, who in their right mind would reject free food and housing in Cape Town, with the world's most exquisite restaurants? Each day the liberal bell of torment against African filmmakers continued to ravish and brutalize us.

One day we went to check out one of the films that were prominently presented at the Film Market. The premise of the film was that there were white South Africans who knew South Africa better than native Africans. This contrived story was created with a very superficial end. There is a young black woman living in the United States. She comes to South Africa and her African culture welcomes her with its outdated proposition of forced marriage. The young Zulu who wants to marry her is presented as a cultural cross-dresser. Temperamental, emotional, and unintelligent, his clan is still primitive. Against the advice of her grandmother, the black woman heads for Mozambique to look for some father lost during the liberation struggle.

As we sat there, the scenario and political message coming out of this kind of white cinema was too much to take. From the minute the film started, some of us wanted to leave; we had seen these Hollywood-concocted movies too many times. But one of our colleagues suggested that we stay for a while and give the film a chance.

On a Land Rover is a New Age white man, a single father who wakes up dancing African. He is so African, he even jazzes up the local dance of the natives by giving it a touch of Buddhism. So this manipulative orphan of a narrative brings the young black woman and this white man together. We are asked to believe that this white man, unlike the African man, is tender and respectful. He asks the African woman the meaning of her name, "Thandi," and the fact that she does not know gives the contrived scenario an opportunity to show a white man being the conduit to our own names.

When he told her the meaning of her name, I knew that it was that old Eurocentric game of the missionaries, who made as if they knew us better than we knew ourselves. So I got up and walked out with the people I had come with. As we were walking, a professor from West Africa stopped in his tracks and said to me: "Haile, we can't leave like this. We have to go back and scream at the screen, at this whole bullshit going on in there." I was totally dumbfounded. This was the most sensitive, the most intellectual person in our group. It was very important for me to feel that I was not the only one enraged. This society's ability to deform our daily existence was not reconcilable and showed the brutal nature of racism. I was so amused that I said to him, "Hell, why scream? Let's go back and throw a bomb." We refrained from acting on our instincts and, in a form of group therapy, escaped into the night streets of Cape Town, laughing.

Two or three days before the end of the Film Market, some fellow Africans asked me to speak to a group of alienated South African filmmakers on the state of African cinema. This group comprised all the colors that apartheid had kept divided. They organized a meeting place away from the Film Market. On the day of my talk, I looked out and saw what spiritual people call the children of God, the true inheritors of the earth. Before I even opened my mouth, I surveyed the eyes staring piercingly at me, eyes that belonged to two hundred individuals. To me they were all African people: the descendants of enslaved Indonesians, Indians, coloreds, and Africans. For some reason their spiritual strength transmitted a kind of force that energized me. From the moment I opened my mouth to the time I finished, I was in a trance. The conflict I was experiencing, the conflict of the insensitiveness of the culture of whiteness, of white supremacy, necessitated this underground meeting.

I began my speech by telling them I felt I was meeting enslaved and alienated individuals in a barn somewhere in the southern part of the United States. I told them that they wanted to meet me because they felt excluded and were angry, and they had a story that they wanted to tell. It was a story that belonged to their ancestors, and it was not being told at the Film Market. When the official power brokers of the "new" South African cinema gathered in Cape Town to organize the event, they did not have Africans in mind. I also told them that our meeting was underground, and that they thus had to synthesize a revolutionary narrative and certainly, at this time, one that had the capacity to heal even the nature of the transgressor. But they had to be prepared to be transmitters of stories, the many untold censored realities of their stories. To truly empower an African film event, they would have to relink back to the thirty-year struggle of African cinema. They would have to participate in workshops and study world cinema, especially early Cuban cinema, Latin American cinema, Asian cinema. And in the end, they must assert their own identity.

I told them not to allow the gathering of the settler white people to make them feel immaterial and nonexistent. We talked about their task in forging the identity of a new South African cinema. And I blasted the propagandist advocates of nonracial cinema. In fact, the new South African cinema is going to be racial cinema, the cinema of every color, without a false imitation of narrative structure. There has always been a South African cinema, all the way to apartheid form and content and grammar, and it was always based on whiteness. Cinema's world history is in thrall to a Eurocentric interpretative idea. Now, are there going to be filmmakers who empower the mothers, fathers, grandfathers, sisters, and brothers transplanted into the wagons of particular aesthetic identities? They would have to be the owners of their stories.

The way the South African settlers had invited the British, Australian, and American filmmakers, they should organize and invite African and African American filmmakers and learn from one another's experiences. Cinema is a powerful weapon when wisely used, I reminded them. But we have to always be students of our narrative film grammar. Do not stop studying film. Don't be diverted by false ivory-tower theoreticians. You are to set the standards, the precedent for other filmmakers in Africa. You, South African filmmakers, have a better climate for production—organize and snatch from the mouth of the crocodile now! Don't wait to fulfill the prerequisites and requirements set by white supremacists on what a film is and how to make and exhibit it. Organize in groups and lobby, invent cinematic institutions in the image and logic of your psyche. You have a resourceful country that can set the example for a productive African cinema structure. But don't be arrogant toward other African nations because you belong to a rich country called South Africa. Factor into your image of South Africa all the children of Africa who fought in your behalf. I don't see them at the dinner table of the new South Africa. I have heard some superficial, lightweight South African filmmakers, who are filmmakers merely by walking the walk and talking the talk, speak badly (without any foundation) about other African filmmakers. You have much to learn from Burkina Faso, which is the poorest country on the African continent.

Their cinematic achievements stand for all of us. Learn the thirty-year struggle of African cinema. Force your government to examine the idea of a national policy on cinema. From Mozambique to Angola all the way to Senegal and South Africa, the footprints of the unfulfilled vision of South African filmmakers need to be resurrected and brought to you, future filmmakers of Africa.

Film is a collaborative process, so hold hands and rise up together. Don't repeat past mistakes; you are entitled to make only new mistakes, and this is something that applies to film language and production institutions and distribution superstructures. Learn from our mistakes and empower your cinematic accent if you want to dynamize the South African psyche. Do not imitate, be innovative; to imitate says, "I was never born." Our cinema has to be reborn, so let's not waste our time. Spare us the "We Africans don't know how to do it." Fight to experiment with your language. We are entitled to make an imperfect cinema, as the Cuban filmmaker García Espinosa wrote a few decades back. All through the hundred years of cinema its practice, everywhere, has always been imperfect. Eurocentric historical cinema fabricates the notion that cinema is perfect by creating a category of film classics. I do not know any film that is not flawed. The best and historically most significant films are all imperfect—because they pushed the boundary of static and arrested cultural establishment. And when filmmakers try to transform it, the medium of expression will automatically manifest imperfection. Don't be hoodwinked out of your opportunity to be an imperfect filmmaker. And in the end, in spite of the brutal circumstances of being excluded always, have your stories based unconditionally on a human face. The day you fail to do that, you will begin to serve fascism, and you will become a mercenary, an exploiter of people; you will be part of the cultural brigades of capitalism. In the years of your retirement, before they close the casket on your face, you do not want to be ravaged by the brutal wrinkles of regrettable acts you committed against other people, even in the form of emotional exploitation.

All this I told them at that underground gathering—a symbolic space illustrating conditions in the new, nonracial South Africa.

The next day the brother who had organized the meeting, Sharif Cullis, I, and a third person were sitting in a coffee shop in the middle of the Film Market. An individual whom I prefer to call the official window dresser of the market (and who speaks with an accent that cross-dresses between English and Afrikaans) approached us. He asked whether I could go somewhere and talk to him, and I said, "About what?" and he replied: "About what happened last night." So I said to him I was not the one who had organized it, that the person he wanted to speak to was in front of me. Sharif Cullis anxiously told him that I was right. The two went aside and came back. Upon returning, Cullis told us that an article had appeared in a film trade newspaper in New York written by someone who had sneaked into the meeting and heard my talk. In the process of writing the article, the pressman had posed some questions to the Film Market organizers and they were offended.

At this point Bridget Thompson, a white South African filmmaker, came and joined our discussion. She commented on how excited people were about my speech, so I asked her why she had not come herself, to which she replied she had not been allowed to attend. I asked her who had told her that and she said, "The people who organized the meeting," and pointed at Cullis. I asked Cullis whether that was true, and he said he hadn't wanted white people there. I told him I do not speak, under any circumstance, where anyone is excluded—whatever the reason. I told him that was not the kind of world I was struggling to bring about. As long as people can appreciate my perspective on world reality, race is a nonissue.

That same afternoon I sat with a brother and a sister who had lived in the United States. With all of their illusion and anticipation, the new reality of South Africa had disappointed them. We met to discuss a script they were writing. The brother actually turned and pointed his finger at whites, Indians, and coloreds and declared, in a frightening tone, that he felt there was no solution for South Africa but to kill all of them. And the sister enthusiastically echoed everything he said. I looked at them and was saddened because I had known the brother in Atlanta, when he was a bright-eyed, passionate, hungry, aspiring filmmaker who could not wait to get back to South Africa. After listening to him and seeing his friend nodding, I saw the whole futile nature of his script. Why films, then? Why give me a script? Why not raise money for guns and bombs?

Right then I knew this was the grotesque manifestation of a person without a validated story; only someone like that could entertain those violent ideas. When he paused for a second, I asked, "Why make films, then?" I went on to tell him that art is not for killing and I quoted him something from Fanon. I asked him to be compassionate with the idea of telling a story. But to me, killing is out of the question. I wouldn't want anyone to think that that is the only manifestation of human expression. Lately I have found out that the struggle to free myself oppresses the oppressors. And if my freedom is to come by means of oppressing other people, I want none of it. We can fight firmly to free ourselves without becoming fascists. And it's with a human face that I want this to happen.

But as I looked at the confused eyes of my friends, we were interrupted by the Film Market's Mafia boss, who apparently had been bothered by my comments at the underground meeting. Under his cowboy hat, his hair was tied in a long ponytail. He sat across from the table and said something to the effect of "What a Kodak moment!" Then, with his hand in the shape of an eyepiece, he framed us. He had probably come across the young filmmakers somewhere in South Africa, though he didn't know me personally. I understood then that his reaction was the by-product of a threatened institution, of his fear about the transformations about to affect South African cinema.

During the Film Market, Caroline Maseko from the SABC organized a screening event for the workshop members from Robben Island. All of them came, as well as a number of invited guests, including international observers. I cannot begin to describe the excitement of these young storytellers waiting to debut their films, their firstborns. At the end of the screening they stood in front of the audience and participated in a discussion that offered validation of their particular stories through contact with an enthusiastic crowd whose members identified their own untold stories in those movies. In the exchange between the audience and the filmmakers, every comment echoed the voice of an empowered people vicariously living through filmmakers who looked like them. To this day, when I think of that moment, I get emotional. A most constructive tension presided over the interaction of the two groups; the exchange was something dramatic on the emotional as well as the intellectual level. I remember how I fought to keep my tears back.

When I was asked to give some comments, I said only that I was grateful to the organizers for introducing me to these young people. I added that all of them had stories to tell, stories that were initially hostage to the formula, and if I'd ever done anything honorable, it was to totally confuse them, which I did purposefully. Once I confused them, the demystification process was set in motion and their particular and independent stories crawled out of their own imagination, imperfectly transported by their own cultural accent. It was a privilege I had enjoyed.

Often, the commercial industry that manufactures our culture has over the years succeeded in traumatizing us, provoking uniform responses to all kinds of human relationships. All of us have been conditioned to love and smile and cry embodying fabricated nods and gestures, and in the process we are people whose response is a captivated response, in the process our emotional feelings have been disempowered and desensitized. But to see these young people creating films that cause original responses from their communities, to see the audience collectivizing and claiming the story as theirs, was a rewarding experience. To this day the emotions I saw radiating out of those young filmmakers remain a pleasantly framed image for me. I can say in no certain terms that this was the most hopeful aspect of cinema culture unfolding in the new South Africa.

A sister who is black (but colored by apartheid classifications) was apparently moved by my presentation and sat across the table to talk to me. Later, from the books she gave me, I found out that she was an outstanding poet. Her voice haunts me today, a voice reminiscent of Billie Holiday's later mournful songs. It didn't sound like it was coming out of a young woman, a single mother. "Apartheid raped and enslaved our ancestors and built fences dividing all of us," she explained. "All you see is a programmed reality of transplanted hate and self-hatred. The fences they built around us, dividing all of us, are well cemented and large. It's hard to cross over without inviting some kind of violence against oneself. The colored wants to kill the African, the Indian wants to kill the colored, and the African wants to kill everyone. And the whites are watching on the sidelines. And those who reject this insane proposition scream across the wilderness of divide-and-rule, often without result." While this may sound like a passionate poetic expression, the racial division illustrated should not be underestimated.

Over the years I have wanted to arrive at the solution to the racism problem through theory, books, professors, psychiatrists, religion, revolution, and revolutionaries, and I have discovered that it is all part of the game. Lately I have found out that all human struggles are based on the ownership and distribution of one's story and the right to tell it. Story is the deeply rooted cause. All human beings want to tell their story. For whatever the circumstances, social, political, or economic, the feeling of one's capacity to tell one's story is the key to the mystery—the mystery of conflict.

In traditional societies all human beings told their stories around the fireplace. Capitalism appropriates the story of a people, packages it, bottles it, and sells it. This violation against human sanctity has destabilized many human beings in brutal ways. When they can't tell their story they create another story by destroying the object of their oppression. A lot of the nonwhite Third World filmmakers I have met throughout my life are asking for one simple thing: the right to tell their own stories. In a capitalist world the immediate beneficiaries have called themselves immediate benefactors of our stories. When we all in our own small ways tell our stories, we overthrow white supremacy. And in so doing we contribute to the consideration of white people as people just like the rest of us, in a world where all of our stories rehabilitate and heal our wounded history.

The day I left Cape Town I was surrounded by most of the young people I had taught at the workshop and by some independent film-makers whom I had known for quite some time. Many people came to the airport to say goodbye, some armed with video cameras and others with meaningful gifts. It was an emotional parting. But at the airport we continued to discuss filmmaking and how to empower our stories, how to distribute them. We huddled and conspired against all odds.

Conclusion

To speak about my impressions of South African cinema I first had to meander through Zimbabwe. At each meandering point, I brought up issues that I felt had direct implications for some aspect of South African cinema, even if by way of personal examples and lessons that are sometimes overlooked in newly independent African countries.

It is easy to disassociate the independence struggle of South Africa from earlier stages of the same struggle in other parts of Africa. For politicians this break is expedient. In the art of deception they always have to think and act in isolation from all of the experiences that the continent has already gone through. I can see the pressures a country the size of South Africa experiences when it looks at the rest of Africa. Especially when considering the economic and technological reality of South Africa, one can easily see why that look may be arrogant and condescending, why this economic reality would be seen as an end, and therefore the "giant" can dismiss the rest of the wretchedly poor African countries. Most of Africa, one way or another, has paid a price for the independence of South Africa. The price is evident in dramatic ways among our continental and Pan-African revolutionaries. Kwame Nkrumah made an international appeal to all children of Africa to join the armed struggle that he envisioned as the only way to dislodge the apartheid system. It would not be possible to enumerate the sacrifices paid at the time of Samora Machel in Mozambique. This point needs to be understood because the idea, when misunderstood, flares into conflict. To say it in much clearer terms, the social change that is taking place in the new South Africa should be carried out with the rest of the continent in mind. The new South Africa owes much to the belief and vision forged by the historical struggle of Pan-Africanism, which was founded on the objective of the total independence of Africa.

A cultural about-face has to occur. And this cultural struggle is not to be relegated to tribal fashion shows and Donald Duck in Zulu or Wolof. It must be so dramatic as to have the capacity to directly confront us with the most fundamental level of our mentality, so thorough as to dislodge our neocolonial mentality. We have to unleash a cultural revolution that dramatizes our continent within the context of its own resources. We cannot buy the CNN version of the New World Order, according to which we are all turned into banana republics. Cultural imperialism is a nerve gas, and if we are to combat it we must dramatize our own humanity. South Africa has two choices: being the vanguard of the millennium's cultural revolution or becoming the platform that disseminates imperialist propaganda to the rest of Africa. The latter is actually taking place on a small scale through outfits such as M-Net.

The technological hype in South Africa seems to be organized on the basis of delivery, distribution, and dissemination, rather than on creating a South African cultural identity. South Africa is the most technologically advanced country; it could bring information to the whole continent at the speed of light. It is from South Africa that Hollywood plans to dominate the rest of Africa economically and culturally. Therefore, many complicated realities affecting Africa also face South Africa. Now the ground is fertile and it is all going to depend on the kind of culture that prevails in South Africa. Already I am personally encouraged by the notion floating around South Africa of the African Renaissance. I feel that this African Renaissance, one way or another, is about dramatizing us Africans. All of us, wherever we are, have to be dramatized, even if it is to restore our individual humanity; we Africans have to energize each other by forging a purposeful vision.

In this, cinema can play a great role. Inherently, within its own operation, cinema possesses a magnetic aura that fixes an idea more effectively than any other technological tool. Inventing images, materializing them in some sense of structure, unleashing the added tension the audience brings into the theater, we can resurrect our own stories, those we have to tell for our own salvation. Any society that suppresses stories and storytellers dies. Filmmakers are nothing but storytellers, and they have to be cultivated and reenergized. The state could play a great role if it only understood that it must support its artists unconditionally. Often African states finance art so long as it remains a mouthpiece for the state, and that is why our cultural development is arrested north, south, east, and west.

Afterword

Earlier I raised the issue of a national policy on cinema. Even if African states consider artists to be among their enemies, in unconditionally supporting the arts they would strengthen themselves and be able to transform, to become progressive nations. National policy on cinema in South Africa is very important. I know that the United States, through the IMF, the World Bank, and its embassies, tries to give the illusion of free enterprise for self-creation, as if creation occurred in a vacuum. The United States has had a developed policy on cinema since day one. All governmental institutions, from state to federal and all the way to the hallways of Congress, consider the cinema industry their ideological ambassador. The state has always contributed through all kinds of support, including financing and technology.

African countries are made to believe that culture is "entertainment" and therefore a luxury. They talk about more urgent priorities such as food and shelter, and I say we Africans need more. Like all human beings we say yes to food, shelter, *and* culture: they go hand in hand. Life does not end with food and clothing. What distinguishes us from the rest of the animal kingdom is our ability to transmit culture; therefore, in South Africa artists should demand unconditional economic support to encourage the formation of cultural institutions, including those that can eventually become independent. They have to fight to gain access to the theaters and television and to become a major cultural fixture of the South African reality—rather than allowing the state to force-feed our people Kevin Costner or Tom Cruise speaking Xhosa.

Filmmakers have to create a culture of coexistence without losing individuality in a communal context. Only then can we stimulate each other's creativity. I know of many egotistical filmmakers who have learned the so-called filmmakers' walk and talk before even having the opportunity to scrutinize the very idea of cinematic narrative and the relationship between our cultural background and cinema.

If I were a South African filmmaker, first I would surrender my ego—not to any power or community, but to my storytelling profession. Then I would meditate and recall the historical evolution of stories within my own individual context. I would go as far back as my childhood and recall childhood stories in all their forms. I would close my eyes and replay those images still buried in memory to reintegrate them with my filmmaking practice. I would remember the village, the community, the dogs, the cows, the fireplace, the monumental turns and twists of my mother's and father's faces, and the wrinkles of my grandparents in order to arm myself for the cinematic venture. (I am

227

not saying people should stop making films, but urging filmmakers to carry out this meditative exercise simultaneously.) All the stories we heard from our neighbors and village elders have their own aesthetic guidelines. We need to consciously know them and bring them to the forefront, for they have much to do with our ideas of becoming film-makers.

Technology must be demystified. Anyone can operate a camera—especially with all of the technological innovation taking place. The technology is going to revolutionize the primitive aspects of filmmaking, it is going to make filming functional in the most expeditious way. But if we do not have stories to tell, the technology will not help. And technology does not come in a good-neighborly fashion. It brings along the ideas and cultural notions of those who invent it. This aspect of technology has its risks, carrying with it the ability to rape our stories. Therefore we have to make the empowerment of the storyteller a priority.

I hope this will be the purpose of such institutions as the Newtown Film and Television School. This is where we have to cultivate the new South African filmmakers. It is unfortunate to see that school struggling from a lack of funds. The Newtown School is sadly underfinanced, still running by the perseverance of committed individuals. Even under these trying conditions, we should promote future South African filmmakers. In 1978 I was asked in Mozambique what I would like to do and I responded: "Give me a film school, a film school where students from all parts of Africa come to be trained in all kinds of filmmaking." And the Newtown Film and Television School dramatically symbolizes that idea.

On several occasions, upon returning from the southern part of Africa, I would meet Ousmane Sembène or Med Hondo in Europe or Africa and they both would ask, "What is going on down there?" And I know that deeply rooted in their question is the issue of what South Africa has to offer to the rest of Africa, especially in terms of cinema. All of us have been disillusioned by the role of cinema in different parts of Africa, and our expectation of South African cinema may seem to many unwarranted. I know most of these filmmakers expect South Africa to offer them funding for their films, but I think their expectations also revolve around our common Pan-African reality and point to two questions. First, can our cinema be distributed as commercial films in the theaters and on the television networks of the "new" South Africa? I certainly saw a dignified presentation of my films in Mozambique. That means a lot to a number of filmmakers who exist on the fringes of the Third World cinema industry. Second, what are the types of films and filmmakers that are being encouraged in the region? Ultimately, most of us African filmmakers want to offer our experiences so that South Africans do not repeat our mistakes, but also so that they learn from our success. To most of us, it is our Pan-African duty; after all, we are children of the same movement.

References

Abrahams, Peter. 1954. *Tell Freedom*. London: Faber and Faber.

————. 1989 [1946]. *Mine Boy*. London: Heinemann.

Achebe, Chinua. 1988. *The African Trilogy: "Things Fall Apart," "No Longer at Ease," "Arrow of God."* London: Picador.

Adorno, Theodor W., and Max Horkheimer. 1944. *Dialectic of Enlightenment*. Translated by J. Cumming. New York: Herder and Herder.

Alexander, Peter F. 1994. *Alan Paton: A Biography*. Oxford: Oxford University Press.

Anderson, Maxwell, and Kurt Weill. 1949. *"Lost in the Stars": The Dramatization of Alan Paton's Novel, "Cry, the Beloved Country."* New York: William Sloane.

A.P.O. (African Political Organisation). South African newspaper published from May 1909 to December 1923. Cape Town.

Baldwin, James. 1968. Sidney Poiter. *Look*, 23 July, 50–58.

Bantu World (known today as *World*). South African newspaper published since April 1903. Johannesburg.

Barnes, John. 1992. *Filming the Boer War*. London: Bishopsgate Press.

Beinart, William, and Saul DuBow. 1995. *Segregation and Apartheid in Twentieth-Century South Africa*. London: Routledge.

Beittel, Mark. 1990. *Mapantsula:* Cinema, Crime, and Politics on the Witwatersrand. *Journal of South African Studies* 16 (4): 751–60.

————. 1996. *Comtsotsi:* Politics and Crime in South African Cinema. Unpublished essay.

Bhabha, Homi K. 1989. The Commitment to Theory. In *Questions of Third Cinema*, edited by Jim Pines and Paul Willemen. London: British Film Institute.

Blignaut, Johan, and Martin P. Botha, eds. 1992. *Movies-Moguls-Mavericks: South African Cinema, 1979–1991*. Johannesburg: Showdata.

BMSC. Bantu Men's Social Centre annual reports. Carter-Karis South African Collection, ca. 1920–71, item no. 8A, film no. 783, reel 17.

Bogle, Donald. 1974. *Toms, Coons, Mulattoes, Mammies, and Bucks: An Interpretive History of Blacks in American Films*. New York: Bantam.

References

Bond, Patrick. 2000. *Elite Transition: From Apartheid to Neoliberalism in South Africa*. London: Pluto Press.

Bonner, Philip. 1982. The Transvaal Native Congress, 1917–1920: The Radicalisation of the Black Petty Bourgeoisie on the Rand. In *Industrialisation and Social Change in South Africa: African Class Formation, Culture and Consciousness, 1870–1930*, edited by S. Marks and R. Rathbone. London: Longman.

Bonner, Philip, Peter Delius, and Deborah Posel. 1993. The Shaping of Apartheid: Contradiction, Continuity, and Popular Struggle. In *Apartheid's Genesis, 1935–1962*, edited by Philip Bonner, Peter Delius, and Deborah Posel. Johannesburg: Witwatersrand University Press.

Botha, Martin P., and Adri van Aswegen. 1992. *Images of South Africa: The Rise of Alternative Film*. Pretoria: Human Sciences Research Council.

Callan, Edward. 1991. *"Cry, the Beloved Country": A Novel of South Africa*. Boston: Twayne.

Cameron, Kenneth M. 1994. *Africa on Film: Beyond Black and White*. New York: Continuum.

Chapman, Michael. 1994a. More than Telling a Story: *Drum* and its Significance in Black South African Writing. In *The Drum Decade: Stories from the 1950s*, edited by Michael Chapman. Pietermaritzburg: University of Natal Press.

———, ed. 1994b. *The Drum Decade: Stories from the 1950s*. Pietermaritzburg: University of Natal Press.

Chatterjee, Partha. 1993. *The Nation and Its Fragments: Colonial and Postcolonial Histories*. Princeton, N.J.: Princeton University Press.

Come Back, Africa. 1960. *Filmfacts* 3 (16): 91–93.

Coplan, David. 1985. *In Township Tonight! South Africa's Black City Music and Theatre*. Johannesburg: Ravan.

Couzens, Tim. 1976. The Social Ethos of Black Writing in South Africa, 1920–1950. In *Aspects of South African Literature*, edited by C. Heywood. New York: Heinemann.

———. 1982. "Moralizing Leisure Time": The Transatlantic Connection and Black Johannesburg. In *Industrialisation and Social Change in South Africa: African Class Formation, Culture and Consciousness, 1870–1930*, edited by S. Marks and R. Rathbone. London: Longman.

Cowie, Elizabeth. 1990. Women as Sign. In *m/f: The Women in Question*, edited by Parveen Adams and Elizabeth Cowie. New York: Verso.

Creed, Barbara. 1989. Horror and the Monstrous Feminine: An Imaginary Abjection. In *Fantasy and the Cinema*, edited by J. Donald. London: British Film Institute.

Cripps, Thomas. 1979. *Black Film as Genre*. Bloomington: Indiana University Press.

Crow, Thomas. 1999. Unwritten Histories of Conceptual Art. In *Conceptual Art: A Critical Anthology*, edited by Alexander Alberro and Blake Stimson. Cambridge: MIT Press.

References

Crowther, Bosley. 1952. Review of *Cry, the Beloved Country. New York Times,* 24 January.

DACST (Department of Arts, Culture, Science and Technology). 1996. "White Paper on the Film Industry." South African government document.

Davies, J. S. A. 1989. Film: A Brief History. *ADA* 6: 32–33.

Davis, J. Merle. 1935. The Bantu Educational Cinema Experiment. *Africa* 8 (3): 384.

Davis, Peter. 1996. *In Darkest Hollywood: Exploring the Jungles of Cinema's South Africa.* Johannesburg: Ravan.

De Lange, Johan. 1991. *The Anglo-Boer War, 1899–1902, on Film.* Pretoria: State Archives Service.

Deleuze, Gilles, and Claire Parnet. 1977. *Dialogues.* Translated by Hugh Tomlinson and Barbara Habberjam. New York: Columbia University Press.

Dhlomo, H. I. E. N.D. Hats. Unpublished essay. Killie Campbell Library, Durban, South Africa.

Diawara, Manthia. 1992. *African Cinema: Politics and Culture.* Bloomington: Indiana University Press.

———. 1995. Black American Cinema: The New Realism. In *Cinemas of the Black Diaspora: Diversity, Dependence, and Oppositionality,* edited by Michael T. Martin. Detroit: Wayne State University Press.

Dikobe, Modikwe. 1981. *The Marabi Dance.* London: Heinemann.

Doane, Mary Ann. 1990. Film and the Masquerade: Theorizing the Female Spectator. In *Issues in Feminist Film Criticism,* edited by Patricia Erens. Bloomington: Indiana University Press.

Dreyer, Peter. 1980. *Martyrs and Fanatics: South Africa and Human Destiny.* London: Secker and Warburg.

Du Bois, W. E. B. 1989 [1903]. *The Souls of Black Folk.* New York: Bantam Books.

Dubow, Saul. 1989. *Racial Segregation and the Origins of Apartheid, 1919–1936.* Oxford: Macmillan.

———. 1995. *Illicit Union: Scientific Racism in Modern South Africa.* Johannesburg: Witwatersrand University Press.

Dunn, Kevin. 1996. Lights . . . Camera . . . Africa: Images of Africa and Africans in Western Popular Films of the 1930s. *African Studies Review* 39 (1): 149–75.

Du Plessis, P. J. 1988. Die Lewe en Werk van Gustav Preller, 1875–1943. Ph.D. diss., University of Pretoria.

Eagleton, Terry. 1990. *The Ideology of the Aesthetic.* London: Basil Blackwell.

Elsaesser, Thomas. 1989. *New German Cinema: A History.* New Brunswick, N.J.: Rutgers University Press.

Fanon, Frantz. 1968. *The Wretched of the Earth.* Translated by Constance Farrington. New York: Grove Wiedenfeld.

Foucault, Michel. 1976. *The History of Sexuality.* Translated by Robert Hurley. London: Penguin.

Gaines, Jane. 1990. White Privilege and Looking Relations: Race and Gender

References

in Feminist Film Theory. In *Issues in Feminist Film Criticism,* edited by Patricia Erens. Bloomington: Indiana University Press.

Gates, Henry Louis Jr. 1989. Introduction. In *The Souls of Black Folk,* by W. E. B. Du Bois. New York: Bantam Books.

Gavshon, Harriet. 1997. Personal discussion. Johannesburg, 6 June.

Geduld, Harry M. 1971. *Focus on D. W. Griffith.* Englewood Cliffs, N.J.: Prentice-Hall.

Glaser, Clive. 1996. "We Must Infiltrate the Tsotsis": School Politics and Youth Gangs in Soweto, 1968–1976. Paper presented at the Centre for African Studies, University of Cape Town, 31 July.

Golden City Post. South African newspaper published since March 1955. Johannesburg.

Gready, Paul. 1990. The Sophiatown Writers of the Fifties: The Unreal Reality of Their World. *Journal of Southern African Studies* 16 (1): 139–64.

Groen, Martine. 1993. Mother-Daughter, the "Black Continent": Is a Multicultural Future Possible? In *Daughtering and Mothering: Female Subjectivity Reanalysed,* edited by Janneke van Mens-Verhulst, Karlein Schreurs, and Liesbeth Woertman. New York: Routledge.

Grundlingh, Albert, and Hilary Sapire. 1989. From Feverish Festival to Repetitive Ritual? The Changing Fortunes of Great Trek Mythology in an Industrializing South Africa, 1938–1988. *South African Historical Journal* 21: 19–37.

Gutsche, Thelma. 1972. *The History and Social Significance of Motion Pictures in South Africa, 1895–1940.* Cape Town: Howard Timmins.

Hall, Stuart. 1989. Cultural Identity and Cinematic Representation. *Framework* 36: 68–81.

———. 1990. The Whites of Their Eyes: Racist Ideologies and the Media. In *The Media Reader,* edited by Manuel Alvorado and John O. Thompson. London: British Film Institute.

———. 1994. Cultural Identity and Diaspora: Identity, Community, Culture, Difference. In *Colonial Discourse and Post-Colonial Theory: A Reader,* edited by P. Williams and Laura Chrisman. New York: Columbia University Press.

Harvey, Ibrahim. 2000. Defender of the ANC and the Presidency. *Mail and Guardian* (Johannesburg), 21–27 July, 31.

Haupt, Adam. 1998. Putting Words into Action. *Mail and Guardian* (Johannesburg), 9 April, 2.

Hayward, Susan. 1996. *Key Concepts in Cinema Studies.* London: Routledge.

Hees, Edward. 1991. *The National Film Board of South Africa.* Stellenbosch: University of Stellenbosch.

Hofmeyr, Isabel. 1987. Building a Nation from Words: Afrikaans Language, Literature, and Ethnic Identity, 1902–1924. In *The Politics of Race, Class, and Nationalism in Twentieth-Century South Africa,* edited by S. Marks and S. Trapido. London: Harlow.

References

————. 1988. Popularizing History: The Case of Gustav Preller. *Journal of African History* 29: 521–35.

————. 1991. Popularizing History: The Case of Gustav Preller. In *Regions and Repertoires: Topics in South African Politics and Culture,* edited by Stephen Clingman. Johannesburg: Ravan.

Hogan, Patrick Colm. 1992–93. Paternalism, Ideology, and Ideological Critique: Teaching *Cry, the Beloved Country. College Literature* 19(3): 206–10.

Holden, Stephen. 1995. Quest through Yesterday's South Africa. *New York Times,* 15 December, B6.

Hooper-Box, Caroline. 1999. South African Film Moves Local Cinema up the Ladder of Acceptance. *Sunday Independent* (Johannesburg), 15 September.

Ilanga lase Natal (The Sun of Natal, a.k.a. *Ilanga*). South African newspaper published since April 1903. Durban.

Imvo Zabantsundu (African Opinion). South African newspaper published since November 1884. King William's Town.

Independent Broadcasting Authority Act. 1993. South Africa.

Irigaray, Luce. 1994. Women - amongst - Themselves: Creating a Woman - to - Woman Sociality. In *The Irigaray Reader,* edited by Margaret Whitford. Oxford: Blackwell.

Izwe La Kiti (Our Nation). South African newspaper published from September 1912 to June 1915. Dundee, Natal.

Jameson, Fredric. 1992. *Late Marxism: Adorno, or, The Persistence of the Dialectic.* London: Verso.

Jay, Martin. 1993. *Downcast Eyes: The Denigration of Vision in Twentieth-Century French Thought.* London: University of California Press.

Johnston, Claire. 1972. Women's Cinema as Counter-Cinema. In *Notes on Women's Cinema,* edited by Claire Johnston. London: Society for Education in Film and Television.

Joubert, Elsa. 1980. *Poppie Nongena.* New York: Henry Holt.

Kass, Judith M. 1981. *Cry, the Beloved Country.* In *Magill's Survey of Cinema: English Language Films,* edited by Frank N. Magill. Englewood Cliffs, N.J.: Salem.

Katz, Ephraim. 1994. *The Film Encyclopedia.* 2d ed. New York: Harper Collins.

Kinder, Marsha. 1993. *Blood Cinema: The Reconstruction of National Identity in Spain.* Berkeley: University of California Press.

Kinghorn, Johan. 1994. Social Cosmology, Religion, and Afrikaner Ethnicity. *Journal of South African Studies* 20 (3): 393–404.

Komai, Felicia. 1955. *Cry, the Beloved Country: A Verse Drama.* New York: Friendship.

Koranta ea Becoana (The Bechoana Gazette). South African newspaper, edited by Sol Plaatje, published from April 1901 to February 1908. Mafeking.

Kristeva, Julia. 1980. *Desire in Language: A Semiotic Approach to Literature and*

Art. Translated by Thomas Gora, Alice Jardine, and Leon S. Roudiez. Edited by Leon S. Roudiez. New York: Columbia University Press.

Kulik, Karol. 1975. *Alexander Korda: The Man Who Could Work Miracles*. London: W. H. Allen-Howard and Wyndham.

Laclau, Ernesto. 1990. *New Reflections on the Revolution of Our Time*. New York: Verso.

Lapsley, R., and M. Westlake. 1988. *Film Theory: An Introduction*. Manchester: Manchester University Press.

Leab, Daniel J. 1975. *From Sambo to Superspade: The Black Experience in Motion Pictures*. London: Secker and Warburg.

Liebenberg, B. J. 1975. Gustav Preller as Historikus. *Tydskrif vir Geestesweten-skappe* 15: 243–50.

Lombaard, M. 1975. Gustav Preller as Historikus. *Tydskrif vir Letterkunde* 13: 10–25.

Lott, Tommy L. 1991. A No-Theory Theory of Contempory Black Cinema. *African American Review* 25 (2): 221–36.

MacCrone, I. D. 1937. *Race Attitudes in South Africa: Historical, Experimental, and Psychological Studies*. London: Oxford University Press.

Maingard, Jacqueline. 1994. New South African Cinema: *Mapantsula* and *Sarafina*. *Screen* 35 (3): 235–43.

———. 1995. Trends in South African Documentary Film and Video: Questions of Identity and Subjectivity. *Journal of Southern African Studies* 21 (4): 657–67.

———. 1997. Transforming Television Broadcasting in a Democratic South Africa. *Screen* 38 (3): 260–74.

———. 1998. Representations of Identity in South African Film and Television: Reflections on the Making of National Cinema in South Africa. Ph.D. diss., University of the Witwatersrand, Johannesburg.

Mandela, Nelson. 1995. Remarks at the Miramax Films World Premiere of *Cry, the Beloved Country*, 23 October, Ziegfeld Theater, New York City. Open Book Systems. http://archives.obs-us.com/obs/english/films/mx/cry/speech4m.htm.

Martin, Michael T., ed. 1995. *Cinemas of the Black Diaspora: Diversity, Dependence, and Oppositionality*. Detroit: Wayne State University Press.

Masemole-Jones, Letebe. 2000. New Directions on Track. *Africa Film and TV Edition*, February–April, 19.

Masilela, Ntongela. 1991. *Come Back, Africa* and South African Film History. *Jump Cut* 36: 61–65.

———. 1999. New Negroism and New Africanism: The Influence of United States Modernity on the Construction of South African Modernity. *Black Renaissance* 2 (2): 46–59.

———. Forthcoming a. *The Modernity and Modernism of H. I. E. Dhlomo: South Africa in the Modern World*. Trenton, N.J.: Africa World Press.

———. Forthcoming b. The TransAtlantic Connections of the New African

References

Movement. In *Black Modernity: Discourses between United States and South Africa,* edited by N. Masilela. Trenton, N.J.: Africa World Press.

Matshikiza, John. 1999. The World of African Film. *Mail and Guardian* (Johannesburg), 2–9 September, 10.

Matshikiza, Todd. 1952. Song of Africa. *Drum,* April.

———. 1985 [1961]. *Chocolates for My Wife.* Cape Town: David Philip.

Mattera, Don. 1987. *Memory Is the Weapon.* Johannesburg: Ravan.

Maxwell, Richard. 1995. *The Spectacle of Democracy: Spanish Television, Nationalism, and Political Transition.* Minneapolis: Minnesota University Press.

Mayne, Judith. 1990. *The Woman at the Keyhole: Feminism and Women's Cinema.* Bloomington: Indiana University Press.

McClintock, Anne. 1990. "The Very House of Difference": Race, Gender, and the Politics of South African Women's Narrative in *Poppie Nongena. Social Text* 25/26: 196–226.

Mercer, Kobena, ed. 1988. *Black Film/British Cinema.* London: Institute of Contemporary Arts.

Merritt, Russell. 1990. D. W. Griffith's *Intolerance*: Reconstructing an Unattainable Text. *Film History* 4: 337–75.

Metz, Christian. 1982. *Psychoanalysis and Cinema: The Imaginary Signifier.* Translated by C. Brittin et al. London: Macmillan.

Modisane, Bloke. 1990 [1963]. *Blame Me on History.* London: Penguin.

Mogotlane, Thomas, and Oliver Schmitz. 1991. "*Mapantsula*": *Screenplay and Interview.* Fordsburg: COSAW.

Mohanty, Chandra. 1988. Under Western Eyes: Feminist Scholarship and Colonial Discourses. *Feminist Review* 30: 61–68.

Morrison, Toni. 1992. *Playing in the Dark: Whiteness and the Literary Imagination.* New York: Vintage.

Mphahlele, Ezekiel [Es'kia]. 1974. *The African Image.* New York: Praeger.

———. 1989 [1959]. *Down Second Avenue.* London: Faber & Faber.

———. Forthcoming. Your History Demands Your Heartbeat: Historical Survey of the Encounter between Africans and African Americans. In *Black Modernity: Discourses between United States and South Africa,* edited by Ntongela Masilela. Trenton, N.J.: Africa World Press.

Mulvey, Laura. 1990. Visual Pleasure and Narrative Cinema. In *Issues in Feminist Criticism,* edited by P. Erens. Bloomington: Indiana University Press.

Mweli Skota, T. D. 1966. *The African Who's Who: An Illustrated Classified Register and National Biographical Dictionary of Africans in the Transvaal.* Johannesburg: C.N.A.

Naidoo, Ravi. 1989. *Tracking Down Historical Myths: Eight South African Cases.* Johannesburg: A. D. Donker.

Nakasa, Nat. 1985 [1975]. *The World of Nat Nakasa.* Johannesburg: Ravan.

Ndebele, Njabulo. 1983. *"Fools" and Other Stories.* Johannesburg: Ravan.

Nichols, Bill. 1983. The Voice of Documentary. *Film Quarterly* 36 (3): 17–29.

————. 1991. *Representing Reality: Issues and Concepts in Documentary.* Bloomington: Indiana University Press.

————. 1994. *Blurred Boundaries: Questions of Meaning in Contemporary Culture.* Bloomington: Indiana University Press.

Nicol, Mike. 1991. *A Good-Looking Corpse.* London: Secker & Warburg.

Nixon, Rob. 1994. *Homelands, Harlem, and Hollywood: South African Culture and the World Beyond.* New York: Routledge.

Nkosi, Lewis. 1959. Why "Bloke" Bailed Out. *Contact,* 11 July.

————. 1960. *Come Back, Africa*: On Making a Film. *Fighting Talk*: 12–13.

————. 1965. *Home and Exile.* London: Longman.

————. 1981. *Tasks and Masks: Themes and Styles of African Literature.* Harlow, Essex: Longman.

————. 1990. Introduction. In *Blame Me on History,* by Bloke Modisane. London: Penguin.

Notcutt, L. A., and G. C. Latham. 1937. *The African and the Cinema.* London: Edinburgh House.

Okoye, Felix. 1969. Dingane: A Reappraisal. *Journal of African History* 10 (2): 221–35.

Open Book Systems. 1995. Cycles of Colonialism: South Africa in Books, Bits, and Film. http://archives.obs-us.com/obs/english/films/mx/cry/aboutov.htm.

Paton, Alan. 1987 [1948]. *Cry, the Beloved Country.* New York: Macmillan.

————. 1988. *Journey Continued: An Autobiography.* New York: Scribner's.

Pearce, Justin. 1995. Feel-Good Film of the Decade? *Weekly Mail and Guardian* (Johannesburg), 27 October–2 November, 33.

Peterson, Bhekizizwe. 2000. *Monarchs, Missionaries, and African Intellectuals: African Theatre and the Unmaking of Colonial Marginality.* Johannesburg: Witwatersrand University Press.

Phelps-Stokes Commission. 1922. *Education in Africa: Report of the African Education Commission.* New York: Phelps-Stokes Fund.

Phelps-Stokes Fund. 1925. *Education in East Africa.* London: Edinburgh House.

Phillips' Newsletter. Day Missions Library, Yale University. Day Missions Collection, record group 31, box 19, folder 135A.

Phillips, R. E. 1930. *The Bantu Are Coming: Phases of South Africa's Race Problem.* London: Student Christian Movement.

————. 1936. *The Bantu in the City: A Study of Cultural Adjustment on the Witwatersrand.* Lovedale: Lovedale Press.

Plaatje, Sol. 1982 [1916]. *Native Life in South Africa.* Johannesburg: Ravan.

————. 1997. *Selected Writings.* Edited by Brian Willan. Johannesburg: Witwatersrand University Press.

Poiter, Sidney. 1980. *This Life.* New York: Ballantine.

Preller, Gustav S. 1988 [1937]. *Andries Pretorius.* Melville: Scripta Africana, Hans Strydom.

————. 1988 [1917]. *Piet Retief.* Melville: Scripta Africana, Hans Strydom.

Pretorius, William. 1994. New Life for an Old Classic. *Weekly Mail and Guardian* (Johannesburg), 9–14 December, 33.

Proctor, A. 1979. Class Struggle, Segregation, and the City: A History of Sophiatown, 1905–1940. In *Labour, Township, and Protest,* edited by B. Bozzoli. Johannesburg: Ravan.

Purkey, Malcolm. 1996. Sophiatown. In *At the Junction: Four Plays by the Junction Avenue Theatre Company,* edited by Michael Orkin. Johannesburg: Witwatersrand University Press.

Reid, Mark A. 1993. *Redefining Black Film.* Berkeley: University of California Press.

Report of the Proceedings of the Fifth General Missionary Conference of South Africa. (Held at Durban, 18–22 July, 1921). 1922. Durban: The Commercial Printing Co.

Rogin, Michael Paul. 1987. *Ronald Reagan, the Movie, and Other Episodes in Political Demonology.* Berkeley: University of California Press.

————. 1992. Blackface, White Noise: The Jewish Jazz Singer Finds His Voice. *Critical Inquiry* 18: 417–53.

Rogosin, Lionel. 1960. Interpreting Reality. *Film Culture*: 20–28.

Rogosin, Lionel, Lewis Nkosi, and Bloke Modisane. 1958. A South African Story. Unpublished film script for *Come Back, Africa.*

Rosen, Philip. 1996. Nation and Anti-Nation: Concepts of National Cinema in the New Media Era. *Diaspora* 5 (3): 375–402.

Rotha, Paul. 1960. Eyes on the World. *Films and Filming* 6 (4): 21, 26.

Sachs, B. 1951. Review of *Cry, the Beloved Country. Trek* 15 (2): 20.

Sandall, Roger, and Cecille Starr. 1960. Come Back, Africa. *Film Quarterly* 13 (4): 34–35.

Saunders, Christopher. 1988. *The Making of the South African Past: Major Historians on Race and Class.* Cape Town: David Philip.

Seepe, Sipho. 2000. How Mbeki Is Hampering the Renaissance. *Mail and Guardian* (Johannesburg), 9–14 June, 28.

Seme, Pixley ka Isaka. 1906. The Regeneration of Africa. *Royal African Society* 5 (20): 404–8.

Silva, Fred, ed. 1971. *Focus on "The Birth of a Nation."* Englewood Cliffs, N.J.: Prentice-Hall.

Snead, James A. 1994. *White Screens, Black Images: Hollywood from the Dark Side.* New York: Routledge.

————. 1995. Images of Blacks in Black Independent Films. In *Cinemas of the Black Diaspora: Diversity, Dependence, and Oppositionality,* edited by Michael T. Martin. Detroit: Wayne State University Press.

Sobchack, Vivian. 1990. "Surge and Splendor": A Phenomenology of the Hollywood Historical Epic. *Representations* 29 (winter): 24–49.

Sorlin, Pierre. 1980. *The Film in History: Restaging the Past.* Oxford: Basil Blackwell.

References

South African Outlook (previously known as *Kaffir Express* and *Christian Express*). South African newspaper. Lovedale.

South Africa's Film and TV Foundation Launched. 2000. *Africa Film and TV Magazine,* February–April.

Soyinka, Wole. 1999. Amid the Slaughter, There Is No African Renaissance. *Mail and Guardian* (Johannesburg), 3–9 September, 23.

Stein, Pippa, and Ruth Jacobson, eds. 1986. *Sophiatown Speaks.* Johannesburg: Junction Avenue.

Stodel, Jack. 1962. *The Audience Is Waiting.* Cape Town: Howard Timmins.

Streble, Elizabeth Grottle. 1977. Primitive Propaganda: The Boer War Films. *Sight and Sound*: 45–47.

———. 1979. The Voortrekkers: A Cinematic Reflection of Rising Afrikaner Nationalism. *Film and History* 9 (2): 25–32.

Taylor, Clyde. 1985. Africa, the Last Cinema. In *Journey across Three Continents,* edited by Renee Tajima. New York: Third World Newsreel.

Theal, George McCall. 1877. *Compendium of South African History and Geography.* 11 vols. 3d ed.

Themba, Can. 1983 [1972]. *The Will to Die.* London: Heinemann.

Thompson, Leonard M. 1960. *The Unification of South Africa, 1902–1910.* Oxford: Clarendon.

———. 1990. *A History of South Africa.* New Haven: Yale University Press.

Tomaselli, Keyan Y. 1980. Class and Ideology: Reflections on South African Cinema. *Critical Arts* 1 (1): 1–13.

———. 1983. Ideology and Cultural Production in South African Cinema. Ph.D. diss., University of the Witwatersrand, Johannesburg.

———. 1986. Capitalism and Culture in South African Cinema: Jingoism, Nationalism, and the Historical Epic. *Wide Angle* 8 (2): 33–43.

———. 1989. *The Cinema of Apartheid: Race and Class in South African Film.* London: Routledge.

———. 1993. "Coloring It In": Films in "Black" or "White"—Reassessing Authorship. *Critical Arts* 7 (1 & 2): 61–77.

Trinh T., Minh-ha. 1989. *Woman, Native, Other: Writing Postcoloniality and Feminism.* Bloomington: Indiana University Press.

Trinh T., Minh-ha (in conversation with Annamaria Morelli). 1996. The Undone Interval. In *The Post-Colonial Question: Common Skies, Divided Horizons,* edited by I. Chambers and L. Curtis. London: Routledge.

Tsala ea Becoana (Friend of the Batswana). South African newspaper, edited by Sol Plaatje, published from June 1910 to June 1912. Mafeking (first six months) then Kimberley.

Tudor, Henry. 1972. *Political Myth.* London: Pall Mall.

Ukadike, Nwachukwu Frank. 1994. *Black African Cinema.* Los Angeles: University of California Press.

———. 1996. Reclaiming Images of Women in Films from Africa and the Black

Diaspora. In *African Experiences of Cinema,* edited by Imruh Bakari and Mbye Cham. London: British Film Institute.

Umteteli wa Bantu (The Mouthpiece of the Native Peoples). South African newspaper published since May 1920. Johannesburg.

Usai, Paulo Cherchi. 1988. *Cabiria,* an Incomplete Masterpiece: The Quest for the Original 1914 Version. *Film History* 2: 155–65.

Van Jaarsveld, F. A. 1990. Gustav Preller: Sy Historiese Bewussyn en Geskiedbeskouing. *Historia* 35 (1): 3–19.

Van Rooyen, Johann. 1994. *Hard Right: The New White Power in South Africa.* London: I. B. Tauris.

Van Zyl, John A. F. 1980. "No God, No Morality, No History": South African Ethnographic Film. *Critical Arts* 1 (1): 32–37.

Venice Film Festival Caption. 1959. *Africa Special Report,* 4, 16.

Videovision Entertainment. 1995. *Cry, the Beloved Country*: Synopsis and Production Notes. http://mbendi.co.za/ve/cry_pmo.htm.

Visser, N. W. 1977. *English in Africa* 4 (2) (special issue on the literary theory and criticism of H. I. E. Dhlomo).

Wallace, Edgar. 1930 [1909]. *Sanders of the River.* New York: Doubleday.

Walshe, Peter. 1987. *The Rise of African Nationalism in South Africa.* Craighall: A. D. Donker.

Wilhelm, Peter. 1999. Wole Soyinka Strikes a Pessimistic Note. *Financial Mail* (Johannesburg), 27 August, 40.

Worsdale, Andrew. 1996. Tales of Township Life. *Mail and Guardian* (Johannesburg), 22–28 May, 3.

Yearwood, Gladstone L., ed. 1982. *Black Cinema Aesthetics.* Athens: Ohio University Center for Afro-American Studies.

Selected Filmography

African Jim (a.k.a. *Jim Comes to Jo'burg*). 1949. Directed by Donald Swanson. Villon Films.

Africa Today. 1927. Directed by T. H. Baxter. Missionary Film Committee.

Allan Quatermain and the Lost City of Gold. 1918. Directed by Gary Nelson. MGM.

The Birth of a Nation. 1992 [1915]. Directed by D. W. Griffith. Connoisseur Video.

Bopha! 1993. Directed by Morgan Freeman. Paramount.

Cabiria. 1914. Directed by Giovanni Pastrone. Itala Films.

Chicken Bizniz: The Whole Story. 1998. Directed by Ntshaveni wa Luruli. M-Net New Directions.

City of Blood. 1983. Directed by Darrell Roodt. New World Pictures.

Come Back, Africa. 1959. Directed by Lionel Rogosin. McGraw-Hill Films.

Come See the Bioscope. 1997. Directed by Lance Gewer. Phakathi Films.

Cry Freedom. 1987. Directed by Richard Attenborough. Universal Pictures.

Cry, the Beloved Country (a.k.a. *African Fury*). 1951. Directed by Zoltan Korda. British Lion Film Corporation and United Artists.

Cry, the Beloved Country. 1995. Directed by Darrell Roodt. Miramax.

A Dry, White Season. 1989. Directed by Euzhan Palcy. MGM.

Dust That Kills. 1921. Directed by A. J. Orenstein. African Film Productions.

Father Hood. 1993. Directed by Darrell Roodt. Buena Vista.

55 Empire Road. In development. Directed by Zachariah Rapola and Michael Mogorosi. Video/Laropa Productions.

Fools. 1997. Directed by Ramadan Suleman. Film Resource Unit.

The Four Feathers. 1939. Directed by Zoltan Korda. United Artists.

Freedom Square and Back of the Moon. 1987. Directed by William Kentridge and Angus Gibson. Free Filmmakers.

Friends. 1994. Directed by Elaine Proctor. First Run Features.

Fruits of Defiance. 1990. Directed by Brian Tilley and Oliver Schmitz. Film Resource Unit.

Game for Vultures. 1979. Directed by James Fargo. Caris Enterprises.

The Great Kimberley Diamond Robbery (a.k.a. *The Star of the South*). 1911. Director unknown. Africa's Amalgamated Theatres.

Selected Filmography

Have You Seen Drum Recently? 1995. Directed by Jürgen Schadeberg. Films for the Humanities and Sciences.

Hlanganani: A Short History of COSATU. 1991. Directed by Brian Tilley and Oliver Schmitz. Film Resource Unit.

In Darkest Hollywood: Cinema and Apartheid. 1993. Directed by Daniel Riesenfeld and Peter Davis. Nightengale/Villon Production.

Jump the Gun. 1996. Directed by Les Blair. Film Four.

Jungle Book. 1942. Directed by Zoltan Korda. United Artists.

King Solomon's Mines. 1918. Directed by H. Lisle Lucoque. African Film Productions.

King Solomon's Mines. 1937. Directed by Robert Stevenson. Gainsborough.

Kini and Adams. 1997. Directed by Idrissa Ouedraogo. Finishing Post Productions.

Lost in the Stars. 1974. Directed by Daniel Mann. American Film Theater.

Mandela: Son of Africa, Father of a Nation. 1995. Directed by Joe Menell and Angus Gibson. Island Pictures.

Mapantsula. 1988. Directed by Oliver Schmitz. Film Resource Unit.

Max in the Crying Business. In development. Directed by Teddy Mattera. Primedia Pictures.

Nonquassi. 1938. Directed by Leon Schauder. Gaumont-British Instructional Ltd.

Ordinary People. 1993–95. Various directors. Mail and Guardian Television.

The Peacemakers. 1993. Directed by Clifford Bestall. First episode of *Ordinary People.* Mail and Guardian Television.

Place of Weeping. 1986. Directed by Darrell Roodt. New World.

Pondo Story. 1948. Directed by Ray Getteman. African Film Productions.

Prester John. 1920. Directed by Dick Cruikshanks. African Film Productions.

Rearview Mirror. In development. Directed by Zachariah Rapola. Video/Laropa Productions.

Rue Princesse. 1993. Directed by Henri Duparc. Film Resource Unit.

Safety First. 1921. Directed by A. J. Orenstein. Transvaal Chamber of Mines.

Sahara. 1943. Directed by Zoltan Korda. Columbia.

Sanders of the River (a.k.a. *Bosambo*). 1935. Directed by Zoltan Korda. United Artists.

Sankofa. 1994. Directed by Haile Gerima. Mypheduh Films.

Sarafina. 1992. Directed by Darrell Roodt. Warner.

The Sexy Girls. 1997. Directed by Russell Thompson. Magic Works.

The Stick. 1987. Directed by Darrell Roodt. Distant Horizons.

Symbol of Sacrifice. 1918. Directed by I. W. Schlesinger, Dick Cruikshanks, and Joseph Albrecht. African Film Productions.

They Built a Nation (a.k.a. *Die Bou van 'n Nasie*). 1938. Directed by Joseph Albrecht. African Film Productions.

Tooth of the Times. 1993. Directed by Clifford Bestall. Third episode of *Ordinary People.* Mail and Guardian Television.

Visages de femmes. 1985. Directed by Désiré Ecaré. Facets Multimedia.

De Voortrekkers (a.k.a. *Winning a Continent*). 1916. Directed by Harold Shaw. African Film Productions.

What's Going On? In development. Directed by Khubu Meth.

The Wild Geese. 1978. Directed by Andrew V. McLaglen. Allied Artists.

Xala. 1974. Directed by Ousmane Sembène. New Yorker Films.

Zeliv (a.k.a. *Witchcraft* and *Siliwa the Zulu*). 1927. Directed by Attilio Gatti. Exploration Ltd.

Zulu Love Letter. In development. Directed by Ramadan Suleman. Natives at Large.

A Zulu's Devotion. 1916. Directed by Joseph Albrecht. African Film Productions.

The Zulu's Heart. 1908. Directed by D. W. Griffith. American Mutascope and Biograph.

Distributors of South African Films

South African Distributors and Resource Centers

African Barter Company
P.O. Box 782497
Sandton, Johannesburg
2146 South Africa
Tel: +27-11 444 4451
Fax: +27-11 444 1302
E-mail: james@africanbarter.co.za
www.africanbarter.com

BMG Africa Video
P.O. Box 91432
Oakland Park, Johannesburg
2006 South Africa
Tel: +27-11 242 3000
Fax: +27-11 242 3070
E-mail: keith.lister@bertelsmann.de

Clear Media and Effect
Tel: +27-11 880 2567
Fax: +27-11 880 2526
E-mail: stan@effectcompany.com

Concorde Films
P.O. Box 8112
Johannesburg
2000 South Africa
Tel: +27-11 337 5581
Fax: +27-11 337 3913
E-mail: concorde@icon.co.za

Film Resource Unit
P.O. Box 11065
Johannesburg
2000 South Africa
Tel: +27-11 838 4280/2
Fax: +27-11 838 4451
E-mail: fru@wn.apc.org
www.sn.apc.org

G.T.V.
Gallo House 6
Hood Avenue
Rosebank, Johannesburg
2196 South Africa
Tel: +27-11 340 9400
Fax: +27-11 340 9355
E-mail: dee@gallotv.com
www.gallotv.com

National Film, Video and Sound Archives
Private Bag X236
Pretoria
0001 South Africa
Tel: +27-12 343 9767
+27-12 323 5300, ext. 204
Fax: +27-12 344 5143

Nu-Metro Entertainment
P.O. Box 392026
Bramley, Johannesburg
2018 South Africa
Tel: +27-11 340 9400
Fax: +27-11 340 9411
E-mail: mikeb@numetro.co.za

Richard Stewart Enterprises
7 Hantamberg Road
Glenvista, Johannesburg
2058 South Africa
Tel: +27-11 432 0371
Fax: +27-11 432 2994
E-mail: rse@global.co.za

South African Broadcasting Corporation
Private Bag X1
Auckland Park
2006 South Africa
www.sabc.co.za

Ster-Kinekor Pictures
Primovie Park
185 Katherine Street (Off Charles Crescent)
Sandton, Johannesburg
2010 South Africa
Tel: +27-11 445 7700
Fax: +27-11 444 6637
www.sterkinekor.com

The University of the Western Cape–Robben Island
Mayibuye Archives/Film and Video Archives
Private Bag X17
Bellville
7535 South Africa
Tel: +27-21 959 2939/2954
Fax: +27-21 959 3411
E-mail: mayib@uwc.ac.za
www.mayibuye.org

Vision Africa
P.O. Box 16427
Doornfontein, Johannesburg
2028 South Africa
Tel: +27-11 402 5477
E-mail: len@visionafrica.co.za

North American Distributors

African Diaspora Images
71 Joralemon Street
Brooklyn, NY 11201
Tel: 1-718-852-8353

California Newsreel
149 Ninth Street #420
San Francisco, CA 94103
Tel: 1-415-621-6196
Fax: 1-415-621-6522
www.newsreel.org

DSR, Inc.
9111 Guilford Road
Columbia, MD 21046
Tel: 1-301-490-3500
Fax: 1-301-490-4146
E-mail: dsr@us.net

Filmmakers Library
124 E. 40 Street
New York, NY 10016
Tel: 1-212-808-4980
Fax: 1-212-808-4983
E-mail: info@filmmaker.com
www.filmmakers.com

Films, Inc.
5547 N. Ravenswood Avenue
Chicago, IL 60640-1199

First Run/Icarus Films
32 Court Street, 21st Floor
Brooklyn, NY 11201
Tel: 1-718-488-8900
Fax: 1-718-488-8642
E-mail: info@frif.com
www.frif.com

Gris-Gris Films
17962 Valley Vista Boulevard
Encino, CA 91318
Tel: 1-818-881-8725
E-mail: grisfilm@ix.netcom.com
www.grisgrisfilms.com

KJM3 Entertainment Group, Inc.
274 Madison Avenue, Suite 501
New York, NY 10016
Tel: 1-212-988 0528
Fax: 1-212-689-6861

Mypheduh Films, Inc.
P.O. Box 10035
Washington, DC 20018-0035
Tel: 1-202-234-4755; 1-800-524-3895
Fax: 1-202-234-5735
E-mail: info@sankofa.com

New Yorker Films
Non-theatrical Dept.
85 Fifth Avenue, 11th Floor
New York, New York 10003
Tel: 1-212-645-4600
Fax: 1-212-645-3030
www.newyorkerfilms.com

Third World Newsreel
545 Eighth Avenue, 10th Floor
New York, NY 10018
Tel: 1-212-947-9277
Fax: 1-212-549-6417
www.twn.org

Villon Films
77 W. 28th Avenue
Vancouver V5Y 2K7
Canada
Tel & Fax: 1-604-879-6042

Index

Index

Caplan, David, 109n. 5
Carnegie Corporation, 46n. 11
Carson, Charles, 73
Carter, Everett, 60
censorship of films, 20, 22–23, 25, 44, 156, 220; opposition to, 43; and portrayal of whites, 40; and showing to blacks, 39, 146. *See also* black audiences
centralization in film production, 134–35
Centre National de la Cinématographie, 133–34
Chaka. *See* Shaka
Champion, A. W., 37
Chaplin, Charlie, 39
Chapman, Michael, 102, 103, 108, 109n. 5, 111n. 20
Chappell, Ernest, 36
Chatterjee, Partha, 153, 159n. 16
Chaucer, 24
Chicken Biznis: The Whole Story, 143, 146
children's television programming, 157n. 1
Christian African elite, 34
Christianity: and censorship, 19; disdain for, 77, 85, 104; and leadership, 78; and segregation, 67n. 13, 79; and social welfare, 34–44, 86, 95
Chronicle of the Ambers, The, 202
churches, independent, 32
cinema: in Algeria, 202; in Caribbean, 153; in Cuba, 202; and education, 19, 20, 24, 28, 38–39, 155, 156 (*see also* Plaatje, Solomon T.); future of, in South Africa, 201–29; in Germany, 141, 142; in Great Britain (*see* British cinema); marginalized, 150; and media, 151; national policy on, 227–29; role of, in South Africa, 133, 155; in Spain, 135, 149; in United

States, 227. *See also* American movies in Africa; cultural history and cinema; filmmakers; films; funding of film production; international competition in cinema; national cinema; South African cinema; storytelling and cinema
cinema of the diaspora, 130, 153
cinema of occupation, 6
cinema verité, 124
Cipriani, Lidio, 41
Cissé, Souleymane, 156, 206
City of Blood, 80–81
Clando, 156
Clansman, The, 21, 43–44
class differences: and social alienation, 33, 37, 88, 137, 148, 204; in South African film, 8–9, 45, 91, 106, 163, 185
classic films, 23–24, 221
Clint (fictional), 164–69, 171, 180–81
Coates, Paul, 55
Cohen, Frank, 39, 40
Cohen, Sande, 69n. 32
colonialism: and cinema industry, 151, 155, 156; in film, 68n. 18, 73–74, 82, 130, 156, 183, 190, 193, 194; as social impetus, 9–10, 43, 49, 53, 135, 136, 156–57, 191
combative cinema, 141
Come Back, Africa, 5–6, 25, 26, 27–28, 88–111
Come See the Bioscope, 30n. 9
commercialization of film, 157
Committee for African Cineasts (CAC), 203
common people and art, 23–24
Communism, 73, 77, 78, 79, 85
Communist Party of South Africa, 78
Compendium of South African History and Geography, 54

Index

Index

Hadji, El, 190, 192, 193, 195, 198
Hall, Stuart, 67n. 11, 129–30, 153–54
Hamlet, 24
Hampton Institute, 36
Harare Film Festival, 205–7
Harlem, 21
Harris, Richard, 81
Harvey, Ibrahim, 137
Harwood, Ronald, 81
Haupt, Adam, 143
Have You Seen Drum Recently?, 109n. 2
Hayward, Susan, 118, 130, 131n. 5
Hees, Edwin, 1, 4
Henry V, 23, 24
Hertzog, Barry, 61, 62, 69n. 27
heterogeneousness, 176–77
historical axis of film, 117
historical context of film, 117. *See also* films, and politics; propaganda in films; realism in film
history and nation building, 56, 153
History of Sexuality, The, 190–91
History of Social Significance of Motion Pictures in South Africa, 1895–1940, 3
Hitler, Adolph, 42
Hlanganani: A Short History of COSATU, 118, 119–23
Hoffman, Carl, 41
Hofmeyr, Isabel, 45, 53, 54, 56, 64, 65
Hogan, Patrick Colm, 77
Holden, Stephen, 5, 71, 87n. 2
homeland policy, 98
homosexuality, 9, 10
Hondo, Med, 204, 206, 228
Hooper-Box, Caroline, 147
Horkheimer, Max, 46n. 19
human rights violations, 152. *See also* apartheid; police brutality; white supremacy, and denying black rights

Hutchinson, Alfred, 29n. 1
hybridity, 125–26, 130, 153

ICE Media, 150
Imaginary realm of language, 176–78, 181, 184
IMF (International Monetary Fund), 137, 227
immigrant experience in Europe, 156
Imvo Zabantsundu, 16, 28
In Darkest Hollywood, 10, 27, 28, 87n. 1, 95, 109n. 2, 111n. 23
Independent Broadcasting Authority (IBA), 134, 157n. 1
independent churches, 32
independent filmmakers, 150, 157, 203, 213, 216; underground meeting of, during South African Film Market, 219–23
Industrial and Commercial Worker's Union, 45n. 9
industrialization, 34–35, 42. *See also* urbanization of Africans
Industrialization of the African, 42
industrial militancy, 140
In the Eye of the Storm, 202
Inkatha Freedom Party (IFP), 124, 128
Interim Film Fund (IFF), 134
international capital in South Africa, 139–40, 151
international competition in cinema, 139, 141, 143, 209
International Congress on the Negro, 16
interviews, 120–22
Irigaray, Luce, 184
Isidingo-The Need, 145
Italian films, 50, 69n. 31, 149
Izwi Labantu, 18

Jabavu, John Tengo, 16, 28
Jacobson, Ruth, 109n. 5
Jameson, Fredric, 46n. 19

Index

Poppie Nongena, 110n. 14
Population Registration Act, 110n. 12
Posel, Deborah, 78
power: female sexual, 189, 190; and sexuality, 190–91, 194
power relations in film, 188. *See also* "male gaze"
Preller, Gustav, 4–5, 46n. 20, 65; and anticolonial views, 5; and *De Voortrekkers*, 49, 50, 54, 64, 67n. 14; and popularizing The Great Trek, 52–53, 55; and white supremacy, 53
Prester John, 41
Pretorius, Andries, 52, 53
private broadcasters, 134, 151, 157n. 1. *See also* M-Net
Proctor, Elaine, 34, 172
production of identity, 130, 131
propaganda in films, 42, 51–52, 54–56, 61, 78, 119, 143, 226
Pudovkin, Vsevolod Illrionovich, 202

race: and polarization, 32, 148; in American film, 21; as reference to white Afrikaners, 58, 63, 68n. 19; and social conflicts, 34; in South African film, 8–9, 28, 44–45, 66n. 6, 67n. 11, 163–64
race consciousness, 17–18, 28, 34, 213
race films, 61, 68n. 24
racial cooperation. *See* nonracial South Africa
racial discrimination, 32–33, 94–95, 137; in film, 59, 79, 82, 97, 104, 185, 188, 203; and laws supporting, 34, 59; and political involvement, 4–5, 54, 68n. 24, 102, 104, 199–200; and viewing films, 19–21, 39, 70. *See also* apartheid, and economic restrictions; black audiences,

prohibition of; National Party; white supremacy
racism, 67n. 10; and blame for disunity, 55; development of, 5, 44, 54, 107; in film industry, 217, 219; opposition to, 34–35, 100; reverse, 6, 136, 137, 208, 222; and sexism, 187. *See also* apartheid; black audiences; colonialism; white supremacy
Radebe, Mark, Sr., 16
Ramaphosa, Cyril, 123
rape in film, 188–89, 191, 193–94, 199
rationalism and New African Movement, 27
realism in film, 51, 64–65, 69n. 31, 72–73, 82, 84–85, 92
Reconstruction and Development Programme (RDP), 138–39, 141
recreation, of Africans as controlled by whites, 33–38. *See also* leisure time
regionalism in film, 134–35
Reid, Mark, 12n. 3, 68n. 24
religion and film, 63–64, 86–87
Renan, Ernest, 56
representation, cinematic, of racial difference, 163–86
Resha, Robert, 27
Retief, Piet (fictional): biography of, 53; as leader of Great Trek, 51, 52, 56, 58; murder of, 52, 58, 61, 67n. 10, 69n. 28
Rhodes, Cecil, 50
Riesenfeld, Daniel, 109n. 2, 111n. 23
Riviere, Joan, 173, 175, 186n. 6
Robben Island workshop, 213–16, 223
Robeson, Paul, 41
Rockefeller Foundation, 148
Rogin, Michael Paul, 61, 62, 64, 66n. 4

Index

Index

Index